Psycho Paths

TRACKING THE SERIAL KILLER THROUGH CONTEMPORARY AMERICAN FILM AND FICTION

Psycho Paths

Philip L. Simpson

SOUTHERN ILLINOIS UNIVERSITY PRESS

Carbondale and Edwardsville

Library of Congress Cataloging-in-Publication Data
Simpson, Philip L., 1964–
Psycho paths : tracking the serial killer through contemporary American
film and fiction / Philip L. Simpson.
    p. cm.
Includes bibliographical references and index.
    1. Serial murderers in motion pictures. 2. Serial murderers in literature.
3. American fiction—20th century—History and criticism. I. Title: Psycho
paths. II. Title.
PN1995.9.S297 S56 2000
791.43'655—dc21   99-056666
ISBN 0-8093-2328-1 (cloth : alk. paper)
ISBN 0-8093-2329-X (pbk. : alk. paper)

To my mother and father

Contents

Preface

My desire to understand the media popularity of serial murder resulted in this book—a general overview of some of the most recognizable American novels and film/television treatments of serial murder, the major literary themes and social context of these treatments, and the critical responses to them. Serial murder, even as overexposed as that term has become, serves as a broad metaphor for a plethora of concerns facing contemporary American society at the start of the twenty-first century. And while serial murder indeed remains a favorite staple of tabloid journalism and cheap fiction, it has also compelled a variety of serious contemporary American writers and film directors to grapple with its philosophical implications. In the pages ahead, I will track the serial killer through some of the most recognizable novels and films—the formative "classics" in the field, if you will—that accompanied the public explosion of interest in serial murder from the 1980s to the present. I will elaborate upon a brief history and key formulations of various structural components of the serial killer text for the express purpose of giving context to the discussion, referring the reader to other studies when appropriate. Then, I will illustrate how these influences work in representative novels and films about serial murder.

The study (as opposed to the tabloid merchandising) of serial murder is already well established in sociological and criminological circles by writers such as Jack Levin, James Fox, and Elliott Leyton, to name only a few. The analysis of the fictional narratives of serial murder, however, is still growing. Those who have accomplished this kind of specialized, in-depth study include Jane Caputi, Deborah Cameron and Elizabeth Fraser, Philip Jenkins, Richard Tithecott, and Mark Seltzer. Each scholar has his or her own insights into the mass appeal of fictional accounts of serial murder. What follows is a brief summary of each of those insights, provided here so that one may better understand the context in which my own work exists.

One predominant school of thought, specific to the 1970s and 1980s, to explain the appeal of fictionalized serial murder has it that patriarchal society, particularly that of the United States, promotes individual masculine terrorism against female victims, even in its fiction. Therefore, the serial killer case study confirms "the links between murder, misogyny, and masculinity," according to Suzanne Moore (71). Most of these "classic" serial killer narratives are set within the resurgence of conservative ideology in the 1980s that created an atmosphere inimical to feminist interests, as Susan Faludi demonstrates in her influential work *Backlash*. Probably the most comprehensive feminist analysis of serial murder and its representation is Jane Caputi's *The Age of Sex Crime*. Her study demonstrates the prevalence of Jack-the-Ripper imagery in popular culture and how many modern serial murderers have appropriated the terms of the Ripper discourse for their own violent agendas. Caputi's book is predated by Judith Walkowitz's feminist study of late Victorian London, *City of Dreadful Delight*, which extensively discusses the Ripper's crimes as emblematic of urban misogyny. Deborah Cameron and Elizabeth Fraser's *The Lust to Kill: A Feminist Investigation of Sexual Murder* proceeds on the thesis that

> although killing for sexual pleasure existed as a form of behaviour well before Jack the Ripper, with sporadic reports going back at least to the fifteenth century, sexual murder as a distinctive category with a meaning for experts and lay members of the culture is a product of the mid- to late nineteenth century and was not completely established in its present form until the early years of this century. (22)

Cameron and Fraser's study concentrates more rigorously than Caputi's (though still sampling from diverse academic disciplines at will) on the philosophical stances, such as those formulated by the Marquis de Sade, André Gide, Jean-Paul Sartre, and Jean Genet, that justify and promulgate violence by men against women. Cameron and Fraser and Caputi argue that serial sexual murder, continually reenacted in our dramatic arts, accompanies the patriarchal backlash reaction to social reforms and advances designed to empower women. In another context, referring back to the prevalence of and fascination with sexual serial homicide in Weimar Germany between the world wars, Maria Tatar equates the male backlash against the female population, which had been granted an unusual degree of social freedom with the widespread domestic absence of men during World War I, to the generalized right-wing nationalist movement that ended in Hitler's brand of fascism.

Engaging in a similar but wider-ranging social-construction approach to the subject's current bankability, Philip Jenkins focuses on the way in which what he calls "claims-makers" benefit from linking certain behaviors "with another phenomenon [serial murder] perceived as far more dangerous" (*Using Murder* 7). As an "ultimate evil" that very few people would actually defend, serial murder serves admirably to enhance the undesirability of any behavior (homosexuality, rape, consumption of pornography) with which it is linked by any claims-maker of any ideological bent. Jenkins notes that those who advocate "expansion of legal sanction and bureaucratic power to combat or suppress a perceived social evil" find the existence of serial murder a convenient rhetorical opportunity. Though quick to caution that linkage of undesirable behavior to serial murder can serve any ideological position, Jenkins nevertheless associates the mid-1970s ascendancy of serial murder to cultural notice with a corresponding highly influential American New Right movement. As Jenkins defines it, the New Right is founded on "the rhetoric of decadence" (8), or discourse that blames growing crime rates and a generalized social malaise on the supposed collapse of fundamental values and self-discipline during the 1960s. The New Right solution is to emphasize the dimension of personal responsibility through metaphysics: to view "wrong-doing and deviancy as issues of personal sin and evil rather than social or economic dysfunction" and to deny "the effectiveness or validity of solutions that emphasized the state or social dimension" (9). The New Right focus on personal responsibility is also definitively patriarchal. It calls for a return to traditional "manly" virtues of "standing tall" and "fighting back," particularly through tough law enforcement measures (10), apparently one institutional expression of "big government" the New Right endorses. However, a strong enemy is needed to justify strong law enforcement, so New Right rhetoric tends to focus on "themes of external threat, national vulnerability, subversion, and internal decadence" (11) made possible not only by the perceived lax morality and hedonism of the 1960s but the judicial and congressional restraints placed on law enforcement. The rhetorical function of the "dangerous outsider" theme, then, is to create an ideological climate in which those restraints are loosened, or dropped altogether, to combat "the enemy" more effectively.

New Right rhetoric has been so successful in achieving social transformation, Jenkins concludes, that even those of leftist or moderate political ideologies in the 1980s and 1990s have adopted and in some cases exceeded the patterns of New Right discourse in an effort to compete for public attention, creating a very unusual alliance between feminist/radical groups and social conservatives. The serial killer, as a dramatic case study of leftist and feminist critique of generalized patriarchal hostility toward marginalized classes during the 1970s, ironically became one of the New Right's favorite bogeymen to illustrate the pernicious effect of the supposed decay of traditional values during the 1980s (12). The ease with which the serial killer prototype suited widely diverse ideological agendas illustrates the polysemous or even ineffable nature of the phenomenon.

Expanding on this idea of the serial killer's rhetorical positioning as an "ultimate evil" standing outside of the observer's own privileged ideology, Richard Tithecott sees the construction of the serial killer in narrative representation as part of a growing cultural tendency to reject intellectual critique of one's own cultural values as contributing factors to violence. As evidence, he points to the culture's frequent use of words such as "motiveless" in constructing serial murder tales. The refusal to entertain a serious discussion of motive, to posit crime as essentially unknowable and thus, at least by some definitions, metaphysically evil, serves to distance the serial killers from the comfortable everyday world and place them in some mythic realm where they are at once profane and sacred. The popularity of the serial killer in fictional narrative, then, is a symptom of a larger cultural denial of responsibility in the production of violence. If nature (or God or destiny) intends one to be a serial killer, and this nature is perceived as unknowable and uncontrollable, as so many of these narratives imply, what is the point of trying to do better as a society? Tithecott wishes to remove the word "nature," with its associations of biological determinism and historical inevitability, from discussions of serial murder (8) so that we may acknowledge our ability to change the parameters of a world we have created (or at least transformed) through narrative representation.

Mark Seltzer, in his book-length study of the representation of serial murder, identifies what he calls "wound culture": "the public fascination with torn and open bodies and torn and opened persons, a collective gathering around shock, trauma, and the wound" (1). The wound, or trauma, is a literal baring of the private interior to the public exterior. As Seltzer tracks it, wound culture is the postindustrial product of the social transformations of the industrial nineteenth century, when private identity became increasingly publicly defined in terms of categories, types, and statistics. The "sex criminal" is perhaps the exemplary statistical person of the past century—one who is individuated by his similarity to others of the same type. One of the "foundational scripts in accounting for the serial killer," Seltzer writes, is the basic psychoanalytic premise that embattled childhood domesticity forms the dangerous future adult (4). The widespread belief that childhood trauma "explains" adult deviance establishes an undercurrent of anxiety in all family settings. This belief also predisposes many people to extrapolate, on the basis of personal experience with domestic pain, that criminality is the universal state of the human psyche. Such hyper-general assumptions lead to intellectual mischief, Seltzer believes. For example, based on the psychoanalytic belief that infantile aggressiveness is a shared universal trait, many argue that extermination or quarantine of the "contagious" deviant is necessary to preserve decent civilization. As Seltzer argues:

> Serial killing is thus represented as at once an horrific departure from normalcy and as abnormally normal: wounds to an idealized and intact American culture that is at the same time seen *as* a wound culture. . . . This style of explanation—like the notions of a "murder epidemic". . . . or "serial murder as an infectious disease" . . . makes visible the tendency to merge the natural and national body, where pathological violence is concerned. (6)

Seltzer furthermore sees this kind of compulsive murderous act as reflective of the machine age itself, where productivity, counting, and replication become their own meanings and

> the yielding of identity to identification proceeds by way of an utter absorption in *technologies of reflection, reduplication, and simulation.* . . . Chameleon-like, the serial killer copies and simulates others; the monochrome man, he melts into place; the minus man, predead, he plays dead and takes life. (20)

Paradoxically, however, the minus man fears nothing more than loss of a core belief that the self is a bounded model. He is terrified of the collapse of his interior boundaries, or what Seltzer calls his "buried inwardness" (139). The serial killer's psyche is characterized by a veering between "the enduring romantic formula of self-making and the contemporary psychoanalytic formula of the self's unmaking: the trauma" (138). Seltzer calls this shifting of boundaries between the interior and the exterior the pathological public sphere. Within this sphere, the besieged romantic identity preserves itself through the annihilation of that which threatens it most but in such a way as to ensure the continued survival of the individual within the wound culture.

Seltzer's theory of a postmodern wound culture complements Andrew Britton's contention that the postmodernist aesthetic in most of its formulations amounts to nothing more than a disingenuous philosophical retreat from, and in some cases a celebration of, capitalist society (10). Annalee Newitz, expanding on Marx's definition of "dead labor" as that period of time during which workers work not for themselves but for the corporate entity in a capitalist state, concludes that serial murder may be the capitalist workers' desperate attempt to restore subjectivity in the machine age by destroying those who represent certain economic classes perceived as enemies (42). In other words, serial murder is a form of capitalist recreation—that is, relief from work, but not a rejection of the system of work itself. Newitz also points to the prevalence of family relationships in serial killer narratives as another symptom of a cultural commodity fetishism, which separates productivity from leisure and family time. Under such a division, one is compelled to view family life as a "haven" from the demands of work. This view, of course, sets one up for disillusionment and bitterness and, in the most extreme cases, murder as a way of relief. Newitz and Seltzer thus provide keys toward understanding the crucial role that microcosmic family life and macrocosmic economic ideology plays in contemporary serial killer narratives.

Rigorous inspection of the sociohistorical context of serial murder is necessary, because as even a cursory examination of the field reveals, no easy distinction between the "fact" (reality) or "fiction" (representation) of serial murder can be drawn: "the fictional and non-fictional texts feed off each other in such a way that they become indistinguishable from each other in the public imagination" (D'Cruz 328). Robert Conrath explains this blurring of boundary as endemic within the contemporary world:

> One of the most glaring tenants [*sic*] of our postmodern popular culture is the collapsing together of traditional epistemological categories of fact and fiction, veracity and verisimilitude. . . . The social matrix which holds, molds, and subsequently defines how we relate to, and process this information, and more importantly how we talk about these events, has now been collapsed into one, a total epistemological leveling. ("The Guys" 149)

Annalee Newitz argues that "because fictional representations of serial killers are often based on biographies of actual killers, one might say the serial killer narrative spans both fictional and non-fictional genres" (39). Joseph Grixti, referring to the American fascination with cannibalistic murderers such as Jeffrey Dahmer, describes the fictionalizing process that accompanies public awareness of a notorious serial killer:

> Fictionalizing figures like . . . [Ted] Bundy as inhuman monsters is one way of coming to terms with the dislocations that they generate in order to preserve the preferred contours of our own identity. Popular fiction, because of its very generic and formulaic nature, frequently acts as a frame of reassurance which allows us to safely engage in this exploratory process. The process involves locating the criminal-outsiders within a tradition, and identifying their affinities with antecedents—which have in their turn been made part of a mythology. What we and our cultures are engaged in when we endeavour to contextualize serial murderers within this broader mythology is an exercise designed to allow them to be habitually perceived in the same unthreatening terms as is the case with domesticated mythic monsters like the werewolf or the vampire. (90)

Grixti's identification of fictional narrative's relocation of the historically contextualized serial murderer into a mythological decontextualized realm is crucial to understanding the current evolution of serial killer fiction into its own subgenre.

Before proceeding into my own analysis of this subgenre, I would like to issue one caveat. It would be tedious and repetitious, not to mention impossible, to attempt to analyze all, or even most, of the works of serial killer fiction that have glutted the marketplace over the past few decades. Even if it were possible, the words of Michael Morrison ring sadly true: that in just a few short years, "a torrent of largely inept and vacuous serial-killer novels have all but exhausted this motif" (24). As is the case with any fictional genre or subgenre, there is a lot of frankly substandard material to sift through before coming to works that reward in-depth analysis. So, I have first chosen to sacrifice a survey or cataloguing approach in favor of in-depth analysis of selected works representative of larger themes within the genre. My second choice has been to limit discussion of this subject that so obsesses America to works by Americans, or at least those with strong American affiliations, such as Paul West. (At the very least, for my purposes here, the work should have an American setting.) Also, for the purpose of audience accessibility, I have chosen novels and films for discussion that have at least some degree of public name recognition or notoriety, as the case may be. More obscure works, of which there are literally hundreds, I will leave for the reader's own discovery.

A project of this magnitude would not be possible without a great deal of help. First of all, I would like to thank my editors at Southern Illinois University Press, especially Karl and Kathy Kageff and John Wilson. I also want to thank three people whose long hours of reading and critiquing have improved the various drafts of this study immeasurably: David Blakesley, Chris Sharrett, and Tony Williams. I would also like to thank Mikita Brottman for her contributions to my intellectual understanding of this topic. To my friends and colleagues at and around Southern Illinois University, Iowa State University, and Brevard Community College, I can only say thank you for your understanding and support as this project evolved over the years. Finally, to my mother, Alice; my father, Les; and my wife, Candace; I would like to express my gratitude for providing me with the unconditional stability, security, and love one needs in this life.

Portions of chapter 2 and chapter 5 were previously published in substantially different form as, respectively, "The Contagion of Murder: Thomas Harris's *Red Dragon," Notes on Contemporary Literature* 25.1 (January 1995): 6–8; and "The Politics of Apocalypse in the Cinema of Serial Murder," *Mythologies of Violence in Postmodern Media,* ed. Christopher Sharrett (Detroit: Wayne State UP, 1999).

Psycho Paths

Introduction

The Serial Killer
in Fiction

The fictional stories of serial murder are only one aspect of a much larger cultural fascination with violent crime in general and serial killing in particular. The phenomenon of serial killing, which involves a number of seemingly unmotivated murders committed by one or more individuals over an extended period of time, has received an increasing amount of attention over the past three decades in the United States. Depending on the proper confluence of publicity and zeitgeist, a select few of these individuals, or serial killers, achieve a great deal of cultural notoriety and hence a qualified kind of immortality. The names of Jeffrey Dahmer, Ted Bundy, and John Wayne Gacy have become part of our national vocabulary. They influence our social dialogue as we attempt to understand and curb violent criminal behavior. Their infamy guarantees an industry of true-crime books, academic studies, and governmental/law-enforcement reports. All manner of social crusades from a variety of political perspectives arise as a result of the struggle to comprehend the damage these people have done. And in our attempt to understand serial killers, we inevitably create myths about them—works of fiction that may superficially portray the serial killer as the ultimate alien outsider or enemy of society but which simultaneously reflect back upon society its own perversions, fears, and murderous desires. Thus, the serial killer is "psycho"—aberrant and depraved—while still remaining a recognizable product of American culture.

In fiction, films, and television, the serial killer has very quickly become an eminently marketable form of contemporary folk legend. Actual serial killers such as Ted Bundy, John Wayne Gacy, Ed Kemper, Jeffrey Dahmer, Ed Gein, Charles Starkweather, Charlie Manson, Henry Lee Lucas, and their ilk are slowly metamorphosing into immortal (and profitable) cultural icons, in much the same way that whoever murdered at least three and probably more Victorian prostitutes on the eve of the mass-media age has become Jack the Ripper. Concomitantly, fiction writers are creating serial killer scenarios loosely based on the media-purveyed exploits of the actual multiple murderers. These real-life antecedents of Uncle Charlie, Norman Bates, Leatherface, Michael Myers, Jason Voorhees, Francis Dolarhyde, Jame Gumb, Hannibal Lecter, and so on, are revitalized and particularized mythic villains for an anomic world that is haunted by the macrocosmic specters of war, genocide, gynocide, terrorism, and random violent crime but ironically constructed from the institutionalized ideologies that make all of these possible. The literature and legends that have coalesced around über-criminals answer the human need to personify free-floating fears, aggravated by the perplexing indeterminacy of the postmodern world, into a specific, potentially confinable, yet still ultimately evil, threat. The marauding serial killers of the late 1970s, 1980s, and 1990s encode, deliberately or otherwise, many of our cultural phobias in their polysemous narrative representation in fiction and film.

The serial killer narratives take many forms of varying levels of complexity and appear in many media. They can be as succinct and brutally straightforward as the much-maligned "serial killer trading cards" of a few years back, or they can be as artistically complex as the metafiction of Paul West. But no matter what shape these narratives are presented in, they are hegemonic. In this country alone, especially since the early to mid-1960s, literally dozens of fiction and nonfiction accounts of serial murder have attracted enough public and critical attention so as to warrant serious academic study.

Serial Murder and Folklore

Historically, tales of multiple murder have always attracted a disproportionate amount of public attention and often appear in oral folklore. Brian Meehan notes, "there is . . . a natural affinity between folklore and savage crime" (3).

This may be so because folklore, essentially verbal in nature, considers repetition of key images and phrases a vital structural component to begin with, and so finds a metaphoric parallel to a series of murders. W. F. H. Nicolaisen professes that counting is equivalent to narrating in the European mind-set (77–89): an applicable concept to explain the kinship between multicide and narrative. Another explanation is that folklore invests otherwise inexplicable phenomena such as multiple murder with significance through the communally shared act of narration.

Whatever the explanation, however, folklore and murder have always been interdependent, as one can readily observe in the wealth of story and rhyme surrounding such notorious historical figures as Gilles de Rais, Vlad Tepes, H. H. Holmes, Lizzie Borden, and Belle Gunness. It is surely no accident that these murderers often become associated with monstrous or supernatural traits drawn from folklore. Philip Jenkins argues that serial killers "provide a means for society to project its worst nightmares and fantasies, images that in other eras or other regions might well be fastened onto supernatural or imaginary folk-devils—vampires, werewolves, witches, evil sorcerers, conspiratorial Jews" (*Using Murder* 112–13). But it took the rise of a modern mass media before specific cases could transcend their singular temporal and sociopolitical contexts to become elements of a truly global contemporary mythology—heinous villainy masquerading behind a Norman Bates– or Ted Bundy–like façade of bland normality. In the contemporary mythic paradigm, the banality and latent ubiquity of evil are cosmological twins.

The supernatural image of the human/monster hybrid is, of course, central to the project of rendering the serial killer into a proper folklore demon. As Lutz Rohrich writes, "in . . . legend the demon is timeless and permanent; it existed before humans and will outlast them. At the legend's end the demon can remain a threat to the future" (24–25). Yet in an age where metaphysical evil has been largely dethroned by notions of psychological dysfunction—where Grendel and his monstrous mother have been narrowly reconfigured into psychosexually troubled Norman Bates and his "castrating" but clearly human mother—it is not easy to preserve the dark grandeur reserved for folkloric monsters. The serial killer nevertheless achieves legendary status, largely through clever textual strategies that relocate the monstrous face behind the human one—the skull fleetingly visible behind Norman Bates's features in the final moments of *Psycho*.

The serial killer is a postmodern shape-shifter or changeling child whose spiritual essence was kidnapped by pornography or bad genes or abusive parents and replaced with the soul of Cain. Any given killer has one pleasant or at least nonthreatening face with which to conduct public negotiations and another evil face with which to terrify helpless victims. This doubling strategy allows inhuman evil to lurk behind human "normalcy," simply because the serial killers' actions by their very nature cannot help but propel them beyond the liminal into what Noel Carroll identifies as the interstitial territory reserved for the most egregious taboo violators. Carroll describes horrific monsters as "the mixture of what is normally distinct" (33), which in turn sounds similar to the devoured/devouring world trope in carnivalesque folk culture, where the limits between human flesh and the rest of the world are blurred or erased altogether. So, in spite of the moral pollution surrounding them and their transgressive actions, and the textual demonization, serial killers remain at least marginally human. Indeed, so have the folk monsters of previous generations, such as werewolves and vampires.

The fictional representations of contemporary serial killers obviously plunder the vampire narratives of the past century and a half, such as those authored by Coleridge, Byron, Polidori, Prest, Wordsworth, Stoker, LeFanu, Wilde, Poe, Emily and Charlotte Brontë, Henry James, and D. H. Lawrence, for suitably lurid and pseudo-supernatural embroidery. These vampire-centered texts, in turn, are conflations of Eastern European vampire folklore and romantic/Gothic narrative conventions. Richard Gottleib and Margaret L. Carter in combination have identified six major features of the earlier vampire folk tradition. First, the vampire is undead and intent on continuing an inherently parasitic relationship with the living. Second, his body is not decayed or decomposed. Third, he is a tormented outcast. Fourth, he experiences conflict over his compulsion to cannibalize the living. Fifth, he destroys with his mouth, creating more vampires even as he nourishes himself. Lastly, he longs for death. One would be hard-pressed to find a better catalog of metaphors for the darker aspects of romanticism—that is, the Gothic. According to Carol Senf's study, nineteenth-century writers freely adapted the folk legends to their dramatic needs, creating characters who were either literal vampires or ordinary human beings modeled on vampires (25–26). In the figure of the serial killer, whether presented in fictional or tabloid "true crime" fashion, we see a similar human monster, textually coded as generically supernatural but, in part, vampiric.

Vampires and serial killers are, in part, metaphors designed for arriving at an intuitive explanation of the human ability to murder other humans for symbolic reasons having nothing to do with literal survival. In many ways, they are low-rent versions of Dostoevsky's fictional treatise on "motiveless" murder, *Crime and Punishment*. Whereas Dostoevsky's novel is essentially an interior monologue remote from the fleshy urgency of nonintellectual existence, the folk demonology represented by the pantheon of shape-shifters and blood-drinking monsters performs its bloody antics on a public stage for public consumption, even as it consumes the public. Mikhail Bakhtin distinguishes the medieval mind-set by its "drama of bodily life (copulation, birth, growth, eating, drinking, defecation)" (88). The survival of this mind-set into the modern age has been made possible by aperiodic exposure to the devouring appetite inherent in what Bakhtin calls the "grotesque body" that "swallows the world and is itself swallowed by the world" (317) in a reciprocal act of energy transfer but with one vital difference. As Maggie Kilgour observes, the modern age reconfigures Bakhtin's "ideal of a cooperative body" into representations of "all relations as not symbiotic but predatory" (145). The gaping mouth (the medieval hellmouth) is the primary symbol of the grotesque body, the same as for the devouring werewolf and vampire. The mouth functions as the portal of consumption that ingests the life force as it rends it. Oral cruelty is inextricably linked to a premodern consciousness, which our modern culture longs for the more technologized we become.

The serial killer, so often associated with biting and eating, serves as the engine that drives our attraction/repulsion toward an elemental existence where one may be free of civilization and its discontents but also possibly killed and eaten. Those killers who evoke this ambivalent frisson the strongest are the ones who will endure in legend: Vlad Tepes, Gilles de Rais, Countess Bathory, Jack the Ripper. In our own modern era, H. H. Holmes's serial wife-killing in his dark castle, Ed Gein's serial grave-robbing, Ted Bundy's biting a hunk of flesh out of a victim's buttocks, and Jeffrey Dahmer's eating a human bicep rouse primitive awareness of the voracious appetite of hellmouth. This arousal of primal emotions is only enhanced by technological advances in communication. When we read about the latest serial killer, or see one posture for the court cameras, we are watching the legend-making process in utero. In any age, fictional narrative steals away the murderer from the source incident and creates a new panoply of incarnations in folklore.

The formal study of folklore makes clear distinctions between myths and legends, rumors and reports. In this context, Bill Ellis's use of the term *contemporary mythologies* "to refer to global scenarios accepted on faith by subcultures who use them to link and give ultimate meaning to puzzling events" is best fitting. The contemporary mythologies arise from "clusters of legends, rumors, and beliefs [that] collaborate with other kinds of stories or bits of information to form global bodies of lore" (43–44). What Jan Harold Brunvand calls an "urban legend" would be a particular legend or rumor that contributes to the global body of lore. In Brunvand's words:

> Urban legends belong to the subclass of folk narratives, legends, that—unlike fairy tales—are believed, or at least believable, and that—unlike myths—are set in the recent past and involve normal human beings rather than ancient gods or demigods. Legends are folk history, or rather quasi-history. As with any folk legends, urban legends gain credibility from specific details of time and place or from references to source authorities. (3)

To elaborate, an urban legend is best understood as a focused narrative expression of a free-floating social anxiety, such as the fear of strangers in a society where physical mobility is essentially unchecked and where the next-door neighbors can do more than drive down the property values. The legendary dimensions of serial killers are thus ensured by their social invisibility, which imparts to them by proxy a pseudo-supernatural, shapeshifting ability carried over from the vampire and werewolf tales of previous generations.

It is also helpful to distinguish between contemporary legend and rumor. A contemporary legend, according to Patricia Turner, is a well-formed narrative held by its performer to be true or at least believable, whereas a rumor is "more open-ended and unspecific and usually lack[s] narrative chronology" (78). In either case, a contemporary mythology is an attempt to incorporate these discrete bits of rumor and legend into a totalizing narrative, or what the hard sciences are fond of calling a "unified field" theory. In other words,

> all cultures have underlying assumptions and it is these assumptions or folk ideas which are the building blocks of any worldview. Any one worldview will be based upon many individual folk ideas and if one is seriously interested in studying worldview, one will need first to describe some of the folk ideas that contribute to the formation of that worldview. (Dundes 96)

Hence, a segment of the population might tie together diverse and demonstrably real (if exaggerated) events like cattle mutilation, child abduction,

and random murder under the rubric of satanism—a foundational, theological explanation of the evil we see in the world and the purpose behind
that evil. Others might explain these same phenomena as clear evidence of
an extraterrestrial presence on earth—another foundational mythology that
accounts for first and last things, as Mircea Eliade might say. Whether the
totalizing narrative is true is less important than whether it can theoretically
account for the puzzling events for a large enough group of people and thus
in some way through the agreed-upon narrative make the unknown known
and less frightening. Brian Meehan concludes that, paradoxically, calling a
human murderer a monster has the result of easing the fear surrounding
the crimes:

> The culture's intention . . . is not to fictionalize the crime, but to
> lessen the threat such irrationality poses to a belief in an ordered
> world. In a universe of angels, devils, and human beings, all over-
> seen by an omnipotent god, vampires are far less disturbing than a
> real Ted Bundy. (4)

A visible, so-called monstrous threat, even if it doesn't exist, can be com-
bated and ritually purged. Along these lines, Philip Jenkins argues that as a
threatening outsider or Other, the serial killer achieves legendary, nearly
mythic status by providing contemporary society with a refreshingly unam-
biguous villain against which nearly everyone can agree to unite (*Using
Murder* 112). The need for immediate legends to explain the unexplainable
drives people to the reassurance of bounded narrative. The seemingly timeless truths implicit in folk narrative provide imaginative relief from the stress
and anxiety of local insecurity. This relief works on the individual as well as
the group level, since any one hearer of a narrative can then assume the empowering function of storyteller and retell it to a guaranteed avid audience.
Murder may indeed serve as a powerful literary metaphor, if we accept one
working definition of literature as "difficult" or elite narrative, but it has its
roots in the easily grasped texts of folklore.

Another of the main reasons the image of the serial murderer services
the folklore narrative so well is the level of fear it generates in a given community. This fear, in turn, is often used as a type of "verbal social control,"
John Widdowson argues (105). Fear, as a negative emotion, has many social
applications, one of which is to threaten people with death should they transgress against community standards. Thus, in many ways, the multicide who

has achieved folkloric dimensions becomes an unacknowledged but nevertheless useful agent of social control, waiting in the shadows to strike down
individuals who stray from the borders of accepted behavior. Widdowson
makes a distinction between two kinds of "bogeymen" in folklore: "A figure
which is intrinsically frightening" or "A figure which is *used* for frightening
others" (105). This latter "threatening" figure has found its way into popular American folklore in many narrative guises. Harold Schechter and David
Everitt list some of them as "The Roommate's Death," "The Assailant in
the Back Seat," and "The Baby-Sitter and the Man Upstairs." Schechter and
Everitt point out that popular media culture, through cinematic figures such
as Michael Myers (*Halloween*) and films such as *When a Stranger Calls,* retell these well-known tales in a more technologically sophisticated form (167–
68). These threatening figures tend to prey on unwary or self-absorbed teen-
agers, most notoriously the sexually promiscuous ones. The "slasher" films,
as the *Halloween* derivatives have come to be known, and their genre brethren atemporalize specific ideological concerns, such as questions of victim
and agency in 1970s feminism in the case of *Halloween,* into a mythic landscape where all transgressions against the collective are brutally punished by
a cultural avenger who is not the alien outsider he initially appears to be.
These killers are among the most conservative figures in a society, answering "liberal" deviations from the mythic norm with murder in a project to
remove those transgressors from specific history and "restore" them to timeless purity.

    Like any "good" monster, the serial killer as a type never really dies in
the narratives of multiple murder. Certainly, an individual murderer in the
typical serial killer narrative may die, but another will invariably rise from
the Gothic setting to take his place. Generally, any one killer's "immortality" is not a physical defiance of death so much as a cultural one. The memory
of the killer's deeds haunts the community through a folktale cycle centering around threatening figures. Of course, in some plots, of which *Halloween* and Wes Craven's *Nightmare on Elm Street* are the most typical, the killer
is at least implicitly coded as, if not specifically acknowledged to be, supernatural and correspondingly immortal. As Amy Taubin observes, "it is the
killer's ability to rise from the dead in film after film—rather than his appearance, his physical strength or even the extreme sadism of his actions—
that demonises him" ("Killing" 16). Taubin's insight into genre formula brings
us from the mytho-historic origins of serial murder to its incarnation within genre texts.

Serial Murder and Genre

The current popularity of serial killer fiction can be further understood through a relocation of the discussion into another area—that of genre texts.[1] The serial killer narrative has developed its own subgeneric conventions and plot formulas, while overlapping with and borrowing from a variety of genres, such as horror and detective noir. However, the fictional serial killer's most appropriate genre home, as Peter Hutchings argues, is horror (91). The horror genre can be best defined as that which depicts monsters for the purpose of disturbing, unsettling, and disorienting its consumers, often for the seemingly paradoxical purpose of reinforcing community identity. Martin Tropp, for example, argues that the horror story's appeal (and its ready adaptability to film as well) can only be comprehended in terms of its audience reception. The horror story is meant to be experienced as a communal event, he insists:

> As a collective experience (made immediate in our century when film enabled us literally to be alone together in the darkness) the popularity of the horror story transformed private nightmares into communal events. . . . [H]orror stories are not nightmares transcribed, but fears recast into safe and communicable forms—a concrete, related, yet separate reality. . . . Horror stories, when they work, construct a fictional edifice of fear and deconstruct it simultaneously, dissipating terror in the act of creating it. And real horrors are filtered through the expectations of readers trained in responding to popular fiction, familiar with a set of images, a language, and pattern of development. Horror fiction gives the reader the tools to "read" experiences that would otherwise, like nightmares, be incommunicable. In that way, the inexpressible and private becomes understandable and communal, shared and safe. (4–5)

Carol Clover, while noting that folklorists usually "disown" horror movies in particular as too profit-oriented and technological in construction, agrees: "horror movies look like nothing so much as folktales—a set of fixed tale types that generate an endless stream of what are in effect variants" (10). James Twitchell similarly argues for an "ethnological approach," as opposed to an auteur one, to understanding horror's appeal: "The critic's first job in explaining the fascination of horror is . . . to trace [horrific images'] migrations to the audience and, only then, try to understand why they have been

crucial enough to pass along" (84). These critics neatly link the horror genre
to the larger experience of community intersubjectivity, from which the interstitial figure of the serial killer arises, both in reality (as it is comprehended
and mediated through language) and fiction.

Horror *can* deal with the explicitly supernatural, as seen in, for example,
the "satanic" Hollywood films of the 1970s, such as *The Exorcist* or *The Omen*.
However, this is an overly restrictive definition. Horror is better understood
as the state of mind induced by one's confrontation with a violation of *cultural categories*. Mary Douglas identifies at least three different types of
violation: pollution, or "matter out of place"; moral, which "involve[s] either the breach of important moral laws or outrages against people, or both";
and invasion of chaos, or the threat of a "lapse into incomprehensibility"
(qtd. in Bridgstock 116). Pollution is integral to Noel Carroll's definition of
horror as an emotion composed of equal parts fear and nausea, elicited by
the sight of the monster: "Within the context of the horror narrative, the
monsters are identified as impure and unclean" (23). The serial killer as
horrific monster *appears* human, but a "hidden" monstrosity radiates a kind
of moral leprosy that taints all who come in contact, much like werewolves
or vampires infect others with their "disease." The serial killers' pollution of
the moral environment marks them as genre monsters. Also in accordance
with another of Douglas's ideas, Susan Stewart identifies the chaotic, destabilizing violation of fixed boundaries "between the human and the other,
between nature and culture" as central to horror's effect (42). Hence, horror's
insistence on doubling "as a polysemy of the self . . . since repetition in this
genre has the effect of cumulative suspense. One repetition is sufficient to
imply an infinity of repetitions" (43). Philip Brophy also isolates repetition
as a key element in horror: "It is a genre which mimics itself mercilessly—
because its statement is coded within its very mimicry" (3). A repetitive series of grisly murders, then, is one of the most appropriate subjects for the
horror genre.

Within this framework of violations, serial killers manage to incarnate
all of them in their fictional treatments. As Andrew Tudor explains, the
murdering "madman" (like Norman Bates) is a relatively recent horror-genre
character:

> Horror-movie madmen are not visionary obsessives, glorying in
> scientific reason as they single-mindedly pursue their researches.
> They are, rather, victims of overpowering impulses that well up from
> within; monsters brought forth by the sleep of reason, not by its

attractions. Horror-movie psychotics murder, terrorize, maim and rape because of some inner compulsion, because the psyche harbours the dangerous excesses of human passion. (*Monsters* 185)

This recognizably human passion, however distorted, is what is so insidious and threatening about serial killers in particular. In spite of cultural attempts at demonization, serial killers resist such distancing efforts.[2] Dana Polan contends that horror narratives "now suggest that the horror is not merely among us, but rather part of us, caused by us" (202). This tendency toward moral equivalency produces an unresolved tension in most serial murder narratives. The killers are coded as monsters, but a tragic personal history of abuse and neglect is also usually foregrounded as part of the narrative, humanizing them to at least some extent and making them capable of earning our sympathy.[3] The overall effect of this tension is to draw our attention to the process of storytelling itself when we see how earlier genre conventions of "monsterdom" are played with and overlaid onto the recognizably human killer.

Yet the serial killers' actions by their very nature cannot help but propel them into the mythic territory reserved for the most extreme taboo violators. Their random murders pollute, in that they often involve gross injury, mutilation, and dismemberment. They morally violate society's laws and affront personal notions of propriety and civilized conduct. They threaten intellectual chaos through sheer inaccessibility of motive. It is little wonder, then, that real-life serial killers incur unprecedented levels of opprobrium, and that their fictional counterparts exemplify an aesthetic decentering of meaning common to horror narrative strategy. Serial murders imply an infinite progression and regression; the murderer's identity is not solidly cast—it will typically be at least doubled in the narrative, if not tripled or quadrupled. Even as serial killers narcissistically seek reflection on the outer screen represented by their victims, they reflect back all attempts to read them.

In another context, Jacques Derrida explains the importance of doubling to perception:

> For what is reflected is split in itself and not only as an addition to itself of its image. The reflection, the image, the double, splits what it doubles. . . . What can look at itself is not one; and the law of the addition of the origin to its representation, of the thing to its image, is that one plus one makes at least three. (36)

Similarly, Michel Foucault points to the Other as a metaphor for what he calls the "unthought," or unconscious mind:

> The unthought (whatever name we give it) is not lodged in man like a shrivelled-up nature or a stratified history; it is, in relation to man, the Other: the Other that is not only a brother but a twin, born, not of man, nor in man, but beside him and at the same time, in an identical newness, in an unavoidable duality. . . . it is both exterior to him and indispensable to him: in one sense, the shadow cast by man as he emerged in the field of knowledge; in another, the blind stain by which it is possible to know him. In any case, the unthought has accompanied man, mutely and uninterruptedly, since the nineteenth century. . . . [It is] the inexhaustible double that presents itself to reflection as the blurred projection of what man is in his truth, but that also plays the role of a preliminary ground upon which man must collect himself and recall himself in order to attain his truth. For though this double may be close, it is alien, and the role, the true undertaking, of thought will be to bring it as close to itself as possible; the whole of modern thinking is imbued with the necessity of thinking the unthought. . . . (326–27)

Given Foucault's basic assertion that the modern consciousness is given shape by a dialectical tension between the rational and nonrational mind, the funhouse-reflective serial murderer is a fitting metaphor for the modern man philosophically in extremis. Modernist serial killers, absorbed into their unthought selves, commit to a dualist project that is at once systematic and messy. They perpetrate a violent penetration of boundaries that upsets epistemological, ontological, and teleological conceptions. Literary and cinematic conventions are distorted but not abandoned to more realistically depict their "madness." The result is fictional narrative that seems at once fractured and seamless in its pursuit of more spectacle. As W. H. Rockett concludes in his study of horrific film narrative:

> Thanks to [those filmmakers] who have returned to the Lovecraft notion of the universe turned upside down and improved upon it to turn the upside down universe sideways through convention twisting and the abandonment of strict Aristotelean narrative conventions, today's audience enters a theater knowing anything can happen. (135)

The horror story where "anything can happen" exists within a larger generic territory comprised of what Linda Williams calls "body genres." The body genre is characterized by its depiction of "the spectacle of a body caught in the grip of intense sensation or emotion" and also "the focus on what could probably best be called a form of ecstacy . . . a quality of uncontrollable convulsion or spasm" ("Film Bodies" 4). The very excess of the images seeks to replicate itself in the reactive, sympathetic body of the spectator. The genre's grossly immediate effects tend to associate it with "low" or "easy" cultural forms—much like the serial format. The body genre can run the gamut from "splatter" like H. G. Lewis's *Blood Feast* to what Williams calls "weepie" women's melodrama. Manohla Dargis identifies a certain type of body-genre narrative as "pulp," ranging from the early-twentieth-century cheap magazines that published multigeneric stories of horror, adventure, and detection; to early noir detective and "roughneck" films of the 1930s and 1940s; to the A-List outlaw and gangster movies of the 1970s; to the 1990s "Tarantino school" self-referential updates of genre favorites (6–9). Most relevant to this discussion are pulp novels such as Jim Thompson's *The Killer Inside Me,* which Mark Seltzer examines in great detail as a prototypical serial killer narrative in his own book. The noir characteristics of pulp can be seen in the tone of paranoia and themes of compromised morality and anti-authoritarianism—what Lee Horsley deems the Dashiell Hammett influence evident, for example, in the contemporary "pulp" mysteries of James Ellroy (142–43).

The links between the general category of pulp/body fiction and the serial killer text, as elucidated by Robert Conrath ("Serial Heroes" 154–55), establish the beginnings of a critical reckoning with the latter. Like horror, noir, pulp, and other such "body genres," the serial killer subgenre is part of a cultural return to the immediacy of a raw sensuality both absolute and dark. These texts dramatize the fears and lusts of the flesh in a modern world undergoing an intellectual crisis of representation.

The Serial Killer Subgenre and Its Conventions

The serial killer story, as a subgeneric movement within the totality of body genres, has evolved its own fairly rigid set of rules that audiences are quite conscious of—a system of narrative obligations and expectations given satirical treatment in Wes Craven's *Scream* movies, or more straight-faced revision in Jon Amiel's 1995 film *Copycat.* But the fictional serial killer, with a "motiveless," idiosyncratic modus operandi, is only the latest manifestation of the homicidal maniacs that have proliferated in American literature and visual media such as cinema and television.

The serial killer subgenre, most strictly speaking, dates from the late 1970s or early 1980s with the coinage and widespread dissemination of the term "serial murder," and so that is where I will concentrate upon selected works of serial killer fiction.[4] In these works, the serial killer is at once transcendental and reductive, literally programmed to commit murder according to some hermetically structured pattern or design, but a pattern that in and of itself magically contains some manifest, nonrational appeal. In praxis, the serial murders are indicative of a sort of atavistic modernism—a totalizing project that works backward to primitivism. Serial killers, through the heinousness of their acts, defy ready understanding and to observers confirm the darkest fears about human nature. This makes them worst-case-scenario characters pliable to any number of authorial ideological agendas from both the left and the right ends of the political spectrum. But it is generally safe to conclude that serial killers in fiction are debased and traumatized visionaries, whose murders privately re-empower them with a pseudo-divine aura. In many of these treatments, the extremely physical method by which the serial killer seeks to achieve a personal apotheosis subtextually implies that individual human nature is somehow bifurcated into a rational self in opposition to an un-rational or Jungian Shadow self. Within this context, the Shadow is the stronger, more compelling, and more corrupting and dangerous of the two. Human nature as foundationally flawed or erring requires an internal censor, which during the dialectic is in constant danger of metaphysical co-option by the desire and sin of the unthought self or, lacking that censor, some form of external governor or constraint. In most works in this subgenre, then, there is a melancholy sense that mankind, because it is always susceptible to committing evil of this magnitude, is ultimately doomed.

In spite of the fairly recent coinage of the term "serial killer," the subgenre is a hybrid with a long pedigree. It is a dark patchwork of earlier genre depictions of multiple murderers and folkloric threatening figures. This confluence of genre elements has been reworked over the years into the contemporary moment and packaged for mass reconsumption in pseudo-demonic forms simultaneously derivative of popular conceptualizations and folk legends of vampires and werewolves but subtly reflective of the peculiar cultural anxieties of America in the late twentieth century. The elegant, aristocratic vampire as a product of nineteenth- and twentieth-century literature, for example, transmogrifies quite easily into the contemporary serial killer beloved of journalistic tabloids, hit movies, and best-selling novels. He is a neo-Gothic villain and demon lover. That the contemporary serial killer inhabits Gothic territory so easily is no accident. The cultural representation of multiple murder, whether presented as fact or fiction, changes its guises from generation to generation but is not new to our recent history, as Philip Jenkins observes ("Serial Murder" 377–92). The current popularity of serial killer narratives can be explained as the latest twentieth-century redressing of the ongoing human fascination with tales of gruesome murders and evil villains finding a receptive audience in a nation galvanized by an escalating dialectic between the Manichean philosophies of both the New Right and the anti–New Right.

The "serial killer" as labeled by the FBI during the American 1980s and passed into the mass-media instruments of popular culture, ever quick to cater to the prevailing ideological winds, is a fantastic confabulation of Gothic/romantic villain, literary vampire and werewolf, detective and "pulp" fiction conceits, film noir outsider, frontier outlaw, folkloric threatening figure, and nineteenth-century pseudo-sociological conceptions of criminal types given contemporary plausibility.[5] All of these, in turn, are mytho-apocalyptic guises of the murdering Other, whose seemingly random but idiosyncratically meaningful, ritualistic invasions of bodies serve as metaphors for and invocations of the generalized, boundary-leveling violence of catastrophic apocalypse itself. The serial killer is a literalization of the devoured/devouring world motif in carnivalesque folk culture. In such a culture, as Mikhail Bakhtin observes, the limits between human flesh and the rest of the world are blurred or erased altogether (317). As an updated version of the murdering bogeyman, the serial killer lurks in the shadows of communal existence, taking down those who stray from the herd. The folk demonology represented in the narrative exploits of shape-shifters and blood-drinking monsters such as vampires, werewolves, and now serial killers dramatizes those rare but spectacular occasions when humans for private reasons have appropriated the state's traditional power to murder humans en masse.

The mass-media purveyors of the serial killer legends in contemporary America respond quickly to their perceptions of the public's interests, fears, and concerns exactly because the media's economic survival is chained so thoroughly to the need to retain an audience that demands an extraordinary mix of the culturally forbidden and the socially conservative—much like the courtly audience for the French fairy tales of the seventeenth century (Zipes 11). Media instruments react to any dramatic social phenomenon in a rumor cycle of ever-inflating narrative claims very recognizable to the folklorist. The net result is the creation of an overarching contemporary mythology where aliens abduct women from their homes in the dead of night and invade their wombs to create human/alien hybrids, where rural satanic cults ritually sacrifice babies and children and eat their hearts, and where serial killers mutilate and devour the lost and unwary travelers in the American mythscape. The killer alien and the serial killer are elements or fragments being coordinated in some as yet unclear but emerging mythology.

But one of the mythology's clearest principles is that the malevolent lurks in the everyday. Our technological, brightly lit America may resemble a postmodern interactive soundstage. But in the contemporary mythology, many of the seemingly ordinary, even boring, actors on its stage retire behind drawn curtains to be abducted by aliens on the passive level. On the more active level, the actors sexually violate or beat their loved ones, stoke masturbatory fantasies with child porn and snuff photos clandestinely purchased from other countries through the Internet when not feverishly seeking underaged sex partners on-line, worship Satan while listening to Nine Inch Nails and Marilyn Manson, and kill strangers in order to keep their heads in the freezer and their sex organs in a pot on the stove. Such are the radically paranoid elements of the mythological worldview that takes a fearful America into the new millennium.

Given this paranoid mythology, I wish to discuss in the pages ahead one of its recurrent themes—multiple murder—as it specifically functions in numerous formative, influential serial killer narratives of the American 1970s, 1980s, and 1990s. The serial killer's recent popularity as monster in this country is an uneasy expression of a superficially apolitical craving for the simple reassurance of seamless and universal myths to mitigate the endless paradoxes and struggles of the present moment. The serial killer of recent American fiction is embarked upon a quest not of self-discovery but of self-recovery—recovery of a lost metaphysical certitude. In this sense, the serial killers are modernists, but where they depart from modernism is their extreme skepticism of Logos, or the yoking of word to meaning. For the more intellectual serial killers of fiction, language is an ironic game or joke to be played with and upon exasperated opponents who from their rationalist, modernist perspectives still believe in meaning as negotiated by language. For the more brutish serial killers, language is to be avoided as much as possible, if not altogether. For both types, only actions—the immediately sensual—carry an urgency or warrant of meaning in the glossy artificiality of the contemporary world.

None of this is to suggest that the serial killer stories haunting our postmodern media are nihilistic or apolitical. In fiction, contemporary American serial killers often still work within the American cultural grand narrative of "frontier individualism." They are actually what some might call affirmative postmodernists. They have accepted a political agenda—popularized during the middle of the twentieth century but partially anticipated in many earlier literary and philosophical formulations—of challenging all epistemological limits, including the "sacred cows" of liberal humanism. But neither have they necessarily deposed or destroyed them as true avant-garde modernists might. This affirmative postmodernism as practiced by serial killers is broad enough to incorporate both liberal and conservative political agendas. However, if one accepts that neoconservatism is the primary American political mood of the 1980s through the twenty-first century, it follows that for the moment, anyway, American individualism will display a distinctly Rightist bent. But whether coming from the Left or Right, postmodernity as a cultural force evokes a crisis-as-spectacle atmosphere (Olsen 13) in which literal violence as well as increasingly sensational narrative representations of it can easily flourish, simply because the postmodern transgression of all boundary is inherently a "violent" act of cognition. Thus, the proliferation of serial murder narratives over the past decade and a half should be perceived as one specialized branching, and not a terribly novel one, of a more generalized movement toward violent spectacle in the arts. It follows, then, that the spectacular criminal, such as the serial killer, will achieve "A-List" status in popular entertainment.

Contemporary serial killers in fiction resonate deeply with the American public because they so literally express what many people feel—an extreme frustration with not only the dehumanizing complexities of mass democracy (Conrath, "Serial Heroes" 151) but the representational ambiguities of the postmodern world. As what Foucault calls an "empirico-transcendental doublet" (319), the serial killer is pathologized by an inability to balance experience and aesthetics, finding purity in neither and so seeking to recover both. The serial killer seeks transcendental meaning in the traditional manner of idealistic truth seekers but is thwarted by the indeterminacy of experience. This frustrated aesthetic eschews or mocks arid intellectualism and turns increasingly toward the primal, often violent and grossly sensual immediacy of prethought or nonrational mythic patterns, including ritualized multiple murder, but in such a clinical and detached fashion that one still sees the modernist inside the beast. The serial killer's murder trajectory aspires toward sociological liberation and higher meaning, even as it drops to the nadir of human behavior. It is a vertiginous project, leading its author into a reductive pattern of compulsive killing that attempts to correspond to an ideal held in the killer's expansive fantasies. It might even be said that the killer is an example of Kenneth Burke's definition of the pious criminal: "If a man who is a criminal lets the criminal trait in him serve as the informing aspect of his character . . . the criminal deterioration which the moralist with another point of view might discover in him is the very opposite of deterioration as regards the test of piety" (77). The romantic linkage of art and divinity to criminality—even murder as Cameron and Fraser have pointed out in de Sade and Genet's works—serves as prerequisite for contemporary narrative obsession with serial murder, which substitutes repetition for creativity, pattern for design, and the spilled blood of corpses for paints.

In addition to a focus on the complexities of artistic representation, it can also be said that serial killer fictions enact an open-ended dialectic between the need to conform to the social system and the secret desire to flout its rules with impunity. Fictional serial killers, who out of necessity conceal their murderous identities from those who would stop them, exhibit "absolute conformism to the system without believing in the system" (Seltzer 163). In one key aspect, however, the killers do exemplify an historic American "virtue"—the reliance on violence as a means of self-expression. Serial killers, deviants extraordinaire, are no deviants at all in their American desire to exempt themselves from the societal restrictions against murder in order to fulfill a higher, consecrated purpose with which many of their countrymen would find sympathy, if not approval.

American serial killer fiction, while primarily concentrating on its pessimism about unrestrained human nature, addresses history and social problems but not in any complex way. Rather, the effort is made to provide one or two easily identified scapegoats as root causes of the violence, or to give contemporary fears of Others a narrative structure for the purpose of making them somewhat manageable, if only by proxy. Other violent media or child abuse often appear as the "culprit" in the subgenre—in much the same way that atomic testing during 1950s "dinosaur/giant insect/mutated human-on-the-loose" films is dangled before the audience as just enough explanation to make the outlandish scenarios plausible. Paradoxically, the violent stories provoke and reassure American middle-class audiences by confirming their commonly held even if rarely publicly vocalized paranoias about class and lifestyle—that yes, their fears of homosexuals and single career women over thirty and male strangers from both the elitist upper classes and the grubby lower classes are quite justified.

Viewed from this perspective, the narratives mostly serve, intentionally or otherwise, to uphold the patriarchal, law-and-order status quo. They also divert narrative attention away from harmful economic and social policies, which do far more violence against persons than the relatively rare phenomenon of serial murder committed by isolated individuals. The serial killer story, in spite of its focus on a malignant social reality, offers little to nothing in the way of genuine social reform. Such a story typically reduces complex issues of modern communal existence into individual Gothic melodrama relayed in a reassuringly traditional, linear narrative form.

However, one must be careful to avoid monolithic and ultimately reductive interpretations of any text, let alone a large grouping of them centered around so polysemous a figure as the serial killer. Because one of postmodernism's key conceits is that it is impossible to suppress completely a text's own internal resistance to a unified authorial voice, very real possibilities of subversion and reform of established order do coexist, side by side, with the countersubversive voice of American serial killer fiction. Maybe the inherent structural complexities of a narrative that casts an inscrutable multiple murderer as a central character saves some of these texts from being polemical rants against a naked singularity. The manner in which these fictional characters are constructed often subverts vested ideological interests and indeed all such boundaries, in a manner typical to contemporary, Gothic-derived horror texts (Modleski 162). Ideological partisanship or advocacy may be obvious at various points in the narrative, but the tone will rarely hold throughout the text before another equally compelling opposition or possibility arises. There is little doubt this internal ideological self-destabilization stems from the serial killer subgenre's enormous debt to Gothic fiction, which David Punter identifies as a "dialectic of comfort and disturbance . . . a continuous oscillation between reassurance and threat" (423).

The reason that the serial killer text usually frustrates any kind of unified, modernist-type ideological analysis lies in its romantic (more accurately, Gothic) legacy of transgression of all boundaries as a conscious narrative agenda. Violation itself becomes the purpose and the meaning of the text rather than a conscious privileging of one distinct ideological system over another. Perhaps the safest ideological conclusion to draw from these narratives is that they are relentlessly pessimistic about human nature, which is seen as polarized into saint and sinner, the two locked in perpetual private struggle for control of the body. The serial killer as metaphor collapses boundaries between good and evil, Left and Right, male and female, high art and kitsch. What is revealed standing in the ruins is not the Noble Savage but the Beastly Cannibal. The killer's behavior is almost always constructed as an acting-out of what everyone else in the narrative feels an urge to do in the first place but is prohibited from only by custom and practice, which illustrates the Gothic's deeply pessimistic underbelly. Admittedly, serial killers through extreme and arguably evil acts lend themselves to extreme interpretations, but one must be very cautious in conclusions so drawn. In serial killer fiction, in spite of its deceptively traditional narrative structure, individual identities reveal their fragile constitutions. Selves blur, conflate, and shift with aggravating fluidity. This indeterminacy of self in relation to Other and environment is a standard of earlier Gothic fiction.

Before this discussion can go much further, it is first necessary to separate the fictional serial killers from the actual ones studied and sensationalized by criminologists and journalists alike. In spite of the destability of rigidly defined fact and fiction in discussions of serial murder, the conventions that shape the serial killer in contemporary American fictional media must be as sharply distinguished as possible from sociological or journalistic definitions of serial murder, however much fiction writers base their murderous creations on the reports of those who chronicle serial-murder case studies. The fictional serial killer bears little relation to his real-life counterparts, such as the psychosexually disturbed Ted Bundy or Ed Gein. In fiction, serial killers are often more exotic in terms of methodology and pathology, as authors seldom resist the temptation to sensationalize them in some uniquely identifiable way, no matter how restrained the narrative treatment overall. They are violent but less impassioned examples of what John Fraser has defined as the violator figure in literature, one who is so obsessed that he or she literally loses self-consciousness in "an intensity of passion" not unrelated to ancient definitions of demonic possession (20–21). However, the fictional serial killer's form of visionary possession expresses itself not so much in a frothing "madman's" rage but rather in chilling abstraction and a deliberate, almost mechanical precision well in keeping with the industrial age, as Mark Seltzer argues in *Wound Culture.* Consequently, the serial killer's "signature" crimes tend to be sensational but rigidly unvarying in practice— mechanical and repetitive. In some treatments of the subject, serial killers are almost literally monochromatic automatons, mindlessly acting out again and again primal traumas and unvarying in their "signatures." They exemplify what Herbert Blau says of repetition: that it is a metaphoric "pregnancy without birth, and thus the end of reproduction, the structure of repetition which is the economy of death" (70). As Blau elucidates, repetition encapsulates a kind of death in life, or a cyclically regressive motion without hope of saving tangents or new influences.[6]

Even given the mechanical nature of their actions, fictional serial killers' motives are usually more metaphysically, psychologically, and culturally grandiose or, inversely, completely nihilistic, than those of their real-life counterparts. They are authorially invested with layers of meaning and metaphor, all of which are destabilized in the course of the narrative. Their character is an elaborate construct designed exclusively to test—in many cases without providing firm answers and in others ludicrously partisan ones—philosophical maxims (free will versus determinism), psychological systems (usually psychoanalytic), socioeconomic models (capitalism in particular), and, of course, the binary nature of good and evil itself. Their inscrutability will invite multiple readings from other characters within the narrative (and from those reading it), who will invariably project their deepest fears and longings onto the blank screen the killers represent. They are broadly allegorical in the sense that Fredric Jameson defines allegory:

> On the global scale, allegory allows the most random, minute, or isolated landscapes to function as a figurative machinery in which questions about the system and its control over the local ceaselessly rise and fall, with a fluidity that has no equivalent . . . a host of partial subjects, fragmentary or schizoid constellations, can often now stand in allegorically for trends and forces in the world system, in a transitional situation in which genuinely transnational classes, such as a new international proletariat and a new density of global management, have not yet anywhere clearly emerged. (*Geopolitical* 5)

In light of Jameson's general definition, B. Ruby Rich's thesis concerning the recent popularity of the serial killer subgenre carries added weight. She argues that serial murderers, at least in their late 1980s and early 1990s incarnations when they gained their current cultural appeal, allegorically represent the domestic tensions inherent in a world that has lost its master narrative of the Cold War (6). These domestic tensions include, but are not limited to, the fear of strangers in a mobile society, the fear of the upper and lower classes, the fear of sexual relationships, and the fear of international capitalist corporations and ruthless management.[7] The serial killer's status as all-purpose cultural bogeyman guarantees a ready audience to any storyteller, no matter how skilled or unskilled, and ensures that the commodi-

fication will continue indefinitely. The serial killer's commodification possibilities are virtually limitless because as literary figure it is easily adaptable
to modern print or visual media. In fact, Richard Dyer argues that capitalistic media itself is based on what he calls seriality:

> the mix of repetition and anticipation, and indeed of the anticipa-
> tion of repetition . . . However, it is only under capitalism that se-
> riality became a reigning principle of cultural production, starting
> with the serialisation of novels and cartoons, then spreading to news
> and movie programming. Its value as a selling device for papers and
> broadcasts is obvious. (14)

Dyer then makes the case that the serial killer is a natural character type for
a modern media based on the pleasure of seriality.

As a fictional character in modern media, the serial killer displays several faces, many within the same narrative: outlaw artist, visionary, hyper-
intelligent gameplayer, masculine hero, or demonic punisher. Most striking
to the observer of the subgenre is its near-obsessive linkage of serial murder
to art, even in the deliberately clinical prose of the social-science and law-
enforcement journals, upon which much of the fiction is based. The literary connection between the murderous impulse and the creative urge dates
back to at least the romantic era. Crime itself, as the term and its connotations of individual transgression against the bourgeois social contract are
commonly understood, is a relatively modern phenomenon. It coincides with
the late-eighteenth-century advent of literary romanticism as part of a general cultural trend to privilege the metaphysical individual sensibility over
what Joel Black calls "conventional morality as encoded in human law" (30).
Thus, the law-breaking criminal and the tradition-shattering artist forge an
individual "vision," as both rebel against the strictures of inherited middle-
class ethics and values. As marginal figures, the artist and criminal share a
real kinship. Black observes that murder "fascinated the romantic sensibility" (56). Murder fascinates the Gothic and postromantic sensibility as well.[8]
The proliferation of texts, both factual and fictional, that combine the sensationalism of serial murder with an often ill-fitting overlay of classical references are an inevitable consequence of a metadiscursive culture where the
modernist concept of "high art" has ironically combined with the boundary-piercing, rebellious agenda of individual romanticism to create mass-
market variations on Thomas De Quincey's now-notorious ideas of "murder as fine art." Thus, it is not surprising that most of our fictional serial

killers are artist manqués. They strive to impose a private and romantic vision of self upon the flow of consensual reality in the time-honored fashion of unappreciated, isolated artists everywhere.

Another common face of the fictional serial killer is that of the game-player of superior, perhaps even genius, intellect. The cultural construction of serial murder, fact or fiction, often emphasizes the intellectual abilities of the killer, positing someone brighter or more cleverly manipulative than the average American. As a trickster, the killer often displays a macabre sense of humor, both in words and actions.[9] As a dramatic device, this intelligence allows the killer to engage in protracted and highly intricate cat-and-mouse games, involving layer upon layer of ruse, deception, red herrings, and encryption with victims and law enforcement alike. Such valorization of the serial killer's supposed genius serves two agendas, as Richard Tithecott argues: "estrangement and celebration" (146). The killers are estranged in the sense that they are again superficially rendered as Other apart from standards of normality, in this case relating to intelligence. But they are also celebrated, in the sense that rationality as virtue exists within them as well, and this makes them recognizably human even if we are incapable of understanding their motives. Tithecott is quick to point out, however, that the rationality and supposed high intelligence of serial killers makes them sane and therefore capable of being incarcerated as an "evil" transgressor in accordance with countersubversive ideological principles.

A third face of the serial killer is the masculine hero, or what Tithecott calls "the warrior knight" (150). Some critics of the subgenre, such as Caputi and Cameron and Fraser, argue that the serial killer is a logical embodiment of masculine values of conquest and rapine, both explicitly expressed and implicitly encoded, within a patriarchal culture built on a foundation of "chivalry." The chivalric knight, at least as the popular culture has defined him, illustrates the self-delusional nature of the conquering/seducing hero. He fancies himself to be a gallant and courteous protector of the weak and courtier of damsels, but in actuality is a paternalist at best and a murdering rapist at worst.

The fictional serial killer also often appears to be a visionary preparing for a unique form of mystic transport through an amalgamation of Christian ritual or primitivist magic based on blood sacrifice. The killer attempts to erase the difference between temporal self and eternity by restoring the ancient practice of ritual sacrifice to the culture's bloodless mouthing of spiritual doctrine—doctrine originally based in what René Girard in another context calls the collective rituals of institutionalized murder designed for the purpose of preventing individual murder (102). Where the serial killer becomes an enemy of society, then, is not necessarily in a desire to murder, which civilization will thoughtfully redirect into socially acceptable manifestations, but rather in a willingness to eschew the approved social channels and instead sacrifice victims of the killer's own choosing. Even then, however, serial killers are imitating the qualities of individual initiative and resourcefulness—qualities highly valued in American society—so they are never as Other as might be supposed at first glance. Indeed, the fact that in most narratives the killer attracts so many zombie-like disciples, or at least compels thoughtful observers to acknowledge their own murderous impulses, only reinforces the notion that serial killers literalize spiritual and nationalistic ideals that most of their fellow Americans share.

A fifth face of the serial killer is that of the demonic messenger and punisher, both of transgressive individuals and civilizations. This guise is potentially the most conservative or socially minded in its intolerance of deviance from traditional norms and values. Simultaneously, it is the most nihilistic or skeptical in its destruction of all communal possibilities. And it is the most personally reaffirming in its merging of the individual with the godhead—the master of all master narratives. The demonic serial killer is a "monster" in the most ancient meaning of the word—as omen of divine favor or disfavor. Many of these narratives establish that the serial killer appears as a nightmarishly literal manifestation of the "normal" protagonist's deepest fears or taboo desires—a "natural" outgrowth of sin. Through intense conflict with this id made flesh, the protagonist either triumphs over base urges or succumbs to them, but in any eventuality is severely traumatized for having harbored or in some cases acted on such desires in the first place. The serial killer's function in such a narrative, then, is to serve as an agent of divine justice sent to punish the protagonist's Original Sin, whatever it may be in the context of the narrative. Such a narrative implies, of course, that destiny or determinism—some outer nature—solely rules human action, and that reactive, not proactive, solutions are the only possible strategies to resolve this crisis of selfhood. On a larger narrative plane, the serial killer may also have been "sent" (or at least believe so, which amounts to the same thing) to destroy—not punish, which implies a future—a society for its evils. In such a text, the demonic serial killer functions as an agent of a catastrophic form of apocalypse that has lost much of its millennial optimism and instead is characterized by despair, not necessarily for the individual but for the society. Because the threat of widespread and nihilistic devastation looms in the near distance, destruction is the primary result of the apocalypse, not rebirth in any redemptive sense. Social reform, then, is impossible. The civilization is destined to die. This argument toward futility on the part of a frustrated reactionary signals the textual presence of perhaps the most skeptical form of contemporary American sensibilities.

These five faces of the serial killer provide a reasonably comprehensive and workable overview of character prototypes within the subgenre. It should be noted that serial killer fiction, as a composite of many genres, finds itself interweaving at least four general structural or thematic patterns: the neo-Gothic, the detective procedural, the "psycho" profile, and the mytho-apocalyptic. Any given narrative may be structured by predominantly one movement or another, but many will employ some proportions of all four in a quadrilateral structuring mechanism.

The first movement, the neo-Gothic, clearly reflects the subgenre's origins in the dark romantic, horror, and melodrama conventions of the nineteenth century by emphasizing the relationship between killer and victim as a type of dangerous seduction taking place in a haunted landscape of taboo violations and border transgressions. The second movement, the detective procedural, focuses heavily on the killer but gives at least equal time to those "detectives," amateur or professional, who have taken it upon themselves to stop him. The third movement, the psycho profile, may adopt any tone or stance toward its subject. Generally speaking, however, it centers upon the killer as protagonist, either placing the audience directly into the murderous point of view or somewhere close by, through friends, lovers, acquaintances, or victims. The mytho-apocalyptic movement recontextualizes or decontextualizes the serial killer from the historical moment in an attempt to give the killer a kind of apotheosis as a demonic messenger whose actions directly or indirectly bring down the "cleansing" fire of apocalypse upon a failed world.

In the chapters ahead, I will respectively discuss and illustrate each of these movements.

I

The
Gothic Legacy and
Serial Murder

The earliest recognizable literary breeding ground for what would become the serial killer fictional narrative is the Gothic tradition. Though the term "Gothic" is overused by critics, nevertheless it remains the most appropriate starting point for this examination of serial killer fiction. Of crucial importance to understanding the destabilizing-of-meaning strategy common to the serial killer subgenre is acknowledgement that its Gothic literary progenitor is devoted to transgression of boundary and breaking of taboo as a textual agenda. Two representative Gothic (or neo-Gothic) texts featuring serial murder will serve as extended illustrations. One is the 1991 Paul West novel *The Women of Whitechapel and Jack the Ripper.* The other is the 1997 Gary Fleder film *Kiss the Girls.*

West's novel is based on an elaborate but largely discredited theory, popularized by the late Stephen Knight in his 1976 book *Jack the Ripper: The Final Solution,* regarding the identity of the Victorian serial murderer nicknamed "Jack the Ripper." According to Knight, the Ripper was not a lone killer but a trio of men who killed five prostitutes who had been blackmailing the British government with their knowledge of Prince Edward's sexual indiscretions and illegitimate daughter. Taking this basic plot outline from Knight's theory, West also portrays three Rippers, each participant representing a different masculine face. The royal physician Sir William Gull is the primary killer—a misogynistic slasher and mutilator who gives the crimes their unmistakable signature. Coachman John Netley and the famous impressionist painter Walter Sickert cooperate, the former gleefully and the latter reluctantly, as corporeal extensions of Gull's formidable but physically incapacitated will. But in and of themselves, none of the three men is "Jack the Ripper." Singular responsibility for the murders is diffused among many contributors and precipitating factors that have joined together at a particular nexus in time, space, and English history.[1]

Gary Fleder's 1997 film *Kiss the Girls,* based on the 1995 novel of the same name by James Patterson, places its two sympathetic protagonists, forensic psychiatrist Alex Cross and medical intern Kate McTiernan, into a deadly confrontation with two serial murderers, "The Gentleman Caller" and "Casanova." In the film, the monomythic Jack the Ripper has split into two neatly compartmentalized, yet complementary, separate killers—one a self-styled "lover" of independent women and the other a vicious mutilator. Both are quite similar, however, in the way they objectify, torture, and murder women. Casanova, for example, who claims to loathe the Gentleman Caller's sexual "sloppiness" as evidenced by his desire to dismember, nevertheless rapes women savagely enough to tear apart their vaginas and leaves them, hair shorn away and limbs bound, to die alone in the forest. When Alex's niece Naomi is kidnapped by Casanova and faces a similar fate, Alex tries to find her in time to save her life. He is aided in his search by Kate, who was also kidnapped by Casanova but escaped from the underground dungeon in which he keeps his female captives. As the investigation continues, Alex discovers that Casanova and the Gentleman Caller actually know each other and are locked in a gruesome rivalry to claim as many victims as possible. The film concludes with both serial killers dead, Naomi rescued, and Alex and Kate victorious.

Serial Murder and the Gothic

A brief historical summary of the boundary-transgressing Gothic genre is necessary to understand how texts such as West's novel and Fleder's film are most accurately labeled as "Gothic." The Gothic mode is not confined exclusively to any one genre or artistic medium. Rather, the conventions break free of their orderly boundaries and filter out into other popular discursive or artistic modes, which in turn later generations of artists and critics alike draw upon for their respective reworkings of inherited formula. David Punter traces the development of the word "Gothic" from its literal meaning of "to do with the Goths" (the Germanic tribes who are said to have precipitated the collapse of the Roman empire) to its more generalized applications in the European eighteenth century, specifically its suggestiveness "of things medieval—in fact, of all things preceding about the middle of the seventeenth century" (5). The barbaric connotations of the word "Gothic" quickly came to invoke a plethora of associations for Europeans: "Gothic was the archaic, the pagan, that which was prior to, or was opposed to, or resisted the establishment of civilised values and a well-regulated society" (6). Writers of fiction, in turn, turned to the precivilized or the "barbaric" as a metaphor for revivifying the supposedly exhausted English culture with a "healthy" injection of primitivism and prelingual awareness. This was a risky operation, of course, as the cure, represented in the ambiguous figure of the mysterious outsider possessed of Dionysian appetites, could just as easily destroy civilization as save it.

In this culturewide turn to "barbarism" as a wild zone apart from the dulling complexities of modern civilization lies the genesis of the Gothic sensibility, which gives rise not only to eponymous literary conventions and architecture but a far more generalized rejection of all things classical. As Punter concludes: "Where the classical was well ordered, the Gothic was chaotic; where simple and pure, Gothic was ornate and convoluted; where the classics offered a set of cultural models to be followed, Gothic represented excess and exaggeration, the product of the wild and the uncivilised" (6). The Gothic is rife with ambiguity, sexual perversion, decenteredness, self-referentiality, repetition, and breakdown of boundary. According to G. R. Thompson, Gothic literature dramatizes the philosophical tension between modern, progressive, and secular notions of man's innate goodness (the romantic influence) and medieval conceptions of man's spiritual corruption. The narrative tantalizes but finally refuses to provide metaphysical illumination or revelation. For Thompson, the purpose of the Gothic narrative ambiguity and occult overtones is to force readers to ask questions about human existence, so that the individual must then rely not on institutional authority but the self for determining moral certitude. Tony Magistrale concludes that the romantic freedom from social constraint is essentially positive because there is an underlying "faith in human nature," whereas the Gothic doubts man's moral faculties—"further suggesting that when their impulses remained unchecked humans were more likely to perform acts of perversity than poetry" (31). The terror of the Gothic (but also its repressed tone of narrative romantic excitement) derives from this kind of intellectual liberation.

The themes of classic Gothic fiction include a strong sense of environmental claustrophobia, the destructive imposition of the past on the present, and a metaphysical internalization of evil for which the Gothic landscape stands as objective correlative. Gothic fiction is also often structured around a menacing but nevertheless captivating villain or monster, which is predecessor to the "attractive" serial killers of 1980s and 1990s fiction, such as Hannibal Lecter (Hutchings 100). In the Gothic, this dark, amoral figure stalks a usually female character through the narrative landscape in a metaphoric seduction.[2] The "dark man" is usually perceived to be a killer, or at least a potential one, but paradoxically, the Gothic villain through his murderer's exile acquires special insight into life, and it is his vision of existence that is narratively privileged, as Judith Wilt has noted in *Ghosts of the Gothic*.

The Gothic, as part of a larger cultural movement of Old World forms and ideologies into the New World, proved readily adaptable to American literature. Not only did the Gothic formulas cross over but so did European romanticism in general, as illustrated by the American reception of the then-popular novels of Sir Walter Scott. Many of the romantic American frontier authors, beginning with James Fenimore Cooper, owed a great debt to Scott. Richard Slotkin elaborates:

> The historical romance was itself a European literary form, and [Cooper] adopted the form as practiced by Walter Scott. . . . The historical romance as practiced by Scott defined history in terms of the conflict between individuals representing nations and classes; and the definition of these class and national types was a primary interest of the writer. Reconciliation between the opposed groups was achieved through the revelation or discovery of a fundamental racial kinship between the parties. . . . The family ties that bind the chief characters of the historical romance provide the metaphorical structure of the work. The division within the family reflects the social disorder of the nation, and the achievement of a familial peace is the conclusion of both the social problem and the family drama. (*Regeneration* 472)

Slotkin then argues that American frontier authors claimed for themselves the notion of "family unity" while simultaneously investing it with a certain irony. The frontier hero usually escapes from the reunited family, fleeing from its constraints out into "the Territory." Huckleberry Finn, of course, is the most famous literary character to do this, but he has his antecedents, such as James Fenimore Cooper's Leatherstocking. Thus, to a greater or lesser extent, the sanctity of the family as refuge is called into question by patriarchal frontier writers because the male escape from family can also be read as a juvenile's escape from a threatening, grown-up woman and the civic virtues and responsibilities she represents.

Leslie Fiedler maintains that the "classic" American novel, while in many ways replicating the tired formulas of European prose fiction, is readily distinguishable by precisely this "pre-adolescent" (4) mentality and its consistent terror of mature sexuality and feminine consciousness. In fact, Fiedler continues, (male) American writers typically shun any adult treatment of heterosexual relations and present their female characters as "monsters of virtue or bitchery, symbols of the rejection or fear of sexuality" (5). Hence, while the female gender looms large (even its narrative absence) in most patriarchal American literature, it exists as a largely impersonal force of nature to be dominated or a pull toward socialization and domestication to be fled.

Nina Baym argues that critical definitions of what constitutes American literature are inherently phallocentric, mythologizing the male individual "divorced from specific social circumstances, with the promise offered by the idea of America" (131). The individual male thus exists before and apart from socialization, and in fact seeks to escape from the "female" entrapment of civilization into the self-affirming, mythic, asocial landscape. Paradoxically, the wilderness is also signified as female in essence, but "no longer subject to the correcting influence of real-life experience" (136) and consequently more and more fantastic and recognizably less contextualized. This realm is ripe for the Gothic treatment. As Baym and Fiedler both observe, the male alone in the asocial wilderness becomes a celibate, infantile wanderer freed from familial obligation and mature sexual relationships. He may have lost his family to hostile outside forces on which he seeks revenge but which have also enacted in reality a murderous agenda he imagined in fantasy (as does the protagonist of Robert Montgomery Bird's *Nick of the Woods,* a prototypical avenger of the sort found in popular films such as *The Searchers* or *Death Wish*). Or, like Cooper's Leatherstocking or Twain's Huck Finn, two celibate perpetual-adolescent figures, he may avoid domesticity altogether.

In such a cultural and literary atmosphere, it is little wonder that murder, that most melodramatic and Gothic expression of the objectification and victimization of the usually feminine or feminized Other, flourishes first in American literature and, later, in cinema. Multiple murder, of a sort roughly comparable to what is now called serial killing, appears quite early in American prose. In addition to the aforementioned *Nick of the Woods* (1835), the novels *Ormond* (1799), *The Partisan* (1835), and *The Quaker City; or, The Monks of Monk Hall* (1845), while mostly derivative of the European Gothic, all present multiple body counts and Shadow villains in which one can see the literary prototypes of the contemporary American serial murderer. For example, George Lippard's *The Quaker City* features a grotesquely deformed multiple murderer named Devil-Bug, who according to David Brion Davis is "interesting primarily as an early ancestor of the countless creatures of horror that infest contemporary comic strips and cheap literature generally" (127). Richard Slotkin in *Gunfighter Nation* makes the same point: "Many [horror/slasher movies] invoke bogeys whose ancestors appear in the literature of the Puritan witch trials, like the Indian or voodoo spirits . . . or murderous backwoodsmen . . . whose literary ancestors are the Harpes and Simon Girtys of early frontier romances" (635).

The kind of cross-fertilization between true-life murder accounts and fictional representation that so troubles contemporary cultural critics is also evident long ago in American letters. No less a luminary than Herman Melville argued in the 1850s that popular literature was overly concerned with the likes of Kentucky's Harpe brothers, two multiple murderers of the 1790s (Jenkins, "Serial Murder" 383). Some of the first nationally prominent cases of "motiveless" or "lust" murder also became known in America during the nineteenth century, such as Thomas Piper's series of child murders in Boston in the 1870s or the murders committed by H. H. Holmes in Chicago during the 1880s and 1890s. Another instance of what we would now call mass murder occurred at a Kansas farm owned by the "Bloody Benders" in the 1870s. All of these cases, in tandem with the popular literature of murder and thuggery, further established a cultural climate in which multiple murder as thematic organizing principle played a minor but definite role.

The Gothic genre's adaptability to film in the twentieth century, made possible by the Gothic reliance on visual imagery (Bunnell 84), ensured the vitality of the fictional murderer to the present cinema-dominated age. The character of the multiple murderer flourished in the new medium. The first cinematic multiple murderers—Cesare in *The Cabinet of Dr. Caligari* (1919), Jack the Ripper in *Waxworks* (1924) and *Pandora's Box* (1929), Franz Becker in *M* (1931), and Count Zaroff in *The Most Dangerous Game* (1932), among others—were European Gothic villains in transition between the premodern romantic era and the modern industrial one. By midcentury, such murderers (Uncle Charlie in *Shadow of a Doubt* [1943] providing the best example) were more unmistakably American in attitude and ideology and much more lethal. In these films and ones to follow, the Gothic has lost many of its superficial trappings (haunted castles and such), but the mythic, ahistorical territory reserved for taboo violators remains central to what many call the neo-Gothic formula—often seen as a category of postmodern fiction.

Allan Lloyd Smith, for one, argues that Gothicism and postmodernism share many parallels, including narrative focus on indeterminacy of meaning, the intrusion of history upon the present, pastiche, criminality, and paranoia of technology and science (6–15). These parallels explain the continued vitality of Gothicism (or neo-Gothicism) within the postmodern world. Barbara Waxman identifies the predominant philosophical conflict in the neo-Gothic as that between the romantic/Gothic imperative of choosing one's actions free of social impediments and the postmodern ironic distance afforded by the recognition that there are always constraints on one's actions. The primary narrative appeal and adaptability of the neo-Gothic resides in its placement of a limited, naïve, but intellectually curious protagonist into a claustrophobic environment. The protagonist is faced with a mysterious, potentially fatal set of circumstances that, while threatening, also educate the innocent seeker, with the "help" of a seducer/mentor, into the destabilizing grayness of worldly experience. This dislocation constitutes a genre variation on what is commonly called the *Erziehungsroman* theme in literature. The various competing and complementary strains of the Gothic-derivative serial killer narrative share in common the *Erziehungsroman* structuring device. Louis Gross identifies this kind of quest for personal education as essentially Gothic in tone and execution:

> Gothic fiction is, first and foremost, literature where fear is the motivating and sustaining emotion. This fear is shared by the characters within the story and the reader. The Gothic thus examines the causes, qualities, and results of terror on both mind and body. It does so in a process of epistemological inquiry, and because it is concerned with the acquisition and internalizing of kinds of knowledge, the Gothic finds an appropriate vehicle in the quest narrative or, more specifically, the *Erziehungsroman* or narrative of education. ... the Gothic journey offers a darkened world where fear, oppression, and madness are the ways to knowledge and the uncontrolled transformation of one's character the quest's epiphany. ... the Gothic quest ends in the shattering of the protagonist's image of his/her social/sexual roles and a legacy of, at best, numbing unease

or, at worst, emotional paralysis and death. The Gothic may then be described as a demonic quest narrative. (1–2)

As contemporary demon and shape-shifter, the American serial killer in fiction moves through the void at the center of what Joe David Bellamy, in his introduction to *Superfiction,* calls the neo-Gothic quest narrative. Irving Malin demonstrates in his study *New American Gothic* that many contemporary American writers in particular use the Gothic images of the haunted castle (transformed into plausibly American settings such as abandoned farmhouses, dark cellars, antebellum plantations, inherited mansions, and so forth) and the forest journey to overlay a veneer of the uncanny on the mundane.

David Punter concurs that the neo-Gothic is a primarily American genre, exemplified by the works of Southern writers Joyce Carol Oates, Flannery O'Connor, and John Hawkes:

> This "New American Gothic" is said to deal in landscapes of the mind, settings which are distorted by the pressure of the principal characters' psychological obsessions. We are given little or no access to an "objective" world; instead we are immersed in the psyche of the protagonist, often through sophisticated use of first-person narrative. It may or may not be coincidence that writers and settings alike have connexions with the American South; in one way or another, feelings of degeneracy abound. The worlds portrayed are ones infested with psychic and social decay, and coloured with the heightened hues of putrescence. Violence, rape and breakdown are the key motifs; the crucial tone is one of desensitised acquiescence in the horror of obsession and prevalent insanity. (3)

As Punter notes, the standard "timeless" trappings of Gothic melodrama—allegedly haunted ruins, womblike caves and subterranean passageways, exotic foreign locales, and so on—are generally carried over into recognizable, contemporary America. The effect on the American reader is to produce the cognitive shock of familiar surroundings unexpectedly rendered threatening and alien. Deeply rural areas, as well as inner-city "war zones," are common settings for the neo-Gothic, although occasionally middle-class suburbia is besieged by invaders from those zones, as happens in Thomas Harris's 1981 novel *Red Dragon.* But most significantly, while "classic" Gothic writers like Ann Radcliffe present apparently supernatural phenomena in order to reveal them, according to Donald Ringe, "as merely delusive appearances" in a world "rationally ordered . . . by natural law" (27), the neo-Gothics are far less sanguine about the stability of the base of natural law. Certain supernatural (or more accurately, extranormal) phenomena may indeed exist for the neo-Gothics, which possibly explains the prevalence of vampiric imagery, apparent precognition, and psychic transference in many neo-Gothic narratives, especially the serial killer ones.[3] Even in narratives that steadfastly resist any true supernatural coding of their murderous protagonists, the characters often receive intuitive, perhaps even psychic flashes of warning regarding the killer's designs on them. The narrative presence of such uncanny external forces suggests that fate controls human action and that human nature is immutably fixed.

Several motifs signify the presence of the neo-Gothic. First of all, the neo-Gothic is consciously metatextual, drawing attention to the process of fiction-making and conspicuously borrowing from other genres (for example, detective fiction) and their conventions when appropriate. Second, the disorienting geography of the fictional realm is haunted by a dark villain and apparently supernatural omens. Third, the neo-Gothic studies gender issues in exquisitely minute detail, frequently emphasizing sexual danger and ambivalence in violent terms. The threatened maiden who learns painful but necessary lessons about life's patriarchal dangers, she of the classic Gothic formula, can now take on a variety of forms, both male and female, as gender conventions blur and reverse in the neo-Gothic with astounding regularity. Paradoxically and destabilizingly enough, the "threatened maiden" may now even be the killer himself in losing flight from his self-destructive sociopathology.[4]

But in all the various permutations of the neo-Gothic formula, of which the serial killer subgenre is only one borrower, the body receives or is threatened by grotesque levels of the extreme violence usually found only in nightmare, to paraphrase Bellamy. The violence, actual or threatened, then functions as the narrative crucible in which character is formed, deformed, or reformed. Knowledge is dearly purchased in the neo-Gothic, as it usually comes at the expense of horrendous and often unbearable levels of fear, pain, and personal ruin. If the characters survive the ordeal, the knowledge they have accrued better enables them to cope with the demands of a fiercely violent and deceptive environment in which the bland normality of chivalric young men masks ravenous monsters. These monsters are not supernatural, of course. Rather, they are postmodern monsters that exist only in terms of how the killers' actions are received by their culture.

It is thus clear that the neo-Gothic sensibility is perhaps the single greatest influence in the development of the patchwork subgenre of serial killer fiction. Most of these works portray their killers as modernized Gothic villains—Shadow seducers who simultaneously live on the margins of society and within it. They stalk victims, mostly women, through a dark mythic landscape teeming with supernatural portents. The threatened women must fight back, with varying degrees of success. But more than any other element, the neo-Gothic serial killer narrative displays an astounding degree of indeterminacy, largely because the killers are such polysemous entities. They defy easy reading as they impose their own reading on an environment all too adaptable to their will. They invite subversive questions the consumers of ideology never before thought to ask, and destabilize pat assumptions about the world even as their threatening presence argues for the strongest possible restoration of protective social institutions. Almost every narrative in the serial killer canon of fiction exhibits this ambivalence toward stability and destability.

Savage Fictions and Serial Murder

One of the most crucial boundaries transgressed by the neo-Gothic protagonist is that between reality and the imagination. The individual internal psyche projects itself on the external environment, and the external environment invades the internal. The result, then, is an externally determining and determined psyche. A corresponding narrative conceit is that the act of writing or creating, normally considered a private action, is a public act, capable of bizarre and evil transformations of environment even if benignly conceived. The neo-Gothic is a critique of the imaginative dangers of human fiction-making. The multiple murderer its most demonic "author," writing his sensual will upon the world in an exaggeration of more "normal" acts of writing. In the neo-Gothic, the mass media in turn perpetuates serial murder by ensuring that a killer's text, with just a touch of the supernatural thrown in for melodramatic chills, reaches the widest possible audience. Caputi calls this process the "propaganda of sex crime/gynocide" (*Age* 30), which attempts nothing less than a universalization of specifically historical, real-life individuals into ahistorical, almost Jungian archetypes for a mass audience. Indeed, Richard Blennerhassett argues that the cinematic serial killer is a manifestation of the Jungian Shadow complex (101–4).

Additionally, many real-life serial killers have been accorded this same mythic status in "objective" press coverage of their deeds. Certainly, one sees a Jungian-like process of universalization in deliberate operation during the press coverage of the Jack the Ripper murders in 1888 London. Jack the Ripper's cultural longevity is due almost entirely to his contemporary press reception, as Clive Bloom notes (123). It is not inappropriate to call Jack the Ripper the first serial killer, simply because the Ripper's advent on the stage of media consciousness happened to coincide with the serial format as popularized in the Victorian press. Periodicals thrived on serial installments, and British newspapers (nearly two hundred of them) imposed the same narrative construct on the flux of existence as they engaged in fierce competition for circulation (Begg 15). The chapter-by-chapter Ripper murders, with the discovery of the sexually mutilated bodies spaced days or weeks apart, were ideal for serial treatment. To fudge further the boundary between fact and fiction, the English press wasted no time framing the murders in the shrill, moralistic conventions of popular stage melodrama. The temptation for the newspapers to editorialize and fictionalize was too great to resist, and any pretensions toward objectivity were completely discarded.

Paul West's novel *The Women of Whitechapel and Jack the Ripper* also touches on the destructive power of human fiction-making and the utter impossibility of maintaining a detached or privileged observer's distance from that which is observed/observing. The collective inherited fictions of myth and communal narrative in the Gothic retain an amazing, transcendentally inhuman ability to cause havoc in the present and distort malignantly the future. These myths are destructive, the neo-Gothic insists, because they tend to erase disharmony or contradiction in the interest of creating a uniform but exclusionary vision of reality. One of these conduits of myth, in the (post)-modern environment, is the mass media, comprised of discrete contributors all working toward production of easily consumable master narratives. These fictions inherently possess the procrustean power to force complex existence within a too-constrictive frame. West's novel indicts mass-produced fictional narrative as a coconspirator in the perpetuation of violent crime, simply because narrative runs the danger of reducing phenomenology to an overly formulaic, too-familiar level.

Following the murder of the first victim, Polly Nichols, the painter Walter Sickert broods that the Ripper's potential victims, currently frightened, will become inured to violence because the human desire to render terror manageable by dramatizing it actually trivializes it to the level of children's-rhyme doggerel:

> The horror would melt into prattle, that was all, and the headlines of the past few days would vanish in their incessant mouths. . . .

London swallowed its horrors daily and made them anew, knowing it could always toss them back with enough gin, enough of a
head-fling. Polly would survive only if they made up a rhyme about
her in the East End and children played jump-rope to it. (254)

At an only slightly more sophisticated level than street rhyme, the London
newspapers immediately leap to sensationalism. They create the Ripper directly from stage conventions and blatantly invent supernatural details for
the purposes of a better story. For example, an East End prostitute, according to the newspapers, "had a vision of Long Liz at the moment of the murder, leaning over her bed in walking-out clothes, telling her not to worry.
How theatrical" (310). Newspapers such as the *Illustrated Police News* recon-
struct details of the crimes for voyeuristic consumers, relying on rhetorically
inflated headlines such as "The Strange Story Told of a Man with a Black
Bag" and "Lured to the Slaughter" (323) to grab reader attention. The newspapers' sensationalism further aggravates civic paranoia as inaccurate and
conflicting descriptions of the "solitary" Ripper are circulated, creating a
transcendent villain "in both reality and myth so generic that he might be
found almost anywhere, which meant that most of male London had killed
Stride and her carnations" (313). Gull, the lead Ripper, gleefully exploits the
media's need to create villains by writing a coarse, pseudo-illiterate series of
letters to the newspapers in which he taunts the police, reveals details of the
crimes, boasts of more carnage to come, and calls himself "Jack the Ripper."
The press instantly seizes on the name, leading Gull to reflect:

> The whole of London . . . had been wandering around in a trance
> for which there was no name, no cause, and now all of a sudden
> the menace had a name to be reviled by; it was as if Brazil had never
> been called anything at all, or Greenland, or Madagascar, always
> there in its amorphous complexity but incapable of being referred
> to. Well, now they had the Ripper to whisper about and scare the
> children off to bed with; it was the most potent-sounding, most
> awful name in London. (320)

Gull's literary creation has the effect of inspiring dozens of copycats to compose and mail similar letters to newspapers, underscoring the desire of the
egocentric human mind to write itself into a good story, however brutal the
subject matter. The cumulative effect of all the Ripper letters is to make "all
murders and mutilations come from the same life-loathing demon, just for

the sake of convenience, focus, and drama. It mattered little who the Ripper was; London needed him, just as it needed its queen and its river, its dock and its music halls" (329). By dramatizing the extent to which writing "Ripper letters" becomes a subgenre all its own in Victorian London, West implies that narrative art, and by extension all the arts, is a pseudo-murderous act.

The women of Whitechapel, who most logically would be expected to resist the illusions of romantic fiction, are no less vulnerable to its blandishments. Annie, for example, at the beginning of her relationship with Eddy, fantasizes that her prince will save her from a life of poverty and drudgery: "To her, [Eddy] was angel, prince, and playmate all in one, and Holy Ghost as well. She thought he would give up his all for her. . . . He was her savior and servitor; she knew now that she would never have to become a mott or go back to the Midlands" (12). In fact, as the relationship progresses and fails to meet Annie's satisfaction, she prefers the romantic dream of a prince to the reality of Eddy: "It was what she had dreamed of, but she wanted the dream to remain a dream: in some ways the moody, impressionable Eddy was too real a man to be dealt with, an imposing presence with a soft inside. Had he remained more of a figurehead, she might have been happier" (70). Mary Kelly, the most attractively earthy of the central female characters, is still powerfully drawn to the ethereal tidiness of fantasy. She calls herself by the French name Marie to put on airs with her peers and proclaims her own version of how to win a prince:

> Princes . . . have a way of graduating to me naturally. I'm a foamy trollop, and they can tell half a mile off. A few of *me* in the so-called royal family, and they'd have to build stronger beds and make bigger pyjamas. I'd have them sweating all night. Anyway, I know what to do now. Get a prince, that's what. (151)

She distances herself from her dreary circumstances by fantasizing about upper-class men as she copulates with the working class in Whitechapel alleys:

> Plying her trade in the street, as she usually had to, she dreamed her way through it, counterpointing the sordid or the rain-sodden with indoor escapades whose male figures sported soft felt hats brought home from Hamburg, shook hands with their elbow held

stiffly against their ribs . . . and undid the bottom button of their waistcoats while sipping the Prince's "cocktail." (156)

She imagines herself with caliphs and yearns "for an aristocratic clientele who, while making perverted demands on her physique at its most private, would ply her with silks and stones, even creating for her some kind of title, to be relished in private, of course, but indelible as a tattoo: Lady Asterik of Pimpernel Pier" (161). Having actually experienced brief exposures to aristocratic life by virtue of sleeping with such men, Mary fancies herself part of their world: "she herself was also a resident of Buckingham Palace, having business there, and Cambridge, Windsor, and Dieppe" (167). This disastrous self-conceit leads Mary into her worst mistake. She composes her own set of letters to Eddy, Lord Salisbury, and the queen in the belief that she knows the ruling class (and their language) well enough to get away with blackmailing them. Once more, the act of writing letters proves to result in murder.

As if to confirm the link between dramatic art and violence, the intellectual focus of the novel is Sickert, an impressionist painter whose aesthetic theory unwittingly propels him into a situation where he sees the logic of his artist's objectification of subject carried out in the most gruesomely literal terms. He finds himself an initially reluctant but ultimately willing partner (brought in as a local expert on the geography and mores of the East End to guide upper-crust Gull) in Gull's plot to "tidy up" Eddy's sexual mess. Sickert is not an active murderer, but he is a passive participant in acts of murder. His artist's temperament in some way finds sympathetic connection to killing. Arthur Saltzman points out the Sickert/Gull bond: "They share a clinical distance crucial to art, surgery, or murder" (par. 33). Sickert speculates on the nature of that connection:

> Painting was a way of altering the visible world, and so was murder, but were these changes in any way alike? The artist was not a murderer, but the murderer was sometimes an artist—hadn't De Quincey written an essay even? . . . [Sickert] was mingling with people who treated human flesh as pigment, life and death as a canvas, the human spine as an easel, and he could not for the life of him look away from it with all of his being: with most of it, yes, but not with the peeping bit of him. (227–28)

Sickert's tragic descent into murder, born from his voyeuristic desire to sample the extremes of the experiences of others, demonstrates again the neo-Gothic's obsessive focus on the dangers of individual fiction-making in fatal interaction with the flow of communal experience. Sickert begins the novel as a mildly decadent aesthete whose favorite haunt is bohemian Cleveland Street, a latently lethal zone of objectification of others:

> [Sickert] had rooms in a large red-brick terrace house on a lively, quaint street. . . . Cleveland Street was an island of art. . . . If London had a Montmartre, this was it, a place for the unrecognized genius to be a notable in, looked up to by rival and shopkeeper alike. It was also Sickert's laboratory, where he ran several experiments having to do with human relations: he liked to make people become more than themselves. (7)

In his art and his daily existence, he takes pleasure in reconfiguring others into bizarre and hideous images not their own—for example, in his studio, he paints Annie Crook "covered with bruises and molasses-like eruptions" to make "her look scarred and scratched" (7). His private transformation of uncontainable feminine reality into scarred, bounded image does not allow for individual differences: "To him a shopgirl, a model, a whore, and a mother were all the same, best expressed in one body" (29). He is simultaneously repulsed and fascinated by the mysterious female biology that his male artistic technique attempts to contain. He mixes in Mary Kelly's bodily effluvia with his paints, for example, in an effort to "get on nodding terms with life raw and bubbly, or he would not be qualified to paint the mysterious with true reverence" (59). Sickert's aesthetic is dictated by his desire to live the extremes of experience so as to enhance his art:

> Always, [Sickert] had instructed himself, he must take on more than he could manage, because doing so was to scramble the mind, make it vulnerable, at the same time demoralizing it and making it alert to combinations it had never known. Only on the brink, he thought, when your mind is all tatters, do you get anywhere near the disheveled shamefulness the artist needs in order to be the true pariah of his genius. (43–44)

Disturbingly, it is this artistic project to experience the boundary-breaking extremes from a detached perspective that sets into motion the sequence of events leading to the Ripper murders.

Sickert's position in the social strata of Cleveland Street brings him into contact with Annie Crook and Mary Kelly, the two pivotal female figures in Knight's theory. Sickert exploits them as nude models and uses them as sexual objects to seek relief from the stifling presence of his fiancée, Ellen. More significantly, he introduces them to the destructively thoughtless and promiscuous Prince Eddy, who is routinely driven to a homosexual brothel on Cleveland Street by John Netley in a royal coach named "the Crusader." Eddy, whose artistic leanings inspire his mother, Princess Alexandra, to ask the famous painter Sickert to "bring him out" on Cleveland Street, poses as Sickert's younger brother and quickly impregnates Annie. Eddy's sexual irresponsibility is another progression along the continuum that will destroy six women.

The destructive result is also attributable, in part, to Sickert's self-confessed status as a good-intentioned but untrustworthy meddler who "would charm people loose from their proper, and quietly assumed, stations in life, then ply them with hopes they could not survive" (41). Again, Sickert's aesthetic theories are inseparable from his manipulation of his surrounding environment. In this case, his introduction of high-born Prince Eddy to lowborn Annie is a kind of romantic experiment to eradicate, or at least ignore, class distinctions in a rigidly stratified society.[5] Annie's pregnancy, a transgression of social taboo, generates a terrifying backlash from forces quite beyond even a prince's control.

Though not consciously cruel, Prince Eddy's indulgences of his immediate passions are contributing factors in the annihilation of the lower-class women who have become emotionally or sexually involved with him. He is also dangerously unmindful of the social reality of his and Annie's respective positions—virtually ensuring a dangerous backlash from the Palace. He cares little for the consequences of their liaison, because "someone had always intervened and settled his problem for him, and he was sure the same would happen with Annie and himself" (76). His doomed lover intuitively recognizes the danger he represents as she makes love to him:

A new confusion grew in her heart, and she suddenly felt endangered, as if he were some deadly tree and to touch him were fatal. What was the name of that tree? The one that turned you into a leper with a single touch? Or the one that burned you with acid and then devoured you where you stood or fell? (17)

Eddy is dangerous because he, like Sickert, straightjackets reality into a frame that fails to live up to its promise to contain flux within its borders. For Eddy, that frame is his desire to rebel against the decorum of his royal obligations without actually giving up his privileged status and protection from the results of his indiscretions:

> If ever, as he might, he heard himself called King Albert Victor Christian Edward, . . . he would have to thin out his rather ample style of living; until then, however, he could afford to fight on several fronts, as he put it, and have several by-blows. He was rehearsing, he said. He was reading widely in the book of life. He was, in fact, preparing to become much the rake his father was. (18)

Eddy's way of reading life (inseparable from performance, as the previous passage suggests) is an act of meddling in the fortunes of others in the same way that Sickert more deliberately initiates. Both men's fictions become, quite easily, reality—but a fluid and irrational reality that they find horrifyingly beyond their control in a manner characteristic of Gothic fictions.

The royal Eddy's witless profligacy, masking itself as a self-aggrandizing romantic rebellion against tradition, complements the fiction-making machinations of the British government. Its representatives, Lord Salisbury and Sir William Gull, in an effort to preserve country and tradition, endeavor to silence permanently those women who hold compromising knowledge of Eddy's illegitimate marriage to Annie. While the intricate kidnap-and-murder plot is sanctioned by Salisbury, it is Gull, with his Masonic affiliation, who provides the frame that bounds the murder series. Elsewhere, before the Ripper murders begin, it is established that Gull loathes the uncertain prognostications of routine medical practice and instead prefers his secret, rigidly controlled surgical experiments on captive dogs and women:

> Gull knew that an experiment was possible in which all the components dovetailed: there would be no waste, no loose ends. He would feed the vivisectionist's dogs on the women who had died, who had been troughing on roast dog—like that. Economy. The closed system recommended in the Holy Bible. (130)

Acting on the framework provided by outside texts, Gull mutilates the Ripper victims according to the Masonic ritual punishments for betrayal. He disposes of the bodies at sites that conform to a linear, parallelogram pattern he imposes on a street map—itself a man-made imposition of order on a much more diffuse reality—or in one case, a site of a previous murder of a woman by a monk during the sixteenth century. He knows that his fellow 33rd-degree Masons will recognize his orderly signature while the public at large will see only the butchery of an invisible madman. David Madden writes that "Gull brings to his destructive mission a curious sense of aesthetic order, a desire to impose a secret structure on what otherwise appears to be random mutilation" (103).

While Gull takes geometrically precise delight in his impromptu surgery, Sickert as his reluctant accomplice tries justifying the proceedings in terms of an aesthetics that has already concentrated to a great extent on the defilement of women's bodily integrity just as Gull's has. Sickert sees his artistic interests and his bourgeois flirtation with proletarian existence as a means of expanding his own borders taken to their utmost extreme. While horrified by the realization of his aesthetics on the bleeding flesh of actual women, he cannot help but accompany Gull on his nocturnal evisceration of the women of Whitechapel. As Sven Birkerts writes, for Sickert, "staring at the gore, the shapes and the colors, there comes a moment when metaphysical curiosity overpowers the regard for the human" (39). While watching Gull and Netley mutilate Mary Kelly, the robust peasant girl he had slept with, he thinks: "This was God's studio in reverse . . . an art of botch, a nest for the poet-peasant with a passion for insides" (365). In the years following the murders, the tragically self-aware Sickert fully comprehends the complicity of fiction-making or representation in actual acts of murder: "Anyone . . . who's lingered on such an act of blood has in a way also committed it, is guilty of it, and God knows I am guilty, of much more than anyone might guess" (419).

Similarly, Gary Fleder's film *Kiss the Girls* is a neo-Gothic study of how fiction-makers choose to project their psyches on their environment, which simultaneously projects back onto them. In other words, they attempt to shape reality to their expectations and, in effect, write themselves upon the world even as the world writes upon them. This act of imaginative alteration of environmental circumstance, given exaggerated form by the serial killer, is viewed as an inherently destructive act. In the film's metaphoric structure, the act of writing to an audience becomes the act of murder writ large upon the corpse of the postmodern mass-media world.

From the opening credits (wherein headline clippings that read "Gentleman Caller Sought by Police" are intercut with graphic crime scene photos and remembered images of a past triple murder as "Casanova" narrates his past to a captive female victim) to the film's concluding scenes (wherein the twin killers' lairs are covered wall-to-wall with similar headlines and newspaper accounts of heinous crimes), the film establishes that the writers of these sensationalistic tales and the real-life authors of these sensationalistic deeds exist in mutual parasitism. Both flourish in the presence of the other. Both copycat each other. Casanova leaves a signed note at the scene of his second murder, knowing that the media will instantly seize on the name of the famous lover and publicize it. Thus, the media grants him a virtual identity behind which he can still remain invisible and anonymous in order to maintain his personal liberty within society.

Knowledge of the murderous link between evildoers and the chroniclers of those evil deeds motivates the film's two main protagonists, Alex and Kate, to exploit the voyeuristic media to their own ends. They know that communicating to the press is equivalent to communicating directly with the killer(s). For example, Kate's press conference, held immediately after her recovery from Casanova's abduction, has been designed by Alex, Kate, and the police to create an electronic conduit between victim and killer in an effort to divert Casanova's rage and frustration at Kate's escape away from his remaining captives toward Kate herself. Kate, as "bait" in the lethal game between dangerous men, does not shrink from her role. She stares into the "killing" cameras' eyes and takes full responsibility for incurring Casanova's wrath, though (as a true performance artist) not forgetting to thank her viewing public for all the "thousands of letters and prayers from across America." By addressing all of her diverse audiences at once and staring back at them simultaneously, Kate both re-empowers herself by stepping bravely into the visual killing zone, yet resubjects herself to the murderous gaze. The conflation of viewing audience and Casanova into one virtually real entity, the object of Kate's address, positions her as an oddly ambiguous figure within that entity's coldly distant, return gaze. She is the objectified and the objectifier, subjected and subjectifier, victim and victimizer, reflected and reflecting. She is the written-upon body seizing the initiative to create her own script, which is then digitized, beamed out, and projected upon the national audience before reflected back at her by Casanova.

Alex is another ambiguously positioned figure in the Gothic hyperreal environment. As a writer of true-crime books, Alex is guilty of betraying his academic credentials and professional confidentiality by pandering to mass-audience demand for voyeuristic thrills and murders-by-proxy. FBI agent Kyle Craig, in his first on-screen exchange with Alex, remarks disparagingly that with Alex's entry into the case of the abducted girls, "the TV crews can't be far behind." Craig deliberately tweaks Alex's internal tensions between his public status as celebrity author and as professional but personally motivated investigator of his niece's abduction. Alex's ambivalence toward the media through which he constructs a successful secondary career will only increase as the narrative progresses. Following a failed capture of the L.A. "Gentleman Caller," Alex ruefully comments on the massive television coverage given to his humiliation: "They sure can document a fuck-up at the speed of light." Yet its speed is the very aspect of the modern media that Alex and Kate, not to mention the two killers, utilize in order to advance their personal agendas and transform their environmental positioning relative to each other. Both killer(s) and victim(s) empower themselves at the expense of the other, but it is a kind of media-connected complicity that makes the bond possible in the first place.

Casanova, the alternate identity of police detective and serial killer Nick Ruskin, stands out as the film's foremost media manipulator and "author" in the postmodern age. He is someone who literally writes his text upon the bodies of female victims with the direct complicity of the Gentleman Caller (Beverly Hills plastic surgeon and serial killer William Rudolph) and the indirect complicity of the media outlets (television and the Internet in particular) that transmit his moral contagion to equally complicit audiences. In scenes such as the one where Ruskin on the East Coast E-mails scanned photographs of the drugged and imprisoned Kate to Rudolph on the West Coast, the film plays on the paranoia of those who view the Internet as the lurking ground of child molesters and serial murderers who hide in plain sight in the vast and ungovernable wastes of cyberspace. The virtual-reality world is the newest Gothicized environment in the American mythscape of monsters.

Ruskin, however technologically cutting-edge he may be, reveals his primary indebtedness is to the communicative modes of the precomputer age, specifically the most hackneyed conventions of romantic literature and a simplistic appropriation of the name Casanova from its historical context. Ruskin is quite literally in thrall to these conventions, mechanically constructing his modus operandi and subterranean Gothic dungeon in accordance with their demands and helplessly unable to conceive of any more open-ended system for constructing identity. As a melodramatic, exaggerated, excessive, and over-the-top Gothic villain self-dubbed Casanova, Ruskin by an act of misapprehension makes brutally manifest the underlying objectification of others implied by romanticism at its most egocentric and paranoid—the Gothic. Ruskin self-deludedly fancies himself quite the sophisticated rake, altering and flattening his distinctive Southern accent into what he believes an aristocratic, European, and pre-twentieth-century lover of beautiful women would sound like. He congratulates himself on his enlightened appreciation of feminine qualities and the arts, even as he tortures and kills women for his own pleasures. His soft voice and courtly manner (the stroking of the hair from the temple of his "lovers," for example) combined with his murder (if they disobey his rules) of the women he claims to love starkly illustrate the hyperliteral degree to which Ruskin conforms his actions to inherited literary convention and cultural systems of etiquette and conduct.

But Ruskin has no true knowledge of or appreciation for the narratives he mimics. One of Kate's female doctors, a Dr. Ruocco, aghast at Kate's medical condition following her escape from Casanova, observes: "He's cunning but he doesn't know his history. The real Casanova would never have approved." Whether or not the real Casanova can ever be known, the doctor's remark compactly conveys one of the more ambiguous ideas common to the Gothic genre—that attempts to recreate the cultural conventions of the past into the present moment are as potentially deadly as they are illuminating. For Naomi's boyfriend, Seth Samuels, his knowledge of the area's colonial history allows Alex to find Ruskin's dungeon (the tunnels beneath an old slave plantation) and thus demonstrates the benevolent use of the malignant past to inform the present. But overall, in a manner typical of the neo-Gothic, the film's overwhelming focus on Ruskin's fatal if superficial reconstruction of the past foregrounds the malevolent quality of the past's intrusion on the present.

As a slavish devotee of a violent literary past who makes explicit its implicit violence, Ruskin believes in the conventions or "rules" of his self-sustaining but unoriginal game quite strongly, to the extent that he will kill, in true "Bluebeard" fashion, any one of his female "wives" who deviates from the rules or defies him. Early in the film, Ruskin marches a tearful, half-clothed woman, Megan Murphy, to her death in the woods outside the dungeon where he keeps his harem. As Megan desperately tries to reestablish emotional connection to Ruskin in words hauntingly reminiscent of a lovers' quarrel based in disenchantment and disillusionment ("Talk to me the way you used to"), it becomes clear that she has broken one of Ruskin's rules of courtly love and must now pay the penalty (rape and murder) for transgression. She tries to convince Ruskin that she loves him, as he demands of his "odalisques." But she fails and screams in despair before the scene ends— thereby graphically establishing for the audience the level of sexually based menace that awaits the narrative's true heroine, Kate.[6]

When Kate finds herself in Megan's old cell as a prisoner among other female prisoners in a subterranean labyrinth, Kate very quickly learns the rules from Ruskin in his masked Casanova identity: "You're here to fall in love. To experience love. . . . I need to tell you the rules. . . . Don't try to escape. Don't cry out for help. . . . Now I'll do what I can to help you not break these rules. But if you do, you will really disappoint me." Ruskin's three rules, the foremost of which is to fall in love with him, illustrate the savage and selfish logic of obsessive romance, and its sub rosa sexual desire, as given mechanically literal life by a "copycat." At a metatextual level of remove from Ruskin, the knowledgeable genre viewer of this film will also recognize Ruskin's style of brutality—the imprisonment of women with the intent of making them love their jailer—as an updated, wildly overblown homage to John Fowles's famous novel *The Collector.* In that novel, Frederick Clegg, having won a fortune in the lottery, uses his newfound wealth to construct a prison in the basement of his country house for a kidnapped young female art student named Miranda Grey, whom he tries to coerce into loving him. In *Kiss the Girls,* Alex reinforces the allusion by invoking the novel's title, deliberately or otherwise, in his profile of Casanova: "I think killing's not his ulterior motive. . . . This guy's a collector." As in *The Collector* or *Shadow of a Doubt,* the legacy of romantic fiction is herein seen as less than beneficial, especially to women. As always, the penalty for transgressing these literary rules, as Ruskin so vividly demonstrates, is pain and death.

The Serial Killer as "Monster"

If the clear boundaries between ways of making and receiving fiction break down in the neo-Gothic, so do the boundaries between internal "nature" and external "super-nature." One of the boundaries most frequently transgressed is that between the natural and the supernatural. A common character type found in the "supernatural" Gothic is the double—what Freud calls the doppelgänger or what R. E. Foust calls "fantasy antagonists." The double is actually two characters. One serves as a point of audience identification. The other is a threatening villain. Both are similar in that they are excluded from a dominant social order. The monstrous killer is the melodramatic stage villain brought in to illustrate the possible consequences of that exclusion. In a very real sense, the killer acts out desires that the more sympathetic double has repressed but nevertheless formulated on his or her own. In a related discussion of horror film, J. P. Telotte states that

> the horror genre typically conjures up monstrous "copies" that, we would prefer to think, have no originals, no correspondence in our world. Their anomalous presence, however, fascinates us even while it challenges our lexicon of everyday images. In this pattern we can discern a subtle desire to remodel the world by projecting into it, cinematically, the doubles of our imagination. It also helps to explain why the most effective threats in the genre are seldom the clearly visible monsters or noonday devils, but dark patches and vague presences which invite projection and suggest an interweaving of specular and blind space—on the screen just as in our psyches. (57)

This type of horror scenario and the Gothic masterplot neatly complement one another. As Louis Gross maintains, Gothic fiction is usually authored by, tailored to, and concerned with marginalized figures (women, gays, colonials) anyway (2). So, when the protagonist (and natural repository of the audience's sympathies) kills or otherwise defeats the murderer in an act of vigilante justice, the willful transgression of legal boundaries such an act represents implicitly allies the protagonist with his enemy through the shared act of murder. As in Poe's "William Wilson," the killing of a narrative double suggests that the surviving twin may assume the burden of carrying on with the first twin's original mission. One monster has created another. It is an infinite progression and regression, again radiating outward and inward, going everywhere and nowhere simultaneously. The past history influences the present moment, which determines the unfolding future. In the Gothic, the future holds little hope except for more violence. The self- and Other-destructive double is a superficial symptom of a genre that is dependent on a fundamental binary opposition—the struggle between good and evil defined by and positioned against one another. Indeed, much of narrative art itself, according to Fredric Jameson (*Political Unconscious* 115), is dependent on exactly this kind of binary positioning of extremes. But an odd thing happens in the positioning—the boundaries between two initially quite distinct characters or philosophies become unstable in the treacherous (neo)Gothic landscape.

This Gothic landscape is also present in Paul West's evocations of dark slum alleyways, narrow streets, cramped rooms, and cellars where women are imprisoned and mutilated by Sir William Gull, villain of *The Women of Whitechapel and Jack the Ripper.* This geographic borderland between urban society and asocial barbarism is literally a hell for those unfortunate denizens of London's slums and bohemian districts. Even before the Ripper murders begin, Sickert often fancies London's East End to be a realm of evil quite capable of twisting and perverting his psyche even as he attempts to manipulate reality for art:

> Constantly trying to catch himself at the onset of an evil move, he saw what he wanted to see, and he always saw a man not quite gone over to the enemy, to the bad, but in need of only a short intense stimulus to get him on the move toward it, to a place where noses bled, loins dried and flaked, dead babies rolled in slush along the gutters, angels ate feces with neuter zeal, and loved ones turned into charcoal before one's eyes. Sometimes he heard a sustained scream coming from the East End, and he knew something dreadful, yet commonplace, was afoot, and he continued on his way home from the music hall, wondering if the death scream was an art form. A paddle steamer had come to a halt in mid-Thames, its wheel fouled by a female corpse no one had yet been able to remove; he had not seen the steamer, nor was he going to look, but the image dogged him, making him wonder how many corpses floated on the river before they sank below. (42–43)

Technological civilization, as represented by the steamer, churns up and is corrupted by the biological pollution of female corpses, either self-drowned or hidden by anonymous murderers in the Thames. The grisly image moves Sickert to contemplate how such hidden foulness can intrude on the surface light of rationality and march of progress at any moment. The bright and pleasant summer before the autumn murders is ruined for Londoners by swarms of flies, for example: "It felt as if some spiteful power had decided to humiliate the lovers of the outdoors, making them sense an itching film descend upon them and then lift away, only to return seconds later with tiny pinpricks" (55). The taboo zone of corruption, just beyond the boundary of daylight appearances and waiting to break through in the messiest of ways, is a defining characteristic of the portentous Gothic landscape and determines the daily lives of West's characters. Sickert believes he has little free will in such an environment:

> What had once been his natural morbidity, his love of the gutter as a subject and a theme, had now become a trap, no longer optional. A style had turned into a footprint of fate, wished upon him as ineluctably as a port-wine nervus on his hand at birth. . . . God was leaning over him, he was certain, getting him ready for the next great wound . . . as a man marked for singular and awesome degradation, no longer a matter of choice. (145)

Sickert is suddenly conscious of being defined by geography. He is obsessed with maps and directions and becoming "lost" by venturing too far past strictly defined borders. Sickert says of his own participation in the Ripper murders: "he had careened off the human map, far behind Gull of course, but trying all the same to strike the very nadir" (285). Clearly, tidy form is what Sickert finds holiest in appearance: "Shape, he saw, was the thing God-given, and not flesh, not offal, not blood. He loved the dry" (289). For the wet blood or offal to overflow its dry shape—for it to be released by Gull's boundary-slicing knife, for example—is the profoundest act of pollution for Sickert, yet one that also fascinates his artist's sensibility. He associates horror with an eruption of liquid, the most pliable yet resistant form of matter to containment. It is symbolic of the inability of straight, masculine lines to frame reality. The Gothic landscape of West's novel consistently melts down forms and dissolves boundaries around its terrified characters. Sickert can speak for all of them in their disorientation in the borderlands:

> Growing up thus, as he was obliged to do now, was like stretching full length into a hitherto unknown region of pain. One touch into that region and there was no withdrawing hand or foot; long, matte strands of its own sticky substance, the devil's magma, came trailing after him, gray and cold. He was enwebbed. (229)

Through this hellish territory of melting forms stalks its demon "Jack the Ripper"—a killer of indeterminate form himself given supernatural shadings by press and public alike. In his narrative incarnation, West's Ripper is a shape-shifter and demonic messenger. He is a harbinger of apocalypse guided by some impersonal but nevertheless malevolent being, perhaps conjured into existence by evil acts. Sickert at one early point sees in Alice Margaret's blank infant face an omen of disaster:

> He just knew . . . that some drear and carnal web hovered over them all, could they but see it and evade it, presided over and mended by some ghastly beast whose origin no one knew, but it had come together from a thousand unguarded acts allowed to stand and so infest the bright promises of yet another swollen summer. (63)

Whereas in narratives such as *Kiss the Girls* the Ripper figure is split into two, West's novel splits the Ripper into infinite replications. There is no literal Ripper, but rather a series of men who directly or indirectly commit murders attributed to a single man. It could be argued that the actions of all of the male protagonists of the novel collectively form the Ripper simulacrum. Each of the internal monologues West writes for each one demonstrates another face of the murderer, constructed as a monster even if ultimately human.

Eddy is a vampiric contaminator, as Annie instinctively feels (17). Similarly, Sickert feels a "wolf unfolding from within" (41) and harbors premonitions of upcoming personal crimes committed not at God's behest but parallel to God's own actions: "He knew that God Almighty had dirty, bloody hands, his own equivalent of which he vaguely detected on the horizon, but without knowing clearly with what raw materials he would work" (48–49). Gull, as a lobotomist of women and vivisector of dogs even before he turns to street murder, is the most monstrous male figure in the novel. He is introduced to the reader as he removes a male cadaver's heart in front of a bereaved sister. Any number of times West explicitly calls Gull a devil— "Salisbury's demon" (141)—or a vampire-like corrupter, slayer, and devourer of women. For example:

> Convicts, the mad, the poor, all made grist for his devil's mill, especially now that he had given up his practice and was free to move about the human body according to whim and fancy, severing and wrecking in the very spirit of the berserk demiurge, say Goya's Saturn, not so much devouring his creatures as blighting them. (100)

He engages in hypnogogy of female victims, like the traditional vampire, except through the more crudely literal device of, first, lancing women's brains in order to make them pliable and certifiably insane and then, later, of drugging them with poisoned grapes before mutilating them. He is capable of miraculous transformations from one identity to another, on the basis that "a sick man, a man quite well, and a monster of health cohabited in him" (203) following an earlier stroke that crippled his mind and body. Sickert notices that Gull is

> always worth watching, not least because the sea changes in his physiognomy were not of his own making nor his knowing; his face brimmed about in front of him, a coat of arms in flux, encouraging now this kind of person, now another kind, until just about everyone he encountered had been won over, to their sometimes infinite cost. (205)

These men are all coded by West as monstrous, who similarly see themselves as monstrous. They are externally directed, or so they believe, to carry out the murderous logic of the borderland's suggestive omens.

The film *Kiss the Girls* also employs pseudo-supernatural imagery not only to demonize the killers but those who come into contact with the killers. This theme of contamination is implicitly deterministic, suggesting that minimal contact with some dark, external force will automatically taint the contactee. The only proper response to such pollution, the film's narrative argues, is either complete avoidance or destruction of the contaminants. The primary contaminants, of course, are the serial killers Casanova and the Gentleman Caller. In spite of a superficial emphasis on the importance of historical awareness and continuity, the narrative conspicuously declines to provide any meaningful analysis, let alone clues, about what may have transpired in the twin killers' personal pasts to bring them to such violence. Jack Mathews, for example, writes: "the movie creates no profile of the eventual villain. . . . All we really know is that the kidnapper collects women he thinks he's in love with and kills them when they disappoint him" (par. 7–8). In contrast, Roger Ebert sees this paucity of clues as one of the film's strengths: "But being left with such a question [about the killers' pasts] is much more satisfactory than being given the answer in shorthand Freudian terms" (par. 8). In one sense, however, the etiology of the killers is secondary at best to the film's main agenda, which is to demonize the human killer into an inhuman monster—or at least a human who is signified in monstrous terms, which achieves roughly the same effect. For example, director Fleder equates his human predator to an inhuman one: "To me, the more you showed

[Casanova], the more he was diminished. So as the shark in 'Jaws' was to the water, Casanova would be to the forest" (*Kiss the Girls* website, par. 8). Casanova's monstrosity, in turn, threatens to create other monsters (those who meet him when he is in "killing mode") because human nature is only superficially civilized, inherently evil and easily "corruptible" to its natural barbaric condition. Narratively, this state of affairs justifies the most extreme reaction (obliteration) possible. Casanova is signified as a type of demon, able not only to kill without remorse but also to change shapes and cloud the human mind at will.

Pseudo-supernatural touches abound in *Kiss the Girls*. For example, Ruskin as Casanova is another unlikely "genius" serial killer, operating both at a higher intellectual capacity than the norm and a lower level of depravity, in exactly the same way that Clive Bloom says of the cultural construction of Jack the Ripper: "[uniting] the lowest and the highest impulses in his society" (126). The almost admiring tone is established early on, when Agent Craig, first taking note of the killer's clever use of one of the most common and thus virtually untraceable brands of rope in the country, calls Casanova "a real student of the game. And he likes to play." As a gameplayer who likes to hide in plain sight—the barbarian beneath the lover's mask— Ruskin slips handwritten notes from "Casanova" to Alex underneath the latter's hotel room door in an attempt to keep Alex close enough to provide competition but not so close as to win the game. Ruskin is clever (and arrogant) enough to toy with capture but not throw the game. He uses his murdering doctor friend on the West Coast to buy quantities of a drug that Ruskin will then use on the East Coast, using enormous distance and a go-between to cover his purchasing tracks. He has the foresight to set up a convincing patsy, or alternate suspect, by targeting female students that a lecherous professor given to bondage games, Dr. Wick Sachs, has been sleeping with. As an intelligent criminal profiler, or supercop, Alex is eventually able to see through each of Ruskin's obfuscations and ruses. (Of course, no "average" law enforcement agent ever would.) The super-criminal versus the super-detective is not a new dramatic convention, of course, but in the serial killer subgenre, the adversarial conflict between geniuses serves to illustrate both the magnitude of the menace and the need for saviors.

More overtly monstrous adornments to Ruskin and William Rudolph's characters exist. Both are, for all practical purposes, "invisible," hiding enormous misdeeds and sexual depravity beneath respectable middle- or upper-class public careers (a police detective, a plastic surgeon) designed to throw off the suspicion of their peers. Alex draws attention to Casanova's practical invisibility, looking around the university campus that Casanova has claimed as a hunting ground and calling it "an environment fit for blending. . . . for him, Paradise." In addition to careers and demeanors that provide capital and invisibility for murder, Ruskin and Rudolph literally change or transform from courteous public servants or professionals to monsters in private. Ruskin dons his white mask and alters his voice, while Rudolph turns into a ranting madman with crazed eye and slashing knife. In their murderous identities, both live outside of civilization in troll-like fashion and are imagistically associated again and again with "wildness." Casanova lives in an underground dungeon in the woods; Rudolph works himself up to a murdering rage in a cabin in the woods. The precivilized forest is dangerous and transgressive by nature, as production designer Nelson Coates makes clear: "We found ways to have nature creep into the buildings through the colors, textures, and organic motifs. It creates a sense that the outdoors is always intruding" (*Kiss the Girls* website, par. 21). The more bestial Rudolph even seems to exhibit some form of extrasensory perception—he feels the presence of Alex and his friend Sampson as they in turn watch him from their vantage point in the forest. Sampson, shuddering at the sight of Rudolph's madness, claims "he's about to scare the wildlife outta this forest."

But perhaps the most important supernatural association between the serial killers and the supernatural is the vampiric. Ruskin, for example, formulates a murderous ritual that resembles the vampire rape/seductions of nineteenth-century literature. As a character, Ruskin retains echoes of the literary "gentleman" vampire. He fancies himself an aristocratic lover of the fine arts in their elitist forms of social expression, such as violin recitals. Though of necessity bound to the fortunes of his fellow killer William Rudolph, "European" Ruskin despises the quintessentially American "yuppie" Rudolph's vulgarity, depravity, lack of self control, and sloppiness. Ruskin's display of class resentment and snobbery is quite ironic, considering that Ruskin is the blue-collar, small-town cop and Rudolph the upper-class, big city doctor. Ruskin affects a deep, rich voice to enhance the illusion of aristocratic origins. As Casanova, he lives in a private Old-World style "castle," full of secret rooms and tunnels and surrounded by a protective forest and moat, where his concubines play music for his audience of one. Most significantly in terms of the vampiric associations, however, he exerts a form of hypnotic command over women. From his perspective, Ruskin first sights his lovers, courts them, hypnotizes them, and finally seduces them in a thrilling (to him) romantic game. However, from the privileged narrative eye, it is clear that Ruskin actually spies on them, stalks them, drugs them, and then rapes and kills them in a postmodern mockery of the vampiric, mesmerizing lover in Gothic literature.[7]

Vampire iconography abounds in *Kiss the Girls,* beginning with the credits sequence, wherein Ruskin's first murders are visually re-created as he speaks of them in flashback. He voyeuristically "possesses" the two daughters and their mother by spying on them from ventilating ducts within their own house. He then comes to them (in his mind, at their invitation) in the dead of night as they sleep. In Ruskin's memory, which structures the topmost layer of the sequence and gives it the "flames of passion" imagistic overlay, his lovers, given over to his spell and penetrated by his masculinity, moan in ecstasy and their eyes close in passion. (The intermingled crimescene photographs and newspaper headlines inform the viewer that these women have actually been first drugged and then raped and murdered.) In the film's second home invasion, where Kate is abducted, the sequence begins with an archetypal setting found in many lurid vampire tales—the halfdressed maiden, the bed, the "dark and stormy" night, the inviting windows, the nocturnal invader with the white, bloodless face (in this case, a mask). All of this iconography establishes for the viewer a link between Ruskin, vampirism, and—most importantly—the vampire's "polluting" or corrupting kiss. The link between serial murder and popular representations of vampirism exists primarily to convince the viewer that Ruskin spreads contagion, and that he will create more killers unless stopped.

The doubling theme is also present in *Kiss the Girls* to an extreme degree. The most obvious doubling, of course, is that of Ruskin and Rudolph, who met when Rudolph as a premed student at the University of North Carolina committed a particularly bloody murder of a 1975 homecoming queen for which policeman Ruskin sheltered him from detection. These kindred yet competitive spirits then keep each posted via E-mail on their individual coast-to-coast murders. In case the point is lost on any viewer, Rudolph repeatedly taunts Ruskin: "If you're here, I'm here" and "You're just like me." But at various points in the narrative, Alex as protagonist will also exhibit, if not a hard-wired affinity for the killing mind-set, at least a tendency to run on parallel tracks. The linkage establishes parity between killer and pursuer and suggests human nature is fundamentally fixed and murderous. Alex, like Casanova and the Gentlemen Caller in their monstrous identities, is socially marginalized, both by virtue of his race and his particular field of expertise (forensic psychology) within law enforcement.

Enhancing his outsider status, Alex leaves his jurisdiction in Washington, D.C., to pursue individual justice for his kidnapped niece, which embroils him in territorial disputes with the Southern whites of the small Durham police department.

Other similarities between Alex and Ruskin proliferate. Both are skilled at social invisibility. Alex boasts of his twenty years of experience "blending in" with his environment—just as Ruskin, another cop, does. Just as Casanova's voice is carefully modulated to soothe women, Alex's soft, reassuring voice is his best professional instrument, as demonstrated in the sequences where he convinces a woman who has murdered her husband not to commit suicide, calms his hyper-tense sister, and reassures the recovering Kate. Like Casanova, he is capable of "entrancing" women—not through drug use but hypnosis induced through soporific tones. He becomes a literal outlaw late in the narrative, when he convinces fellow black officer Sampson to secretly provide him with police equipment and another cop to maintain illegal (or at least unsanctioned) surveillance of Rudolph so as to not endanger the imprisoned Naomi's life if something happens to Rudolph. Alex's gambit goes catastrophically wrong and places two other police officers in jeopardy of their lives (not to mention their careers). All of these twists are narrative ploys to distance Alex, increasingly obsessed and thus tainted by his contact with Casanova's madness, from social affiliations and identity out into the realm of true self. From the Gothic perspective, this realm is decidedly unfriendly territory where "blending in" means not getting lost, but rather rediscovering the monstrous hidden self.

The parallels between Alex and Ruskin intensify until the climactic face-to-face confrontation with the unmasked monster. Ruskin, chained and bloody and definitely degraded from his suave Casanova identity, reveals his true bestial nature by snarling at Alex: "Truth is looking at a beautiful woman . . . and saying to yourself . . . I gotta break her down. It's your basest animal self. Dig deep, Alex, you'll recognize him. He's ugly." Alex next acknowledges the basic validity of Ruskin's philosophical perspective on monstrous human nature: "I've run into him now and then." He denies that he is like Ruskin, but he proves himself a liar when Ruskin deliberately taunts him about Naomi's sexuality. Ruskin further suggests that Alex envies Ruskin's personal encounter with that sexuality (a tactic that Ruskin's patsy, Dr. Sachs, also uses to enrage Alex during a police interrogation). The narrative does not dwell on Alex's uncomfortable recognition of his possible sexual desire for his niece. However, his discomfort with the issue of Naomi's sexuality on two separate occasions nevertheless illustrates his fear that it might be true. This transgression, in thought if not deed, brings its practitioner into the mythic realm of the most primal forms of corruption. Faced with this unacceptable mirroring of self, Alex fatally shoots Ruskin and becomes, ironically, a murderer for individual reasons, not for the public good. The final import of the parallels between Alex and Ruskin is designed not to humanize Ruskin but to demonize Alex and Ruskin both. Their dual monstrosity demonstrates the degree to which a copycat murderer can supposedly influence thinly civilized human beings to act in similar fashion. In this neo-Gothic narrative, social identity is an extremely dangerous yet evanescent abstraction that paradoxically receives the gist of narrative opprobrium. Yet the socialized self pales before the sublime terror and corruptive influence of the unfettered and monstrous individual self.

Sexual Terrorism and Serial Murder

One of the most obvious plot features of the above texts is their emphasis on female characters facing desperate physical danger and psychological trauma. One must look to the history of the Gothic to understand how texts centered on serial killers who predominantly target women can appeal to a mass audience weaned on American domestic romances. Cameron and Fraser's study again proves instrumental in understanding the attraction of what they dub "sexual murder" in contemporary culture. The murdering "sex beast" as hero, Cameron and Fraser argue, is a logical outgrowth of inherited genre conventions such as those found not only in "true-crime" broadsheet-type narratives of criminal case histories and their attendant moralistic tones (such as the *National Police Gazette*) but the more literary European Gothic novels of authors such as M. G. Lewis and Horace Walpole. The authors elaborate:

> [A] more recent influence is the Gothic genre and indeed the Romantic movement of which it was a part. From this development of the late eighteenth and nineteenth centuries we get a characteristic ambience: a fascination with terror, with the evil and repulsive, and a persistent conjecture of transgression, sex and death which is associated in particular with the Marquis de Sade. (36–37)

In the Gothic, the romantic individual rebellion against conventional morality and vested authority finds itself most fully embodied in Sadeian figures who regularly transgress the taboos against not only sexual license but also against rape, incest, and murder.

The targets of the murdering Gothic libertine are usually female. One of the primary symbols of isolated individualism in the Gothic narrative is the Maiden in Flight. Leslie Fiedler calls her the anima, a feminized representation of the artist's soul dispossessed from his or her moral complacency. Another is the Jungian Shadow, "the villain who pursues the Maiden and presides over turrets and dungeon keep alike" and who represents the animus, "that masculine archetype in which the feminine psyche projects all it has denied. But he is the animus regarded as forgivable victim of passion and circumstance, an admirable sufferer" (Fiedler 119). The Shadow is a double of the Maiden (and vice versa) in the Gothic tale of terror, Fiedler concludes. Both are alienated from bourgeois society. Through that distant perspective they can see how fragile and illusory bourgeois values really are. Furthermore, even as they threaten one another in the dark Gothic landscape, they exhibit an odd understanding, even sympathy, for the other's lonely plight. This pairing of outsiders is demonstrated quite overtly in the fiction of Thomas Harris, through the developing Lecter/Starling alliance in *The Silence of the Lambs* and its logical sexual conclusion in *Hannibal*. According to Jungian psychology, this type of pairing symbolizes the reconciliation of dualities within the individual personality. The Maiden and the Shadow share terror as well as sexuality, each arousing it within the other.

Observation of the terrors of sexuality in fiction leads Fiedler to make his famous pronouncement that American "classic literature is a literature of horror for boys" (9), to which, in the case of contemporary literature and cinema, I would also add "girls." Complex issues of romance and sexuality generally assume a minor role in much of our popular literature, while the sadistic and melodramatic terror-fantasies typical of an adolescent's fear of sex eclipse other narrative considerations. In the general context of American literature as Fiedler defines it, gruesome murder (or at least the threat of it) stands as one of the primary governing themes. A series of murders, for sheer melodramatic impact alone, serves our national literature even better. It should not then be surprising that, in the contemporary serial killer subgenre, evolved from Gothic conventions, the Shadow pursues a feminized representative of the anima through the bulk of the narrative. This happens, for example, in Tobe Hooper's *The Texas Chainsaw Massacre* (Leatherface and Sally) or in John Carpenter's *Halloween* (Michael Myers and Laurie). It is seemingly inevitable that these two alienated Gothic figures should ultimately forge a mutually respectful alliance, as happens in *The Silence of the Lambs* between Clarice Starling and Hannibal Lecter. In some cases, they sexually join in monsterdom, as between Starling and Lecter in *Hannibal* or Helen Lyle and the title character in Bernard Rose's film *Candyman*. Together, these monstrous couples reject socially defined boundaries of normality and explore the taboo territory of their true selves together, fated never to return to normality.

The monstrous male psyche receives a devastating critique in West's novel, especially as masculinity is contrasted with the female psyche. As is typical of the neo-Gothic, the distinct line between social constructions of gender blurs and shifts. Sickert exhibits a "feminine" sensitivity toward experience and Mary Kelly demonstrates "masculine" independence. But at some deeper primal level the masculine principle reasserts itself with a destroying vengeance and is fundamentally different than femaleness. For Sickert, the female essence is fluid and biologically "messy"—fascinating in its abundance but horrible in its liberation. His ambivalent response toward the female body is in no small measure one of the reasons he is attracted to painting, which begins as wetness and then hardens to dryness or semi-dryness. Painting is an artistic medium through which he can safely explore and contain the uncontainable. By this symbolic logic, the female body becomes a wild zone that Sickert commits himself to manipulating and conquering. As his fiancée Ellen says to him: "A woman's body is a workbench for you" (81). He literally mixes the irrepressible and "open" Mary Kelly's sexual secretions into his paints.

West suggests this kind of dogged and linear literalness in the transformation of reality to representation is one of Sickert's greatest weaknesses. Sickert confesses to himself that as an impressionist painter, "All I am, truly, is a copycat. I do impressions of people and things" (45). Yoked so stringently to slavish recreations of his perceived linear reality, Sickert has very little choice but to leave himself paradoxically open to the strongest systemized influence to come his way. He calls himself "a patchwork man, aching to have several of me killed off so I can be constant to myself" (141). This statement suggests both his openness to impression and his linear desire to shut off those impressions and find a constant, impenetrable male self. First, he is attracted to the female open-ended and all-inclusive system. He envies, for example, women's ability to give birth: "What he wanted—what all men lacked—was an experience like this, basic to life and indeed love, that was slimy and unstoppable. The idea of the afterbirth appealed to him as a mass of God's will" (57). But, as a male, he is deterministically doomed to fall back upon his innate masculine love of what Gull calls closed, self-containing systems. The contrast between male and female systems is clearly spelled out by Sickert:

> Of the two types, the female sex was the more mysterious vessel by far, therefore to be the more profaned, the more abused. It made sense to him that the superior mystery attracted the greater rage. People hated God more than they hated the queen, didn't they? A queen could be made, appointed, but a god could not, nor a buttercup, an ant, a glacier. No, *cunnus* was algebra or something incalculably worse, *penis* was arithmetic. A rising or standing prick, he had heard, had no conscience, whereas that other thing, all mucous petals and tiny red linked onions of futurity, capable of nine months' harboring and nurturing after five minutes of tupping, that was miraculous: to come up with so completely orchestrated a commitment after a splash from just about any indifferent johnny. . . . It was more miraculous than land or air or sea, it was the holiest thing he knew, but he wished its incessant profanation did not stalk his nights. (169)

Gull's murders fascinate Sickert and compel his voyeuristic participation because Gull is willing to explore and reshape female anatomy along more familiar lines. Compare Sickert's observations of female profundity and fecundity with Gull's:

> Gull sometimes found himself brooding on the formal magic of female anatomy, reminding himself that women were partly slit open to begin with. What man worth his salt would not wish to complete the job with a razor or surgical knife and make a proper glory-hole of it? What he did was sculpting; and, although he bowed mentally toward the Masons, Salisbury and the Queen, he knew that something barbaric and heartless, even if only secondarily lascivious, tugged him on, almost as if he wanted to enter women headfirst in some comfort, not through a God-given aperture but through a gaping wound. . . . Every man in England has a touch of this gashing fancy. It is appropriate, just as, perhaps, all women harbour a desire to take a razor to the male member and make of it

a trophy. Yet it is we who haunt the streets, whetted, lurking, every bit the boss. (231)

As the passage suggests, Gull is not alone in despising and reconfiguring female openness. All men are susceptible to it. West editorializes that the hundreds of Whitechapel prostitutes are

> raw meat for those who, nameless and uncontainable, hung around with knives and razors, clubs and thuggee cords, acids and pitchforks, bayonets and steel-tipped boots, to do them in and bring them down, not the Gulls but the impromptu madmen of London with not a Masonic thought in their heads. (249)

True to Gothic paranoia, this misogyny is found at all social levels. Eddy's royal father Bertie, sporting with Mary Kelly, is suddenly horrified of her monstrous biology:

> He had just crossed over into spectator hell, where, if the spectacle failed to arouse it became abominable, and the woman Kelly swelled above them, all barnacles and greasy flanks, her cavities releasing seaweed and her mouth heaving into view a viscous ectoplasm amid which ptarmigans, cakes, and trifles lost their shapely, tactful nature and became a hell-dame's droppings. (159)

As a representative of his sex, Gull's most masculine-directed act of hatred against femaleness, then, is not necessarily his killing them but his obliteration of their uniquely female organs—those mysteriously reproductive wet zones that Sickert covets but fears. West says of Gull that he changes Annie, for example, by cutting "the effusiveness out of her, the gaiety that always preceded whatever attitude she formed about someone" (105).

Yet of the two, and for all his crimes against women, it is Sickert who shows moments of potential deviation from the tyranny of closed systems and straight lines. He always empathizes with women's complicated biology:

> Did women, he caught himself wondering, always link this kind of suffering [giving birth] to the so-called deed of kind? When they let any man, never mind a prince, "have his way with" them, did they always have this horror in mind as a possible outcome? And were they always prepared to pay for a moment's pleasure thus? (57)

On the basis of this kind of empathy, he begins to conceive of a more indeterminate world:

> He had begun to divine a world in which exact relationships of a
> formal kind did not matter, so long as compatible people kept to-
> gether. Never mind who was whose whatever, the main thing was
> to be someone's anything, if you were devoted to them, as he had
> been with Annie, whose fate did not square with his notion. He
> found it hard to believe that Annie was a permanent loser, never to
> surface like Eddy. (137)

He recognizes that the appearance of solidity or fixed-ness is an illusion: "No
picture was static, he was convinced; the paint was always on the move, never
mind how dry, or seemingly so" (214). His sexual encounter with Liz Stride
and Mary Kelly, shortly before their murders, restores his faith in the integrity of seemingly uncontrolled systems: "Surely, if there could be a reason
for doing what Gull did, it was the defenselessness of flesh, its openness to
wounding. Left to their own devices, however, flesh and skin made a superb
job of staying together, rarely coming apart" (283). Justifiably full of self-
loathing and self-contempt following his participation in the murders,
Sickert nevertheless resolves to readjust his method of ordering reality:

> He knew now that to get rid of something you did not externalize
> it in a work of art, for that work of art hung around your neck. What
> he had to do . . . was to transpose things, always relating a dead
> individual to a class of the dead, a specific murderer to a class of
> murderers, and a voyeuristic painter to a class of those . . . to whom
> he felt closer and closer. It was as if his life were shifting sideways;
> he limped along a diagonal. (379)

Though still crippled by linearity, he vows to think multidimensionally.
Whether he will succeed is questionable, but he recognizes the need.

In West's Gothic environment, women also dread and envy men's biological and social zones. Attempts to cross the borders create not only disappointment but, in the case of the Whitechapel women's plot against the
patriarchy, a murderous backlash from the offended males. The female ability
to construct alinear systems backfires in the case of Mary Kelly, who deliberately disseminates an exaggerated narrative of Eddy's indiscretions among
her prostitute allies. She then enlists their aid in challenging the social sys-

tem for financial restitution and a restoration of women's names to historical notice by means of a letter written to a figurehead of a queen. By venturing into the forbidden male realm of power, she and her female friends
directly confront Salisbury, who up until that point had been willing to let
matters go with Annie's lobotomy. The women's desperate ploy to gain au-
tonomy is foolhardy but understandable. They are weary of their vulnerability to masculine malfeasance. Kelly complains to Sickert after Annie is
lobotomized by Gull: "Women are women, and men is what kills them off.
All the time" (108). West's female characters tend to reduce this fear to a
deterministic biological basis, in this instance the openness of female geni-
talia. Ellen, for example, laments her body's susceptibility to invasion:

> If only, she thought, women had tighter zones: less open, less prey
> to rubbish; but that would make them less open to men, which in
> the end would defeat all purposes. It had to be so, but she often
> wished she were a man, able to cut off all traffic with the outside
> world by simply trapping the end of it in a clothespin or squeezing
> tight between finger and thumb. Nothing entered them. Their
> troubles came from the surface and lurked in the cheesy folds. She
> did not shrink from the facts of life, but she wanted them revised.
> . . . The sperm-bearers, she decided, are full of redundancies: that's
> why they go whoring off to make more of sex than it really is, add-
> ing filth and frenzy to something that's, for them, over in a trice,
> and, for us, easy to do at home, in a hammock or just about any-
> where. We need their seepages, that's all. (67, 69)

Ellen, though economic and social worlds apart from the murder victims
of Whitechapel, is nevertheless part of their sisterhood not only because
boundary-transgressing Sickert sleeps with all of them but because she shares,
if nothing else, their female vulnerability to exploitation.

What distinguishes West's novel from most other Ripper retellings is
precisely this restoration of the Ripper's female victims as key players in the
Gothic narrative of gender jeopardy.[8] West's elevation of a formerly repressed
or marginalized subplot in the Ripper narrative provides the novel its true
complexity, and a nuanced sensitivity missing from most fictional treatments
of the Whitechapel murders. Rather than attempting to universalize the
Ripper and the prostitute victims into archetypes of Victimizer and Victims,
West creates layered characterizations of the victims as well as the killers to
demonstrate their interconnectedness. As Madden observes:

West examines these figures to display an intricate phenomenology of victimization. In every case victimizers are themselves victims. No one appears to exert any genuine control in this world; even those with the greatest authority—the queen and her prime minister—must answer to forces that supersede and manipulate them, and the invisible role of the Masons provides the novel's air of mystery. (102)

Rather, all of these characters are continually acted on even as acting. Their active attempts to influence events routinely meet with disaster from outside forces, which gives the narrative its Gothic horror. Sickert's manipulation of Eddy, Eddy's manipulation of Annie, Mary Kelly's manipulation of the government, even Gull's manipulation of civilian London—all efforts end in destruction of the self and others. But West's novel is something other than nihilistic in its suggestion that, while death is inevitable, meaning and identity and physical appetite can benignly manifest themselves without renouncing all notions of community or solidarity.

For example, the women of Whitechapel, Mary Kelly's little band of struggling victims, attempt a politically negotiated escape from their oppressive circumstances and bring death upon themselves. However, this tragic outcome does not negate the fact that their smaller female community is a nourishing, vital, and loosely structured (thus more pliable and durable) one. Mary Kelly shows a refreshing candor and lack of sentimentality when answering Sickert's question about what drives women to prostitution:

> Mostly by inclination. . . . Don't be sentimental, my old lad. Don't you forget that what the ladies have between their legs is every bit as bad as what the gentlemen have. Just as hot to trot, my dear, mark my words. Just as wet and wobbly when the moment strikes, so much you don't rightly know what you're a-doing of. So long as it gets what it wants. (140)

Mary Kelly, in the same spirit of acceptance, reflects at one point upon her drunken revelries with her fellow prostitutes. She calls their collective "an only slightly divided family, half a dozen or so among some twelve hundred prostitutes in Whitechapel, all of them women on the edge, making no kind of living but eking out a cobweb of an existence, undecided what to do next, if anything" and a "loose clique of the loose" (163). Their alternative family is a viable defensive structure in a larger society that allows them no participation or protection and frequently shows them no mercy.[9] God is no help to her folk either, as Mary Kelly knows:

> It was strange: all the time, like a properly brought-up Irish girl, she listened for the voice of God, Who did not always have His prick in His fist, but all she ever heard were the voices of the women of Whitechapel, going more and more to booze to quell their pain or obscure time, and mispronouncing more and more the words that life depended on. (245)

After the murders begin striking down her coconspirators, Mary Kelly decides "that a woman had no chance, not unless she went about with a friend or two, preferably with a pointed umbrella" (264). Another marginalized figure in London's social hierarchy, a Jewish socialist, thinks along similar lines following his discovery of Liz Stride's corpse: "if you were a member of *nothing* you were nobody at all, were you? Safety in numbers had something to commend it, he decided, and the bigger the number the better" (306).

West proposes that interconnecting relationships are the solution to meaningful existence within the master narrative of a monolithic and dehumanizing political system, even if that system musters its resources to quash its ideological enemies. Mary Kelly therefore consistently seeks a sisterhood as a survival strategy, which dooms her (the blackmail plot) yet keeps her true to her open nature. Though she ironically confides her fears to Ripper-accomplice Sickert, she does not reject personal responsibility and seek protection from a stronger male, unlike more traditionally structured narratives of this subgenre. Sickert himself, on the eve of the murder series, realizes that "the women of Whitechapel would have to look after themselves like foxes hunted" (212). While this narrative focus on victimization could have been little more than another imaginative trampling of female initiative, in West's scenario it is an elegiac indictment of those who victimize. And in a patriarchal society where men control the institutions of power, even though Queen Victoria may be the figurehead, it is the impoverished, particularly the females, who will bear the brunt of victimization. Some of the victimization is individually originated, but most of it is institutional. Prince Eddy, for example, has no idea

> how badly the poor were treated in his precious England, or how severely, in that massive group, women were dealt with just because they were women—vessels of slop, as he had heard his father refer

to them, whereas the tonic tone of the time was to be closed, sealed, upright, dry, and aloof. (102)

Passages such as these lead Gary Davenport to the conclusion that the novel "would delight a Marxist critic. It is among other things a political novel and can even be strident at times about the gulf between the 'two nations' of Victorian England" (302). It is also a feminist novel, according to Andrea Dworkin in *Ms.*, because of its rewriting of the Ripper legend from, at times, the female point of view and its scathing denunciation of patriarchal objectification of living females. Josh Rubins points to Mary Kelly in particular as "a bona fide radical feminist hero of sorts" (12).

Gender boundaries in *Kiss the Girls* also break down in the presence of the elemental, precivilized human identity. However, the film's emphasis is markedly different than West's. *Kiss the Girls* destabilizes gender for the primary purpose of reconstructing gender within a traditional masculinist framework. In the narrative's mythic territory, the elemental human identity into which the social female identity must be subsumed is undeniably masculine. Only Alex, not Kate, can defeat Ruskin's phallic power by becoming, in effect, a stronger male murderer. The film's claustrophobic Gothic environment is full of men like Alex competing physically and mentally for their own inviolate patch of space. "Territoriality" is the guiding masculine principle in this narrative. The principle is expressed through male participation in games of superiority over other men (and, of course, women). The film's opening minutes establish that Alex, by way of seeking "relief" from his professional duties, coaches boxing for young men who beat one another for dominance of the few square yards of roped-off boxing ring. Dr. Sachs, the lecherous patsy set up by Ruskin for arrest, is introduced to the audience as a superb swimmer who pushes his older body to surpass the athletic abilities of college students half his age and to exceed their sexual prowess by bedding as many young women as possible. Naomi's boyfriend Seth is first seen by Alex playing sweaty, physically raw basketball with his fellow black males. Castillo, a police detective, is not an athlete, but nevertheless bores Kate on a stakeout with his quoting of baseball statistics and zealous favoring of a specific team on the basis of regional loyalty. All of these sporting rituals are conducted within an enclosed geographic space—the boxing ring, the swimming lane, the basketball court—whose limits exclude outside participation and allow individualized control from those most physically able to do so.

By extension, through repeated narrative reference to "jurisdiction," the professional activities of the male police investigators are also seen primarily as a game conducted within precisely defined geographic parameters. The rules have been expressly designed to box in and "beat" not only the subject of the investigation but also to exclude other investigators from participation. The film establishes that this jealous territoriality is the masculine norm. Those who penetrate the precisely defined borders of the game (like Alex) are stigmatized and punished. Alex, for example, leaves his home turf to investigate Naomi's kidnapping, and so encounters rudeness and incivility from the North Carolina police. On his arrival they keep him waiting in the outer office for two hours. The North Carolina police chief says to Alex, "Don't mess around in the kitchen"—an interestingly feminine metaphor indicative of the film's contradictory desires to blend individual domains (the masculine crime scene, the feminine domestic sphere) and then finally to restore their sanctity. "Not messing around in the kitchen" becomes the metaphor for understanding the degree to which the film insists that border crossers, who don't respect the rules, must be beaten down. In such a jealously territorial male world, Ruskin and Rudolph's competitive rivalry and private killing zones are only slightly exaggerated forms of the will to dominance, traditionally a male-gendered prerogative.

The most brutal males in the narrative are Ruskin and Rudolph, but Ruskin ironically believes himself to be the most sensitive—"the greatest lover." He transforms himself into a mutedly androgynous figure, capable of disarming female fear (so he thinks) of over-strong masculinity with his soft voice, appreciation of the arts, and lover's manner. But in the precivilized world of naked power differentials in *Kiss the Girls,* Ruskin's penchant for "feminine" tastes (art, music, poetry, romance) is not a respectful appreciation of female and "civilized" difference. Rather, his "appreciation" is an attempt to incorporate femininity into his own masculinist realm of power, where Casanova can completely possess the minds and bodies of his lovers in a harem subject to his autocratic sexual desires. Unlike Rudolph, whose relatively uncomplicated fear and revulsion of women as Other combine murderously but briefly with his sexual desire for them, Ruskin attempts to conquer his fear of female sexuality by lengthy exposure to it—taking prisoners. He then breaks individual female identities for the express purpose of asserting his own power over them for as long as possible—until they break "the rules." Of course, just as the police need a worthy adversary to make their victory sweeter and more appreciated, Ruskin needs worthy female opponents to beat, so that his one-upmanship of Rudolph can also be more personally satisfying.

Toward this goal, Ruskin selects, as Alex puts it, "extraordinary" women as his "lovers." His eight abductees are professionally aspiring young women drawn from his hunting territory—the ultramodern Research Triangle cluster of colleges and institutes in North Carolina. They are also quite assertive, as Agent Craig says: "They're all strong-willed. They're all defiant." The point is underscored by the narrative focus on Kate, the only one of Casanova's victims to escape from his dungeon on her own "masculine" abilities—verbal aggressiveness and physical strength. Following her escape and near-death, Kate enters the public masculine domain to issue a *mano a mano* challenge to Casanova via television. She begins a partnership with Alex, Sampson, and Castillo to track down her tormentor. In these and similar actions, Kate enters the male domain of power willfully and creatively, as a more-or-less equal partner, but is ultimately beaten into submission for her trespasses.

Kate, as a female doctor, is already a masculinized trespasser into male territory as the film begins. A scene where she is unable to express compassion to the family of a young female coma victim works on a couple of levels to confirm gender stereotypes. Aspiring toward a male profession, she seems at odds with her "natural" female compassion. Her awkward attempt to be a strong, silent male suggests not only her unsuitability for the job but also evokes audience stereotypes of male doctors as less empathetic and less articulate than females. She is also a kick-boxer (a parallel to masculine Alex), whose athletic endeavors are seen by herself and a female colleague as a "poor substitute for sex." Her comment is in some way a validation for audience members inclined to see Kate's masculine endeavors as perversions of women's natural station in life as sexual vessels. Casanova's consequent invasion of her "proper" domestic sphere to kidnap and threaten her sexually is the most fitting expression of the film's symbolic logic—that female transgression of proper gender boundaries must be punished by sexually potent male authority.[10] The film's final scene completes the symbolic arc. Ruskin, knowing his game is almost over, decides to return to Kate's domestic territory—literally, the kitchen—and kill her. His violent battering and stabbing of Kate wears her down and punishes her for her disobedience of his private masculine rules and, by extension, the patriarchal authority he represents as policeman.

The victimized maiden is only saved by Alex's timely arrival. Alex is the film's approved patriarch, because he is capable of redeeming masculine social control as a morally unimpeachable (i.e., black) former victim of its excesses.

He kills the white male rapist/killer and accepts his proper gender role as protector and comforter of the thoroughly broken and now submissive Kate. The narrative has anticipated this function for Alex all along. In his role as psychologist first and police detective second, he favors empathy and intuition rather than rational, logical analysis. Before entering the serial killer investigation, Alex convinces an abused woman that her murder of her drunken and violent husband was justifiable and thus keeps her from killing herself with a pointedly phallic choice of weapons—a gun—crammed into her submissive and open mouth. Alex is thus immediately associated with a repudiation of male violence. He further shows a "feminine" willingness to cross proper boundaries by taking on an essentially private investigation, in defiance of male social protocol, to find his kidnapped niece. His reliance on words more than action is evident in his soothing treatment of the suicidal wife, his distraught sister, and recovering Kate.

But Alex is also a strong male, capable of moving freely through all social spheres with fewer penalties than Kate. He is perfectly willing to meet force with force. He is a boxing coach, after all, and also very good with a gun when "reluctantly" forced to use it at the film's bloody climax. But the masculine hero of 1990s fiction must be empathetic in order to redeem masculinity, as decades of cultural critique have illustrated glaringly the deficiencies in traditional philosophies and applications of male-gendered force. So, when Kate's female physician implausibly fails to recognize the effects of a drug named Sistol while Alex does, he literally brings Kate back to life in a way her physician cannot after her first escape from Casanova's lair. He then preserves that life by recognizing Ruskin's alternate identity as Casanova just in time to stop Ruskin before he can kill Kate. Alex first tries the empathic and "feminine" approach to stopping Ruskin's violence, a gambit that Ruskin, protecting his own metaphoric masculine boundaries, definitively refutes: "Don't mindfuck me!" The narrative thus leaves Alex no choice except to shoot Ruskin to save the weaker, sobbing Kate. Alex's solution is the traditional physical force of patriarchy. Alex is an androgynous figure, true, but androgynous only to the degree he needs to be to restore patriarchal force to some semblance of its previous credibility.

The
Psycho Profilers
and the Influence of
Thomas Harris

It is little exaggeration to say that Thomas Harris, for all practical purposes, created the current formula for mainstream serial killer fiction back in 1981 with the publication of *Red Dragon*. His 1988 follow-up, *The Silence of the Lambs,* solidified the formula (controlling Gothic tone, two killers, a dark and troubled law-enforcement outsider in uneasy alliance with a murderer) and ensured his status as the foremost writer of serial killer fiction.[1] A film adaptation of *Red Dragon,* re-titled *Manhunter,* was released to limited notice in 1986. However, the 1991 film version of *The Silence of the Lambs,* directed by Jonathan Demme, became a certified box-office hit, won five major Academy Awards including Best Picture, and firmly ensconced the cannibalistic psychiatrist, Hannibal Lecter, into pop demonology.

Harris's imitators in various media since 1991 have been numerous and many have met with success, proving the durability of the formula. One need only look to the television programs *The X Files,* the now-canceled *Millennium,* or *Profiler* to see the Harris influence still at work. Harris's narratives, and most of those to follow, play with any number of genre conventions—Gothic romance, police procedural, murder mystery, hard-boiled detective fiction, horror, and so on—even while he bases them on careful research of the FBI's theories and databases regarding serial murder,[2] which in turn have evolved from decades of collaborative work between police officers and psychologists to produce "personality profiles" of unknown criminal perpetrators.

Two of the most famous and media-savvy FBI profilers frequently mention their associations with Thomas Harris's fiction and the films made from it. John Douglas, coauthor of two popular books on what he calls "mindhunting," makes a point of mentioning that Jack Crawford, Harris's fictitious FBI section chief, is modeled after him (*Mindhunter* 172). Kristi Zea, production designer on the film adaptation of *The Silence of the Lambs,* also credits Douglas with significant input into the creative process (Persons 16). Actor Scott Glenn, who portrays Crawford, was reportedly traumatized into renouncing his long-held opposition to the death penalty after hearing Douglas play confiscated tape recordings of two serial killers torturing teenaged girls (Goodman 70). Retired FBI agent and author Robert Ressler, the man who claims to be most directly responsible for popularization of the phrase "serial killer," relays the story of how on two occasions in the 1980s, at the request of the FBI public-affairs office, he showed Harris around the offices of the Behavioral Science Unit. During these visits, Ressler gave Harris case profiles on such notable serial killers as Edmund Kemper, Richard Chase, and Ed Gein and introduced him on his second visit to the only female agent then working at the BSU. The strong implication is that Ressler provided him his worldly inspiration for Clarice Starling (Ressler and Shachtman 272–73). One of Harris's confidantes confirms the FBI influence on Harris: "[Harris has] *been* to Quantico. . . . He's *talked* to that FBI man" (qtd. in Hoban, "Silence" 50). In Ressler's meetings with Harris, the Möbius strip of what Jean-François Baudrillard refers to as "simulacra" plays out. The FBI profilers draw on nineteenth-century detective fiction to create a database of "fact" that Harris incorporates into his "reality"-based twentieth-century detective fiction.

It is not too surprising that the FBI institutional authority is generally supportive of authors such as Harris because the resulting narratives on one level sanctify, even glorify, the law-enforcement reactive approach to violent crime. No doubt part of this institutional acceptance derives from the superficial media depiction of the profilers as the guardians—"the thin blue line"—between civilization and anarchy. In terms of the popular narrative being communally created, Ressler and his fellow experts are suit-and-tie variants of the folk legend hero as categorized by Lutz Rohrich and the fairy-tale hero as identified by Vladimir Propp. These heroes make a risky, lone journey into the enemy's territory to combat an evil beyond the comprehension or warrior's abilities of ordinary men. In accordance with Propp's structural analysis of the fairy tale, which can be extended to include folk legend, the profiler is constructed as a "prophetic hero" who "gets along without any helpers. . . . One of the most important attributes of a helper is his prophetic wisdom: the prophetic horse, the prophetic wife, the wise lad, etc. When a helper is absent from the tale, this quality is transferred to the hero" (82–83). The fictionalized profilers are "prophetic" in this sense because as American individualists, they claim no helpers and possess an insight into the killing mind so acute that it enables the profilers to divine the identities of the invisible killers. The Gothic legacy and the inherent destabilization strategies of the serial killer tale work against the scientific, rationalist methodology of the state law enforcement apparatus by instead focusing on individual profilers whose connection with their intuitive selves verges on the extrasensory or supernatural. Harris's novels (especially his latest, *Hannibal*) are not unqualified celebrations of the modern law enforcement wizardry of the state or its status as protector of middle-class civilization. Instead, the novels valorize the pseudo-supernatural abilities of skillful individuals to defy orthodoxy and flawed institutional procedure in the service of some greater good—in itself a classically orthodox, populist mythology of American selfhood in rebellion against the posers and bureaucrats whose stewardship of cherished institutions is treasonously flawed. Harris's fictionalized profilers do make use of the FBI definitions and computers, of course, but at the same time they quickly realize the limitations of narrowly defined academic knowledge when faced with "the real thing"—the evil and unknowable serial killer.

For example, Jack Crawford, Harris's depiction of a prominent FBI Behavioral Science agent, is shrewd enough to draft intelligent but academically unorthodox "outsiders" such as Will Graham and Clarice Starling into service to combat the more elusive serial murderers, particularly Francis Dolarhyde and Jame Gumb. The distant perspectives of Graham and Starling allow them to approach the cases "fresh," as Graham puts it. These two profilers have read the FBI papers (Starling calls them "fundamental" in the most reductive sense of that word—see *Lambs* 17) but remain largely unconvinced by FBI orthodoxy. Nor does the FBI bureaucracy want these maverick profilers around: that is, until an extraordinary serial killer eludes capture. At such times, the narratives suggest, the American public is damned lucky to have resourceful free agents such as Graham and Starling who can operate unhindered by the restrictions of formal institutional affiliation. Though Graham and Starling are not vigilantes, they nevertheless appeal to a certain aspect—the desire to police one's own area of responsibility without interference from the distant machinery of due process—of the American individualist character. The same fierce ideology of the asocial individual also produces, of course, the serial killer. The psycho profiler and the profiler are two sides of the same belief system. This doubling is a constant in the subgenre, as I will discuss in relation to Harris's first two serial killer works and one of the films based on them.

The dialectical tensions in Harris's contributions to the serial killer subgenre are even more self-destabilizing than most, because the Gothic conventions he adopts are in opposition to the rationalist assumptions of the detective genre in which he also works. Harris's score of imitators, though usually far less artful, similarly adopt this strategy of destabilization of meaning. A brief history of the detective genre and FBI theories about profiling is illuminating, not only because Harris and all of his imitators are so obviously influenced by these texts but also because their debt to earlier genre fiction is striking.

The Detective Genre and Criminal Profiling

The serial killer in fiction is a product of the Gothic literary movement; so, too, is the killer's adversary—the profiler/detective. Maurine Reddy argues in *Sisters in Crime* that detective fiction finds its roots in the Gothic. Geraldine Pederson-Krag identifies another influence on the detective story: the "witch-hunting" tales of the sixteenth, seventeenth, and eighteenth centuries, wherein "there was a need to discover witches lurking in everyday surroundings" (16). Thus, the serial killer narrative comes naturally by its sense of a lurking menace to be discovered behind the veil of appearance, and has found its full flower in the United States, where a Calvinist heritage predisposes many Americans to "read" their environment for clues regarding their "elected" or privileged status.

The mystery or detective genre is notoriously difficult to define in the sense that almost any novelist at one time or another structures a narrative around a crime or criminal and yet remains outside the boundaries of genre. Even for those working within the genre, classification is complicated by the existence of various narrative subsets: the police procedural, the classic "puzzle" story, the hardboiled detective story, and so on. In spite of the difficulties, however, David Lehman has broadly defined the genre in this way:

The detective novel, as a condition of its being, took murder out of the ethical realm and put it into that of aesthetics. By analogy, murder in a murder mystery becomes a kind of poetic conceit, often quite a baroque one; the criminal is an artist, the detective an aesthete and a critic, and the blundering policeman a philistine. (xvii)

The detective genre, then, like the Gothic, resembles nothing more or less than a fictional commentary on the process of sign-reading itself, with the detective discovering "the significance of these [signs] and forg[ing] them into a chain of clues that leads to the criminal and finally binds him" (Pederson-Krag 14). As Lehman goes on to say, the detective story's "narrative line flows backward, from effect to cause, causing the reader to become a participant or co-conspirator" (xvii) as he or she constructs hypothetical scenarios of what may have happened on the basis of a few clues. Poe's Dupin and Doyle's Sherlock Holmes excel at this style of critical reading—so much so, in fact, that they become as separate from the plodding mass of dull professional detectives, or critics, as the criminals they all theoretically oppose. The intellectual mastery of a Dupin or a Holmes naturally compels reader sympathy, which has the corollary (and troubling) effect of implicating the voyeuristic reader in the criminal mind that the equally voyeuristic fictional detective exerts so much mental effort attempting to enter. As is evident in a novel like Harris's *Red Dragon* or the Michael Mann film *Manhunter* that is based on it, implication of the viewer into the criminal mind-set occupies an ascendant position in the serial killer narrative—a trait it has inherited from the story of detection.

The objectification that this implies has landed the detective genre, as it has evolved from Poe and Doyle's original contributions, squarely in the arena of feminist debate. Kathleen Klein argues in *The Woman Detective* that female detectives in fiction seldom challenge patriarchal norms, and therefore the genre itself is inherently antithetical to feminist interests. Barbara Lawrence traces the detective story's sexism back to its most famous male character, Sherlock Holmes. Holmes's emotional detachment, as she characterizes it,

has been exaggerated by later writers until the tough American private-eye emerged, using, abusing, scorning the women who draped themselves over him, lurked in his bed or started undressing before he even knew their names. The writers and readers of these stories are, of course, indulging in sexual fantasy. But the emphasis on male dominance cannot be ignored: women are objects; they are unthinking, emotional creatures whose sole reason for existence is to serve men's needs, even when those needs are, perhaps, abnormal, as are Philip Marlowe's or Mike Hammer's. (40)

In response to this genre development, Lawrence continues, women writers created more emotionally engaged female detectives (like Agatha Christie's Miss Marple) who initially were older spinsters but gradually became more integrated into traditionally masculine spheres of activity. Today, there are fictional female private detectives (like P. D. James's Cordelia Grey) or law-enforcement professionals (Patricia Cornwell's Dr. Kay Scarpetta) who directly work, or compete, with their male counterparts.[3] Maggie Humm in her article "Feminist Detective Fiction" argues that the detective genre does indeed challenge gender norms. Carolyn Heilbrun goes so far as to say that the detective genre, in spite of its phallocentric legacy or maybe because of it, has been in the cultural forefront of revising sexist attitudes and patriarchal tradition:

> [The] move toward androgyny and away from stereotypical sex roles—away, more importantly, from the ridiculing and condemning of those who do not conform to stereotypical sex roles—has, I am proud to say, found greater momentum in the detective story than in any other genre, and has recently gone further in the United States than elsewhere. (5)

The serial killer narrative, for all its dehumanizing and gory excesses, is also centrally facing these issues Heilbrun speaks of. In fact, it could be argued that gender concern over the representation of serial murder has been an outgrowth of the feminist concern with and rewriting of the originally masculine-dominated detective genre—a controversy that cannot help but be reflected in the serial killer/detective story.[4]

These kinds of stories, regardless of their gender shadings, reflect a distinctly separate, and more recent, development in the detective genre: the police procedural. The police procedural, according to Julian Symons, "concentrates upon the detailed investigation of a crime from the point of view of the police, and . . . does so with considerable realism" (193). In contrast to the labyrinthine plotting and intellectual complexity of the puzzle story, the police procedural seeks to ground itself in the mundane, often sordid, reality of criminal behavior. Such behavior typically involves spontaneous or "motiveless" crimes of passion that do not require inspired guesswork to solve so much as plodding adherence to the routine procedures of police-work.[5] Ratiocination is secondary to persistence. Also, rather than one crime or murder dominating the narrative, several (usually unrelated) crimes compete for the detective's strained attention in an attempt to make the puzzle story more realistic. The lone detective is depicted in his relationships with other police professionals, all of whom are suffering under their own bur-densome caseloads. Multiplicity of crime generates multiple storylines (Bin-yan 109). Puzzle solving is replaced by crime solving. This twentieth-century genre development was a prerequisite for the serial killer narrative as demonstrated, say, in the NBC television series *Profiler.* The often-graphic nature of the multiple murders and the emphasis on investigative detail, pro-fessional alliances or rivalries, and "realism" are legacies of the naturalistic conventions of the police procedural.

However, attention to realism does not prevent the detective story from exploring the metaphysical realm associated with Gothic destabilization. The detective story's reliance on the powers of the mind to make order of com-plexity is often called into question, as Michael Holquist argues. On the basis of precedents set by Robbe-Grillet and Borges, both of whom have worked decidedly postmodern turns on the detective genre, Holquist concludes that

> the metaphysical detective story does not have the narcotizing ef-fect of its progenitor; instead of familiarity, it gives strangeness, a strangeness which more often than not is the result of jumbling the well-known patterns of classical detective stories. Instead of reas-suring, they disturb. They are not an escape, but an attack. By ex-ploiting the conventions of the detective story such men as Borges and Robbe-Grillet have fought against the modernist attempt to fill the void of the world with rediscovered mythical symbols. Rather, they dramatize the void. (173)

The serial killer story more than most projects its subjects (characters and readers) into this metaphysical void. This destabilization of solid systems and symbols is the true narratological agenda in the story of serial killer versus detective—not puzzle solving or crime solving, though these conventions are played with, often to ironic effect. Questions of the void, called forth by the killer's deliberate penetration into it, preoccupy the characters within the narrative. Because of its emphasis on ontology and the inability to come to definite conclusions concerning it, the revealed identity of the murderer, which is in flux anyway, is not as important to the reader, though obviously still a concern for the characters within the story.

This kind of unstable, constantly shifting narrative is not a murder mystery in the classic sense, but rather what David Richter terms an "anti-mystery" and Stefano Tani calls "anti-detective." The police still seek to unmask a murderer. However, in many cases the killer is revealed to the audience, by isolated point-of-view psychological portraits if not by actual named identity, long before the police find him or her. In contrast to the traditional mystery, the victims of this murderer are usually chosen precisely because no traditional investigation centering on suspects with a hidden but ultimately clear motive will succeed. The victims generally have little to no prior connection to their murderer. No motive, as the classic mystery defines it, exists here for the police to uncover in plodding, linear fashion. Richter contends that

> serial murder serves to break up even more successfully the narrative's diegetic flow, the sense of linearity, of a movement between beginning and end. In the process, of course, the serial victims . . . become random targets rather than individualized persons. . . . [W]e read the blood only as a code, an exercise in spatial form. (108)

The modernist highbrow mystery has transmuted into this typically postmodern form of anti-mystery, Richter concludes.

This kind of metafictional project, or anti-mystery, has always been a subsidiary of the mystery genre. Rather than reading a plot, the anti-mystery reader reads a metadiscourse on how plots are written and then consumed by readers. Tani further identifies three distinct narrative strategies of the anti-detective story: *innovation,* in which an early, unsatisfactory solution to the mystery is complicated by a later, more puzzling one, or the solution "does not imply the punishment of the culprit," or "a solution is found by chance"; *deconstruction,* in which "instead of a solution there is a suspension of the solution"; and *metafiction,* in which "detection is present in the relation between the writer who deviously writes ('hides') his own text and the reader who wants to make sense out of it" (43). To varying degrees, most of these elements are present in those serial killer narratives that emphasize a pursuit of the murderer. Serial killers as metafictional gameplayers conceal, move, and reconceal their texts in an effort to stymie the detective "readers" who may be looking right at the text and still be unable to decode it—until the last few pages of the novel or last few scenes of the film.

Incidentally, the term "detective" as applied to the procedural movement is used quite loosely, as the protagonist is often not a professional law-enforcement figure at all. In fact, the detectives in serial killer fiction are usually academics or intellectuals in only the loosest of confederations with law enforcement (as in Caleb Carr's 1994 novel *The Alienist*) or, in some cases, no alliance at all.[6] Lest this idea of pursuit, with its bipolar situating of hunter and quarry in opposition to one another, sound too morally clear-cut, the procedural theme as combined with the Gothic genre influence usually works very hard to implicate the detectives, at least to some extent, in the killer's crimes, or the cultural attitudes that make them possible. Frequently, moral surety is completely lost or severely undermined as both killer and detective conceptualize their relationship in terms of a complex, multirole game, where abstract, binary notions of right and wrong become tenuous at best. The procedural narrative operates within an ominously Gothic environment where the daily practice of morality and justice constantly slides away from idealistic centers, epitomizing a destabilizing strategy common to Gothic fiction.

One of the most characteristic destabilizing operations of literary Gothicism is its refusal to honor the traditional demarcation between "fact" and "fiction." Rather, all texts or linguistic constructs become "fictions" subject to reading or interpretation. The body itself becomes a text to be read. In fact, Roland Barthes calls the text "an anagram for our body" (17). In the serial killer narrative, the crime scenes that harbor the bodies of slaughtered women and children are texts left behind by "authors," which the literary critic—that is, the detective—must then decode. In the anxiety-ridden milieu of crime-obsessed America, the profiler has become a cultural archetype of the ancient detective figure. The most obvious source of this archetype as disseminated to the nation by fiction writers is, oddly, a federal police organization guided by what it considers to be eminently scientific and rational principles. The tense marriage of rationalist philosophy and postmodern indeterminacy bears a closer look.

Instead of directly investigating crimes or arresting suspects, profilers attempt to provide psychological sketches of murderers, rapists, arsonists, bombers, and so on, based on an interpretation or "reading" of the crime scene left behind. The law enforcement literature on profiling provides an insider's view of how the profilers view their job. According to Hazelwood and Douglas, "the profiler is searching for clues which indicate the probable personality configuration of the responsible individual" (22). Ault and Reese add that this kind of speculative profile is designed to make the task of finding an individual within a suspect pool of thousands or even millions of people easier: "The goal of the profiler is to provide enough information to investigators to enable them to limit or better direct their investigations" (23). In spite of these eminently practical-sounding mission statements, however, profiling resembles, more than anything else, fiction writing. It is a particularly empty or hollow style of writing at that, revealing little to nothing of social complexities and almost offensively self-laudatory or self-confirming, as Mark Seltzer says (131). Regardless of how intellectually unsatisfying it may be, however, profiling still fits within a long literary and cultural tradition of what Joel Black calls the "aesthetics of murder."

Close examination of any one of the manifestos of criminal investigative analysis, or profiling, reveals that they are not only paeans to a need for control rivaled only by that of a serial killer but also what Colin Campbell deems "romances of science" (113). More specifically, the ontology of the entire hyperrational profiling process as canonized by the Federal Bureau of Investigation lies in detective fiction, as a crucial passage in Ressler, Burgess, and Douglas's homicide primer reads:

> Although Lunde has stated that the murders of fiction bear no resemblance to the murders of reality . . . a connection between fictional detective techniques and modern profiling methods may indeed exist. For example, it is an attention to detail that is the hallmark of famous fictional detectives; the smallest item at a crime scene does not escape their notice. [This] is stated by the famous Sergeant Cuff in Wilkie Collins's 1868 novel *The Moonstone,* widely acknowledged as the first full-length detective story. . . . [A]ttention to detail is equally as essential to present-day profiling. No piece of information is too small; each detail is scrutinized for its contribution to a profile of the killer. (11)

The authors' veneration of nineteenth-century detective fiction, and more significantly its good-faith reliance on the ability of clues to form a solid deductive chain of logic leading to the author of a crime scene, is clear. The authors are aware of their breaking of disciplinary barriers, as John Douglas and Alan Burgess elsewhere write: "Criminal profiling . . . combine[s] the results of studies in other disciplines with more traditional techniques" (9).

John Douglas and Mark Olshaker make the point explicit: "And though books that dramatize and glorify what we do, such as Thomas Harris's memorable *The Silence of the Lambs,* are somewhat fanciful and prone to dramatic license, our antecedents actually do go back to crime fiction more than crime fact" (*Mindhunter* 19). Passages such as these not only cross disciplinary boundaries but also tacitly admit the interweaving of empiricism and representation in much the same way as Gothic literature does. The main departure from the Gothic tradition is that the profilers and detectives are typically much more confident, with little basis in actual results, in their abilities to discern reality from chimera.

The profiling strategy proceeds on the optimistic, rationalist assumptions that there is a one-to-one, fixed or true correspondence between sign and signified, and that close enough reading by a skilled enough "critic" will strip away ambiguity and coax forth the secrets of the signified.[7] Ironically, however, profiling as an act of reading is based on a foundation of fiction. This seems like a fairly self-evident statement until one remembers the profilers' professed agenda is so doggedly yoked to empirical data.[8] Profiling is a curiously abstract approach for those who elsewhere deny a professional interest in theory, such as FBI agent Roy Hazelwood: "We don't get hung up on why the killer does the things he does . . . What we're interested in is that he does it, and that he does it in a way that leads us to him" (qtd. in Porter 50).

The act of reading carried out by profiling represents a pseudoscientific attempt at mastery or control of the unknown author's "literary" project. In fact, profiling is an attempt to appropriate the text's language in order to identify the author. The reader must interact with the text and, in a way, supplant the author. The profiler enters into an oddly personal power struggle with a completely imaginary enemy as manifested in the physical traces left behind by a real but anonymous individual. At times, the profiler imaginatively becomes the killer he or she is seeking. One of the most disturbing examples of this in the true-crime literature is found in the opening section of one of Douglas and Olshaker's books. In this introduction, Douglas speculates in the first person about what a particularly savage rapist/murderer might have been thinking as he stalked, captured, and brutalized his victim (*Journey* 1–5). This sympathetic bond between detective and criminal illustrates the literature of serial murder's easy merging with the Gothic romance of doubling.

"Serial killer" itself, as a term, reveals a fundamentally slippery relationship between signifier and signified when we consider that a profiler, by attempting to halt an ongoing series of crimes, becomes a killer of serials. But because the serial killer is the primary author of the "text" or serial under construction, the profiler is at a grave disadvantage. The profiler does his or her best to offset the imbalance with high-tech computers and databases (all of which must be funded by a corpus of taxpayers who must be frightened enough of serial murder to approve the expenditures) and a formidable arsenal of impressive-sounding but almost uselessly vague psychological jargon. The power differential between profiler and killer is intolerable to the profiler, so the killer's protective anonymity must be stripped away as soon as possible. The lack of any demonstrably clear motive renders this a next-to-impossible task in reality, largely because the serial murder profile can only propose a hypothetical or "statistical" (Seltzer 130) criminal—a fictive construct or system—into which specific suspects must be "framed." The profilers, such as Roy Hazelwood, often admit that this imaginative drawing of frames resembles art more than science (Porter 52). However, the messy distinctions and contradictions are concealed behind clinical language.[9]

The media and the public characteristically celebrate profiling as an almost magical method of detection, but one that is nevertheless yoked to scientific method and the rational daytime world in which legend must exist. The trouble is, even when not blatantly off the mark, a typical profile's language is usually so general as to apply to dozens, hundreds, perhaps thousands of people.[10] None of this matters, however, to the cultural purveyors of the serial killer legend. They have a vested dramaturgical interest in establishing the profilers as the "good guys" in the postmodern mystery play.[11] Richard Tithecott elaborates:

> The struggle with evil elevates the FBI to a community service, above politics. As fighters of evil, the FBI can assume the powers of a priesthood: that is, the power of being both attached to the law and above it, the power of the confessor, the power of possessing the right to regard an individual as a battleground between Satanic and godly forces. (22)

Colin Campbell suggests an explanation for profiling's enduring appeal:

> The problem is not so much that these profiles are sometimes wrong—anyone can be wrong—but that they're usually irrelevant, and vastly overtouted. The police do not really need them. Yet psychological manhunts are fascinating mysteries to many Americans,

including some psychologists and detectives. So the press keeps writing about them and the public keeps reading them. Psychological manhunts thrive partly on account of their entertainment value. (113)

The serial murder profile can only narrow down to a hypothesized *type:* a fictive construct or system not unlike a computer-generated model. Furthermore, profiling's ascendancy as a potent public-relations tool for law enforcement is intimately linked to the increasing utility of computer technology in all areas of modern existence. This linkage suggests that the cultural mania for mathematical and computer modeling of life's flux (the very heart of the popular appropriation of formerly obscure chaos theory and fractal imaging) is given specialized expression in the realm of profiling. Jon Stratton contends that profiling as a "new form of detection decentres the individual and aims instead to construct a simulacrum based on assumptions of normative patterns of behavior" (13), those patterns in and of themselves fictions problematically masquerading as reality.

Seizing on law enforcement's unacknowledged but tacitly confessed breakdown of boundary between reality and fiction, Thomas Harris in his own fiction quickly points out the inherent contradiction in the FBI's attempts at scientific classification and categorization even as the profilers embrace the ambiguity of fiction. He does this primarily through the creation of serial killers who, as Ressler complains, combine into one individual many of the traits the FBI has assigned to various categories of real murderers: "personality dynamics that would be highly unlikely to coexist in one person in the real world" (Ressler and Shachtman 273). The irony, of course, is that Ressler's categories clearly do not exist in the "real world" either. Harris also directly criticizes some of the most accepted tenets of the profiling manifestos. For example, the serial lust murderer as a Freudian subset of the general class of multiple murderers was perhaps the one most studied by the FBI's then-named Behavorial Science Unit (BSU). The BSU further bifurcated the lust murderer into the rather simplistic polar opposites of disorganized asocial offender and organized nonsocial offender (Hazelwood and Douglas 18). Hannibal Lecter, whose improbable genius seems largely created to complicate most of the FBI's categorizations of serial murder, calls this particular distinction "simplistic" and concludes that "most psychology is puerile, . . . and that practiced in Behavioral Science is on a level with phrenology" (*Lambs* 17).

On the basis of the observation of such textual freeplay between the FBI's actual theories and Harris's fictional characters, it should be evident that the cultural recycling of the genre narratives of serial murder cuts across the boundaries between fact and fiction.[12] In this instance, the founders of the FBI profiling program admit that they model their process in part after nineteenth-century detective fiction, which in its turn is an outgrowth of the Gothic formulas of the century before that. Harris, recognizing the artifice of the FBI construction, uses its conclusions as raw material for his own permutations of the Gothic genre. Now fiction and fact are emulating Harris, particularly in cross-generic replications of his powerful scenes involving a series of increasingly psychologically intimate prison-house interviews between killer and detective nemesis.[13] Just as Ressler and the former BSU (now Investigative Support Unit, or ISU) can claim some credit for inventing the media serial killer, Harris is perhaps the man most directly responsible for the 1980s and 1990s explosion of interest in serial killers, the current cycle of fictional narratives of serial murder, and the future shape of the mythos itself. It remains to be seen what influence Harris's 1999 critically controversial novel *Hannibal* will have on writers to come, so extended analysis of Harris's latest will wait until a later time.

Dragons and Lambs: The Fiction of Thomas Harris

Francis Dolarhyde, Hannibal Lecter, Jame Gumb: the featured serial killers of Thomas Harris's second and third novels (*Red Dragon* and *The Silence of the Lambs,* respectively) present an array of violent but highly distinctive behaviors. Lecter cannibalizes his victims to incorporate them into his body. Dolarhyde murders entire families to possess his mutilated, bitten female victims in front of posed audiences consisting of slaughtered husbands and children. Gumb removes the skins of his female victims and sews the remnants into a literal bodysuit that helps him enact his fantasy of transformation into feminine beauty. In effect, each killer has a *signature,* or method of killing (and postmortem disposal or display of the corpses) unique to that individual. The signature is so individual and elaborate, in fact, as to resemble a work of art rather than a mindless act of brutality. As Edith Borchardt points out in reference to the character of Jame Gumb, Harris's serial killers are examples of deviant modern artists who "destroy human beings for the sake of their objectification in art rather than destroying the illusion of art for the sake of life, as happens in Romanticism" (126–27). Consequently, the plots of Harris's novels depict the efforts of various FBI agents and af-filiates to identify or reveal the artist behind the criminal signature. Harris's is a murder-mystery narratological strategy Stefano Tani identifies as specif-ically metafictional. In Harris's fiction, profiling places the investigators at physical and psychic risk because they must operate in the killer's territory. In this mythological and asocial domain, identities are destabilized, moral-ity suspended, and societal codes subverted in a manner common to the en-tire Gothic genre to which Harris is indebted (Magistrale 27–41). Yet some degree of closure is granted to the frustrated reader in search of narrative stability. Harris's artistic project in composing each of the novels is an inter-weaving of dual narratives, the killer's and the detective's, which inevitably converge as the detective successfully identifies the killer from his signature and then tracks him to his "lair."

Although neither of Harris's novels is a murder mystery in the classic sense, each is representative of the anti-mystery, in David Richter's termi-nology. While each investigator (Will Graham or Clarice Starling) still seeks to unmask a murderer, the killer is known far in advance by the reader. And in contrast to the traditional mystery, victims are chosen by the killer in such a way that a traditional investigation that centers on suspects with hidden but ultimately clear motives will not succeed. The victim has little or no prior connection to the killer. There is no "practical" motive for the police to un-cover. In Harris's novels investigative success depends more upon intuition and empathy than pure logic. But the need to enter the killer's mind-set threatens to bring the detective into conflict with society's prohibition against manifestation of murderous urges. In the serial killer story, these urges are often considered to be a part of nature, ultimately beyond human control or knowledge. Similarly, Harris's novels clearly argue that man the beast has very little hope of bettering civilization.

In *Red Dragon,* the law-enforcement representative is Will Graham, a retired FBI academy forensics instructor (a civilian, not an agent) with two previous experiences in capturing serial killers. He is beckoned from his early retirement to lead the search for yet another such killer. In the course of this third investigation, he loses his family and nearly his life. *The Silence of the Lambs* moves the mutilated and defeated Graham offstage and introduces Clarice Starling. She is a young FBI academy student who quietly, almost surreptitiously, identifies and finds the serial killer "Buffalo Bill" while the mammoth FBI pursuit, rendered ungainly by its very size and complexity, sweeps by them until well after their confrontation is finished. She initially fares better than Graham does, surviving her initiation into Gothic ambiguity. However, she achieves a level of professional and media notoriety (the tabloids call her the "Bride of Frankenstein") destined to destroy her future career and isolate her enough to turn her into the "bride" of Lecter in *Hannibal*.[14]

What distinguishes all of Harris's fictional narratives is their reliance on maverick outsiders to operate beyond the FBI's bureaucratic constraints and thus reduce the killers' lead time. Will Graham is a temporary special investigator, not an FBI agent. Clarice Starling is a student, not yet an FBI agent, and most significantly, a woman in a traditionally hypermasculine environment. While neither of these two is a Dirty Harry–style vigilante, both are relatively free to work at the margins of FBI procedure. They utilize their technological resources and social freedom of passage but skirt around institutional regulations and paperwork with a fair degree of invisibility and impunity. They are also alienated in some way from the ideologies and attitudes of their professional coworkers. Graham is widely considered to be insane by his colleagues (as well as by the tabloid press) because of his empathic ability to visualize a killer's fantasies from crime-scene evidence. Starling is a woman whose strength, competence, and physical attractiveness make her immediately suspect to most of her male peers, who alternately resent her and lust for her.

Thus, Harris proposes an updated variation on a fairly conservative, time-honored American dictum. In order for things to get done, in this case law enforcement, competent professionals need to be unfettered by timid state legislation and interference. Unfortunately, these mavericks, who embody the contradictory notion of "authentic" nationalistic American values of individualism, will be shunned by the more traditional rank and file institutional drones—either by those who envy their achievements or misunderstand their methods. Working either alone or with a minimum of intrusion from probably well-meaning but bungling state authority, Graham and Starling can be trusted to accomplish what a massive bureaucracy cannot. Circumventing established procedures and codes with streamlined efficiency, Harris's simultaneously amateur and professional detectives are, literally, outlaws. They are different from their quarry only in degree and manner of transgression. (Starling even becomes a cannibal herself, though under the dual influence of drugs and hypnosis, in *Hannibal*.) Joel Black elaborates:

> A convention of the [detective fiction] genre [is] to portray the sleuth at odds with the established police force. In fact, the literary figure of the detective typically was and continues to be an extraordinary,

marginal figure who frequently bears a closer resemblance to the criminal he pursues than to the police officers with whom he supposedly collaborates. (43)

This alienation from society is true for both Starling and Graham.

Will Graham's name sounds suspiciously like "Pilgrim," the moniker Hannibal Lecter assigns to the "Tooth Fairy," as the press calls the unknown serial killer (or, alternatively, "Red Dragon," as Dolarhyde calls himself). Graham's intuitive ability to create psychiatric profiles from crime-scene evidence is far beyond that of his colleagues. His skill frightens and revolts Graham as well as many of those who know him. His uncanny ability to "read" crime scenes borders on the supernatural, threatening to pierce the boundary between the mundane and the fantastic. Even his professional confidantes, Crawford and forensic psychiatrist Dr. Bloom, speak of his ability in hushed and secretive tones, and Crawford has gone so far in the past as to ask Bloom to write a study on Graham's unique mentality. To Crawford, Bloom diagnoses Graham as not only an *eideteker*, someone possessed of a "remarkable visual memory," but an empath: "He can assume your point of view, or mine—and maybe some other points of view that scare and sicken him. It's an uncomfortable gift, Jack" (152).

Graham reflects on his "gift" as he inspects the crime scene at the Leeds house:

> Graham had a lot of trouble with taste. Often his thoughts were not tasty. There were no effective partitions in his mind. What he saw and learned touched everything else he knew. Some of the combinations were hard to live with. But he could not anticipate them, could not block and repress. His learned values of decency and propriety tagged along, shocked at his associations, appalled at his dreams; sorry that in the bone arena of his skull there were no forts for what he loved. His associations came at the speed of light. His value judgments were at the pace of a responsive reading. They could never keep up and direct his thinking. (15)

Civilization and primitivism are established in opposition to one another, the passage argues. Graham's violent or base "associations" are elemental or natural. His decency is learned. His psyche is a battlefield within a metaphoric arena. It is implied that he finds it all too easy to visualize violence against his loved ones. Passages such as this one demonstrate the ideological tension that pervades Harris's works, in particular *Red Dragon,* with its first-act mystification of Dolarhyde and second-act humanizing of him through a flashback to his emotionally deprived childhood.[15]

In Harris's novels, the morally ambiguous Gothic landscape jarringly destabilizes the often conservative values of his protagonists. In this instance, unlike the asocial loners of classic American literature, Graham longs for the stability of family. However, like those literary loners, he deliberately exiles himself from his wife and stepson and places himself (and by extension, them) in increasingly dangerous situations until he and they are nearly killed by his Gothic double, Dolarhyde. In effect, he spurns (however reluctantly) what the desperately alone Dolarhyde covets, a more subtle variation of the intrafamilial horrors dramatized by Harris through the primary character of family-slayer Dolarhyde. When Graham attempts to return to Molly and Willy (renamed Kevin in the film adaptation) after everyone believes Dolarhyde to have killed himself, their relationships have altered irrevocably for the worse under the stress of Graham's long investigation: "When they saw that it was not the same, the unspoken knowledge lived with them like unwanted company in the house. The mutual assurances they tried to exchange in the dark and in the day passed through some refraction that made them miss the mark" (343).

Dolarhyde's psychic effect on Graham and his family is disastrous enough at this point, but the novel is not over yet. The "unwanted company" metaphor soon literalizes itself in the troubled Graham household. Dolarhyde, having obtained Graham's home address from Lecter in a coded message placed in the *National Tattler,* stalks Graham's family with the intent of killing them in revenge for Graham's uncovering his identity. While Dolarhyde does not initially succeed and is in fact killed by Molly, in the long run he has destroyed the Grahams as surely as he has the Leedses and Jacobis. At the novel's end, Graham, his face ripped apart by Dolarhyde's knife, lies wounded in a hospital bed as Molly prepares to leave him to go to Oregon to her parents' house, probably never to return.[16] Through Dolarhyde's psychological destruction of the Graham family, Harris suggests that family life, no matter how apparently stable or based on love and mutual respect, is inherently fragile and probably pathological for those concerned. This is a distinctly subversive idea given the 1980s public obsession with family values.

Graham's troubling sacrifice, no matter how unintentional, of family to his work is not the only example of his decidedly ambiguous status as narrative "hero." His empathic abilities, stopping just short of "true" psy-

chic insight, gravitate more toward murder than kindness. Though he attempts to connect with the phantoms evoked by inspection of the dead families' belongings (Mrs. Leeds's diary, for example), his true gift lies in empathizing with the killer. In a drunken state, he imagines he can see the faceless
shadow of the Dragon sitting across from him in an empty chair. He tells it
comfortingly: "I know it's tough." Then, as he reaches out to touch the
shadow, it disappears, leaving him to muse upon his tenuous connection to
the murderer:

> Graham had tried hard to understand the Dragon. . . . Sometimes
> Graham felt close to him. A feeling he remembered from other
> investigations had settled over him in recent days: the taunting sense
> that he and the Dragon were doing the same things at various times
> of the day, that there were parallels in the quotidian details of their
> lives. Somewhere the Dragon was eating, or showering, or sleeping
> at the same time as he was. (194)

This sense of doubling will finally reveal the Dragon's identity to Graham,
but only after Graham has compromised his safe boundary of distance from
the murderer to a costly degree. He and Dolarhyde exemplify a disastrous
twinning between equally matched super-detective and arch-criminal, most
famously anticipated by the Holmes/Moriarty conflict in Arthur Conan
Doyle's corpus of work.

Graham can establish the empathic link to a murderer because he realizes he will always be more hunter than prey—a dragon more than a lamb.
The most "intense and savage joy" (340) he has ever experienced comes when
he realizes from watching the Leedses and Jacobis' home movies, and cross-
correlating details visible in the films to his *eideteker* memory of evidence
from the crime scenes, that the Red Dragon must have seen these same films.
Thus, in order to find the murderer, Graham merely has to find out where
these two sets of home movies were developed. In retrospect, Graham finds
this intellectual joy of revelation a troubling, pseudomurderous act: "It was
unsettling to know that the happiest moment of his life had come then, in
that stuffy jury room in the city of Chicago. *When even before he knew, he
knew*" (340). The point is further driven home by the knowledge that his
insight was derived from voyeuristic absorption into the same celluloid
images Dolarhyde used in his job—film processor at Gateway Labs—as murderous imagistic foreplay. Moreover, Graham worries that his own murderous urges may be unduly stimulated by his contact with killers.

The worry is not ill-founded in the philosophical terms established by Harris's text. Harris implies that the Tooth Fairy's murder of reporter Freddy Lounds is at least a sort of wish-fulfillment for Graham. Graham detests Lounds because of the latter's sensationalistic coverage of Graham's previous involvement in the Lecter case. Lounds, who has been taunting the killer in the *National Tattler* at Graham's request, is gruesomely and painfully murdered when an FBI trap conceived by Graham leaves the reporter unprotected. Lounds dies believing that Graham set him up for a "hit" because in an earlier posed *Tattler* photo Graham placed his hand on Lounds's shoulder, as if Lounds were one of the family pets that the Tooth Fairy ritually kills prior to slaughtering a family.[17] From his asylum cell, Lecter congratulates Graham for "the job you did on Mr. Lounds. I admired it enormously. What a cunning boy you are!" (270). Graham wonders about his possible complicity in Lounds's murder and comes to no firm conclusions: "He had put his hand on Freddy's shoulder . . . to establish that he really had told Freddy those insulting things about the Dragon. Or had he wanted to put Freddy at risk, just a little?" (271). The reader him/herself is also implicated in Lounds's murder, simply by virtue of the fact that Lounds, while exhibiting a certain pathetic vulnerability in his subordinate relationship with the mothering prostitute Wendy and in keeping his wits about him during his torture by Dolarhyde, is primarily an unpleasant, manipulative character. Lounds does his best to exploit Graham's weaknesses (as well as the police investigation's) for personal gain within the ranks of the tabloid press. As author of quickie true-crime paperbacks on Lecter and the Tooth Fairy, he is a genre predecessor of Wayne Gale, another sleaze-journalism schlockmeister destined to be murdered by his story subjects in Oliver Stone's *Natural Born Killers*.

Through a sort of sharing of the murder act targeted against a common enemy, Graham and Dolarhyde become thematic doubles whose separate identities become hopelessly compromised, a convention seen in many nineteenth-century vampire and Gothic narratives. Francis Dolarhyde, while undeniably human, parallels many literary vampires in his nocturnal invasions of houses to claim female victims who, from his point of view, have "invited" him in through their voluntary submission of their photographic images to Dolarhyde's film developing laboratory. Graham, through close pursuit of this seductive "monster," risks contracting the infection he studies, as illustrated in his possible complicity in the Lounds murder. The virus metaphor is made clear by the novel's conclusion when Graham meditates on the subject of murder: "He wondered if . . . the vicious urges we control in ourselves function like the crippling virus the body arms against" (354).[18] The "vaccine" that only partially restores Graham to psychic equilibrium is the knowledge of his capacity for murder and the purging confrontation with his "secret sharer," the neo-Gothic vampire Francis Dolarhyde.

Thus, Harris is working within familiar genre territory when he characterizes Graham as an emotional chameleon whose exposure to murderers may have turned him into one himself. In the later novels, Starling also becomes a monster. She begins as an ambitious female student whose eagerness for professional advancement and fortuitous link to helpful male mentors and father figures (one of them, ironically, a serial murderer) removes her from the routine career track her fellow trainees follow, isolates her professionally and personally, and finally turns her into Hannibal Lecter's cannibalistic lover. In a real sense, Harris's individualistic detectives and the equally alienated killers they chase are acting out, in contemporary industrialized America, a frontier drama analogous to the earlier genre war between Indians and Indian fighters. These ideological wars rely heavily on a privileging of the individual's strengths and abilities over those of the social institutions originally charged with protecting the traditional family unit. Yet the strong individual is also a potential monster.

Not that Harris offers panegyric tribute to the moral virtues of the nuclear family—in fact, just the opposite. For Harris, the family is a site of deep ambiguity, emotional hazard, psychic scarring, and hair-trigger potential for physical violence. More often than not, its crucial importance in his characters' lives will result in as much pain as solace, with the extreme cases producing serial killers such as Francis Dolarhyde. Tony Williams examines the textual incidences of abuse in young Dolarhyde's life (abandonment by an uncaring and sexually promiscuous mother, threats of literal castration by a domineering grandmother) and concludes:

> Due to years of abuse by grandmother, he is traumatically fixated in the mirror stage under a self-created, socially generated, monstrous super-ego named Red Dragon. He works out before a mirror, often concealing his face behind a mask, unwilling to undergo separation from the maternal order no matter how much it has traumatized him. ("Dark Mirror" 9)

Dolarhyde's compulsive need to target substitute victims, or scapegoats, in a repetitious strategy vainly designed to master his primal trauma of abuse is related to the 1980s psychoanalytic-derivative focus on child abuse as the chief factor in the perpetuation of adult violence. This "family values" theme is reflected in the FBI studies of serial murder, which in turn have been absorbed into Harris's fiction.[19] The threat to idyllic American domestic existence posed by the vengeful return of the repressed, in this case the adult survivor of child abuse, must be stopped.

Harris announces the narrative concern with protecting the mainstream family early on in *Red Dragon*. The reader learns in the opening chapter that the offstage serial killer has slaughtered two traditional nuclear families, the Leedses and the Jacobis, as they slept in their formerly safe suburban homes. Both families had been affluent, respected, and blessed with many children. But in the dead of night, a lone murderer has violated this holiest of American institutions, killing in one act of mayhem per house a husband, wife, children, and the family pet, and thus metaphorically rendered the entire country unsafe. Recognizing at once a mortal threat to the domestic interests of the state, the FBI is quick to seize control of the investigations away from the local police jurisdictions and assign them to Jack Crawford, who with Graham's help has successfully resolved two previous serial murder cases. Crawford exhibits ruthless managerial efficiency by pressuring an extremely resistant Graham to return to work. As Tony Williams argues, at this point the manipulated Graham "almost resembles a helpless child in a dysfunctional family" ("Dark Mirror" 8), another parallel to Dolarhyde. Graham must temporarily abandon his wife and stepson, eventually place them in danger, and, as the novel ends, probably lose them. Graham's loss is a supreme irony, considering that Graham has been re-recruited in order to preserve his society's traditional family values but cannot save his own.

The lost family occupies a central position in *The Silence of the Lambs* as well, which is essentially the previous novel rewritten from the point of view of a young female. Clarice Starling searches for a surrogate family to replace the one she lost as a child. Her own father, a rural marshal whom she remembers as a policeman but who was really a night watchman, was killed during a fumbling shoot-out with a couple of thieves he surprised coming out of a drugstore. At that time, she was eight years old. Two years after that, her mother admitted her inability to raise her and sent her to live with her cousin at a Montana ranch, where Clarice's new family slaughtered horses and lambs in order to survive. After Starling was impelled by the ghastly screaming of slaughtered spring lambs to run away with her favorite horse, Hannah, she was sent away again, this time to a Lutheran orphanage. Hannah went with her, where the heavy, nearsighted horse lived out her days peacefully pulling children in a cart around a track; but Clarice's physical connections with family were gone. She spent her juvenile years in institutional facilities, materially well provided for (more than her mother or her mother's cousin could do, it is implied) but emotionally remote. Her only continuing family connection is an abstract knowledge of her genealogy (paternally reckoned, of course):

> Starling was an isolated member of a fierce tribe with no formal genealogy but the honors list and the penal register. Dispossessed in Scotland, starved out of Ireland, a lot of them were inclined to the dangerous trades. Many generic Starlings had been used up this way, had thumped on the bottom of narrow holes or slid off planks with a shot at their feet, or were commended to glory with a cracked "Taps" in the cold when everyone wanted to go home. A few may have been recalled tearily by the officers on regimental mess nights, the way a man in drink remembers a good bird dog. Faded names in a Bible. (266)

As the passage suggests, Starling's major childhood memories are ones of loss, abandonment, and grief. These memories include her father's hospital stay after his shooting; the death rattle in his throat; her mother washing blood from her father's hat and tearfully insisting that everything will be all right; her mother in her motel maid's uniform sitting Clarice (who must accompany her to work) down on a bed and telling her that she will be going to Montana, while outside an ominous crow soils the clean linens on her mother's laundry cart; the screaming of slaughtered lambs; the flight with Hannah; the second displacement to the orphanage in Bozeman.

The emotional privation of her childhood parallels her to Jame Gumb, who was born out of wedlock to an alcoholic failed actress and sent to a Los Angeles County foster home at the age of two. Starling is also a victim of maternal inability or unwillingness to cope with the burden of child-rearing. Additionally, Gumb's grandparents took him in when he was ten, the same age as Clarice's entrance into her mother's cousin's home. Here is another instance of Gothic character doubling, given a gender twist. Starling and Gumb each aspire to the traditional social sphere of the other. Both are single-minded, even ruthless, in pursuit of their goal, both defy patriarchal institutions, and both kill. Starling and Gumb bear out Linda Williams's hypothesis that the woman and the monster in horror narrative, because of their shared status as "biological freaks" in patriarchal society, share a "surprising (and at times subversive) affinity" ("Woman" 90). Starling is a recognizably Gothic heroine whose moral education—that is, her awakening to the existence of evil—is obtained in the grueling and sexually dangerous manner of all threatened Gothic heroines.

As part of her education, Starling learns of the human sins of passion and appetite, particularly the human susceptibility to violence. Like her predecessor Graham, she comes to possess uncomfortable insight into the "joy of the hunt." Her quiet moment of solitary epiphany, when she realizes that the oddly distinctive manner in which Buffalo Bill has mutilated the victim Kimberly will lead Starling directly to him, is a deliberate recreation on Harris's part of Graham's similar epiphanal moment in *Red Dragon*:

> Staring into the lighted closet, Starling saw the triangles on Kimberly's shoulders outlined in the blue dashes of a dressmaking pattern. The idea swam away and circled and came again, came close enough for her to grab it this time and she did with a fierce pulse of joy: THEY'RE DARTS—HE TOOK THOSE TRIANGLES TO MAKE DARTS SO HE COULD LET OUT HER WAIST. MOTHER FUCKER CAN SEW. BUFFALO BILL'S TRAINED TO SERIOUSLY SEW—HE'S NOT JUST PICKING OUT READY-TO-WEAR. . . . Starling put her head back, closed her eyes for one second. Problem-solving is hunting; it is savage pleasure and we are born to it. (294)

The intellectual will to power drives not only the urge to solve problems but to kill, Harris implies here, as did Arthur Conan Doyle through his creation of Holmes and Moriarty. Harris argues that our tendency to murder one another is biologically predestined through our intellectual hyperdevelopment. From the deterministic perspective, we are "born to it"—or, as Oliver Stone's mass-murderer Mickey Knox says, "Shit, man. I'm a natural-born killer." It is not an exclusively masculine faculty, as Starling's possession of it demonstrates.

This drive toward violence predates modern behavioral science dogma or the Christian dogma that preceded it, as Lecter chides Starling:

> Nothing happened to me, Officer Starling. *I* happened. You can't reduce me to a set of influences. You've given up good and evil for behaviorism, Officer Starling. You've got everybody in moral dignity pants—nothing is ever anybody's fault. Look at me, Officer Starling. Can you stand to say I'm evil? Am I evil, Officer Starling?

. . . Evil's just destructive? Then *storms* are evil, if it's that simple.
And we have *fire,* and then there's *hail.* Underwriters lump it all
under "Acts of God." . . . I collect church collapses, recreationally.
Did you see the recent one in Sicily? Marvelous! The facade fell on
sixty-five grandmothers at a special Mass. Was that evil? If so, who
did it? If He's up there, He just loves it, Officer Starling. Typhoid
and swans—it all comes from the same place. (19)

Lecter here attempts to shift Starling's focus away from inherited modes of
discourse—the psychoanalytic, the religious, even the jargon of insurance
underwriters—and onto a reckoning with the cultural question of evil and
its resistance to definition. Lecter, in his role as monstrous mentor/therapist,
forces her to confront the issue of teleology itself. Is there design, as Robert
Frost once asked, or mere accident in nature? Why does God drop church
roofs on His worshippers? Is Lecter evil, a freakish monster with maroon eyes
and a six-fingered hand, or an adult victim of child abuse like Gumb and
Dolarhyde? Lecter refuses to provide pat answers, unlike the FBI.[20] He points
out the crumbling façades of failing ontological systems (the church-roof
collapses) and lets Starling make of them what she will. Lecter's is a Gothic
strategy (though of course it is not called that in the novel), and one that
horror fiction in particular frequently adopts.

But in yet another dialectical tension, Lecter's apocalyptically flavored
methodology, far from being an act of individual nihilism, actually complements the populist ideology of the culture he lives in. Though he consciously
affects the elitist guise of a pretentiously inaccessible and "evil" modernist,
Lecter relies more than he will admit on the mass reactions of others and is,
indeed, an adult survivor of childhood trauma like all of Harris's other killers. For one thing, his pre-incarceration professional life demanded at least
the appearance of empathy. For another, his distinguishing traits are his
courtesy and his artistic pretensions—characteristics usually associated in
the popular imagination with highbrow culture. Yet his courtesy parodies
the calculated game of social maneuvering and his art tends toward the
kitschy, such as crucifixion watches and origami chickens. He publishes in
the professional journals he professes to despise.

Lecter is the consummate "negative" man, a living embodiment of the
shadow presence the drunk Will Graham confronts in his hotel room. Lecter
is defined only in relation to the nullifying effect he has on the energy level
of others. Like the death's-head moth, he lives parasitically on the salt found
in the tears of mammals.[21] He fancies himself to be beyond history and

context, somewhere in the mythic realm of precivilization. Harris early on links any social acknowledgment of Lecter to a sudden collapse of the sense-making structure of language: "A brief silence follows the name [Hannibal Lecter], always, in any civilized gathering" (4). Lecter's ability to withdraw completely from others into that silent void leads Joe Sanders to conclude that Lecter is a "reader . . . who refuses to be read" (5), but this observation is only partially true. Lecter does manifest an extreme sensitivity to attempts to quantify or demystify him (as when he kills and eats a census taker for merely asking him biographical data), but *is* willing to play theater for his audience and hence is open to a reading, at least on his own terms.

More than anything, Lecter resists reduction. He consciously plays at self-aggrandizement. Crawford tells Starling that Lecter's only real weakness is that he must appear to be smarter than everyone else (86). Paradoxically, Lecter has achieved the ultimate in name recognition in his culture by becoming a serial killer. Though his murders physically isolate him from society, he continues to thrive on the hyperreal effect he has on others. Someone will always seek him out, he smugly knows, but only if he continues to play the game of the Professor Moriarty of serial killers to its furthest possible extreme. This is why his Cainlike exile is a sham. Lecter would not exist without a herd to terrorize and he knows it. He hints at this through his admonition to Starling to reject prefabricated discursive models, including the FBI distinction between organized and disorganized offenders, and comprehend the primitive fears of the massed herd (symbolized by the groveling worshippers who die in church collapses). Lecter is the perfect high priest of mythical thinking because as a cannibal he represents one of the strongest of all primal fears. The will to power that Lecter embodies defines itself in relation to mastery of the herd. His lordship also implies psychological separation from the herd in order to manipulate its timid social structure all the more easily.

Those who would understand him, Lecter hints, must distance themselves from (but not entirely abandon) the approved codes of civilized behavior as he has. He mocks the conventions of courtesy while adopting them, simply because his methodology of existence depends on the very cruelty that courtesy masks. His profilers must be open, as he is, to both grossly extreme (relishing the taste of human flesh) and finely nuanced (identifying Starling's perfume and smelling her blood through the vents in his cell) sensory input as a way of repudiating civilization's verbal obsessiveness. Lecter's reactions to two of his fellow inmates are quite revealing of his values. Miggs, whom Lecter verbally coerces into suicide because of his rude carnal remark to Starling that he could "smell [her] cunt" (12), enacts only the grossly sen-sual aspect of Lecter's prescription and so fatally transgresses Lecter's ideal. In contrast, Lecter provides effective jailhouse therapy to Sammie. Sammie is a religious schizophrenic who beheaded his mother and placed the head in a collection plate at a rural Baptist church. Sammie's sacrifice of the nic-est person in his life was designed to please Jesus Christ, quicken the Sec-ond Coming (134), and thus serve a loftier spiritual purpose than do Miggs's masturbatory fantasies. The savagery of Sammie's symbolic gesture, com-bined with its spirituality, places him beyond the pale of civilization and out in Lecter country.

Because of Starling's past alienating experience with spring lambs and horses slaughtered by representatives of a blindly consuming society, Lecter finds Starling a receptive student. Graham, too, reacts to Lecter's primitiv-ism, but Graham is in far more danger of succumbing to it than Starling. Joe Sanders observes that the key difference between Starling and Graham is the depth to which they must enter the killing mind-set. Though Star-ling kills Jame Gumb, much like Graham kills Garret Jacob Hobbs, "she focuses her attention on victims, trying to determine how they became vul-nerable to Buffalo Bill" (4). (In *Hannibal,* Starling's isolation becomes so profound that she eventually allies herself with Lecter, the only human be-ing who can satisfy her needs.)

On the other hand, Graham's isolation more closely parallels that of Dolarhyde, until Graham becomes so alone in and receptive to the objecti-fying, two-dimensional world of the image that he can suddenly grasp the pathology of the Red Dragon during his viewing of victims' home movies. Graham's link to this particular subjectivity, however, destroys him because it paradoxically leaves him incapable of empathizing with any other view than its solipsistic self. Gavin Smith calls the cinematic version of Graham a "Method cop" ("Mann" 75), a brilliant summary of Graham's risky ap-proach to detection, wherein acting like a killer for a long enough period of time becomes indistinguishable from actually killing. The meaning is the performance. It matters little that Graham never actually kills anyone dur-ing the course of the Red Dragon investigation. He has destroyed himself. He is a casualty of the hazards of simulacratic confusion of representation and actuality. Graham's destruction graphically demonstrates the psycho-logical dangers, as well as the physical, in entering the serial killer's mind-set, however peripherally.

In either case, Graham and Starling's boundary-piercing quests parallel those of their intended quarries and also provide a way of understanding the serial killer narrative as a whole. Whether structured around the killer or the detective, the narrative is typically a kind of dark bildungsroman. The killer practices and learns his craft, while the detective masters the art of sign-reading. In any event, the narrative landscape both move through is distinguished by its Gothic proliferation of signs or clues, which in turn expresses its accessibility (or in some cases, as with the 1986 film *Henry: Portrait of a Serial Killer,* its resistance) to reading by those who are privy to the encryption code. Thus, in spite of the structural ambiguities derived from Gothicism, Harris's novels about FBI profilers affirm the possibility that given enough information and intelligence on the part of the profiler, signs can be read and the anonymous murderers revealed. As Steffen Hantke concludes of *The Silence of the Lambs:* "[It] decides, despite the narrative ambivalence of its ending, in favor of a moral assertion that provides the reader at least with a powerful ideological sense of closure" (46). As Hantke further observes, this closure is not typical of the more controversial entries in the serial killer subgenre, such as *Henry* or *American Psycho.* Tony Magistrale remarks that in Harris's fiction, "'the virtues of the norm' are inevitably reaffirmed with a sigh of relief" (40). Harris's guardedly optimistic version of the neo-Gothic, as did the film adaptations of Harris's novels, thus appealed to a very large audience.

"Reflections, Mirrors, Images": *Manhunter*

Much ink has elsewhere been spilled in extended analysis of Jonathan Demme's 1991 film adaptation of *The Silence of the Lambs.*[22] Little purpose would be served in redundantly examining the film here. Rather, it is more valuable to turn to the lesser-known *Manhunter,* a film adaptation of *Red Dragon.* Directed by Michael Mann, the 1986 film remains largely neglected by academic critics. Probably the most extended analysis of the film so far is by Tony Williams. He champions *Manhunter* and laments the acclaim given to the film version of *The Silence of the Lambs,* calling the latter "a repugnant example of post-Reaganite cinema, narrowly opening patriarchal gates to allow ideologically conditioned feminists inside" (*Hearths* 255–56). He prefers *Manhunter* as a "far more subtle" work wherein the killers are simultaneously victims and victimizers and the law-enforcement protagonist achieves "self-knowledge and retreat from a corrupt system" (255) to a degree that Special Agent Starling, graduating into the patriarchal FBI, never does (at least until the events detailed in *Hannibal*). Williams focuses on the "undermining" of "convenient barriers between monster and human counterparts" (255) to conclude that *Manhunter* is a skillful examination of the links between normality and monstrosity. Gavin Smith concurs, pointing to "*Manhunter*'s ultimately compassionate empathy with the killer-who-is-also-a-victim" ("Mann" 77), which offsets the inherent reactionary themes established earlier in the film "when the civilized world is confronted by the antisocial forces at its margins" (75). Another destabilization centers around what I might call, taking a lead from Smith, the victim-who-is-also-a-killer: Will Graham. As center of audience identification and sympathy—a survivor of a near-disembowelment by Hannibal Lecter—Graham also displays murderous hatred toward Lounds, the offensive tabloid journalist, and has directly killed two other men by the time the narrative closes. However, Graham does so in such a way as to not preclude continued audience support. Oddly, audience sympathy is also skewed dramatically toward the killer in the last third of the film, when Reba enters the story. Noting this balancing of sympathies in the film, Ross Wetzsteon writes of the casting of William Petersen as Graham: "Petersen plunges into the disreputable side of his characters yet makes the audience root for him every minute of the way" (34). Mann's film, in spite of its icy and futuristic look, plunges its characters and audience headfirst into a Gothic environment where the sympathetic lead sign-reader, Graham, works to decipher the code presented to him in frustratingly plain sight by fellow-traveler Francis Dolarhyde.[23]

Manhunter is a profoundly ambiguous and destabilizing film. The dialectical tensions between binary oppositions are quite pronounced, creating uncomfortable affinities between protagonist and antagonist(s), especially the ways in which they are threatened and exploited by others. The most obvious victims in the narrative are the dead families, the Leedses and Jacobis. However, plot developments suggest that paternal relationships themselves are the culprit in the production of future "monsters." All of the three main male characters, who constitute what Kathleen Murphy calls a "perverse [trinity of] father, son, and holy ghost" (31), are literally punished, physically or psychologically, by other stronger males or patriarchal forces and pressures. Graham, in spite of his soft manner, uses all of his institutional authority to threaten and brutalize Lecter and Dolarhyde. Lecter and Dolarhyde threaten and brutalize Graham in individual retaliation. Graham's ostensible boss Jack Crawford shames prodigal-son Graham into "behaving" by coming back to work for the FBI. Male-female romantic relationships fare little better, with the onus of narrative blame for violence attaching to the sexually threatened male. The "normal" relationship between Graham and Molly is threatened by Graham's increasing remoteness. The potentially redemptive relationship between Dolarhyde and Reba is shattered by Dolar-hyde's jealousy—ironically, a completely unfounded jealousy based on mis-interpretation of a coworker's condescending but well-meaning escorting of Reba to her front door. Institutional affiliations, as a metaphoric substitute for the heterosexual family structure, are also subject to destabilization. Gra-ham, returning to work at paternalist Crawford's behest after a temporary retirement, finds only alienation and danger awaiting him.

Graham's complicated familial relationship with the FBI is worth fur-ther exploration. As a surrogate family for its investigators, Crawford's FBI is a professional technocrat's dream. As a privileged member of this extremely wealthy family, Graham has literally millions of dollars worth of crime-fight-ing equipment and expertise at his command. Extensive laboratories devoted to the minute analysis of hair and fiber, tools, documents, and latent prints and staffed by zealous and supremely self-confident technicians (document examiner Baumann, for example, says of Lecter, "You're so sly, but so am I") gear up into efficient action when provided with Graham's leads, such as the cut branch and the mah-jongg sign carved into the tree in the Jacobis' backyard. The FBI can place Graham onto a commercial flight anywhere he deems it necessary to go in the country. Lacking that, the agency can load him into a helicopter or a private jet. A state-of-the-art communications sys-tem renders the limitations of time and space irrelevant, as Graham in Bir-mingham can simultaneously talk to Crawford in D.C. and Dr. Chilton, Lecter's "jailer," in Baltimore regarding the message from the Tooth Fairy discovered in a book in Lecter's cell. An extensively outfitted mobile crime lab awaits word of the next family murder, so that Graham can get a "fresh" crime scene, as Crawford puts it. The FBI can appropriate personnel and resources from other federal agencies as necessary. For example, a painstak-ingly established Secret Service letter drop becomes central to a plan to cap-ture the Tooth Fairy as he attempts to pick up souvenirs supposedly sent through the mails by correspondent Lecter.

Yet, for all of this wizardry, the state monolith of the FBI routinely fails. The ploy to tap into the Lecter-Dolarhyde conduit of communication through the tabloid personal ads fails miserably, ending in the death of Lounds and the further disintegration of the Graham family. They must go into protective hiding when Lecter's personal ad to Dolarhyde translates as Graham's home address and the chilling coda: "Save yourself. Kill them all." The FBI experts, intimidating in sheer numbers and availability of resources, are all impotent in the face of Dolarhyde's larger solo potency. Fingerprint expert Jimmy Price has a fingerprint but no matchable suspect in his multigigabyte database. Nor can Price fume Dolarhyde's note to Lecter for prints without revealing his manipulation of the note to Lecter and thus giving away the game. Document analyst Baumann cannot decipher the note in time to save Lounds's life. Nor can he substitute another message that would have kept the Graham family address safely secret from Dolarhyde. The elaborate FBI traps come to nothing. An innocent black jogger is assaulted and nearly shot in Dolarhyde's place, and an obnoxious but basically inconsequential reporter is gruesomely mutilated (his lips bitten off) and burned to death in Graham's place.

Most egregiously of all, from Graham's point of view, the FBI is incapable of living up to its father figure Crawford's promise to keep Graham "as far away from it [the field investigation] as I can." Graham, honoring Crawford's request to return, promises Molly that he will not become "deeply involved" in the investigation but rather will stay safely at the margins examining crime-scene evidence. This promise is quickly broken through a combination of personal willfulness, such as the ill-advised consultation with Lecter, and unhappy but foreseeable circumstance, such as Lounds's paparazzi-style stalking of Graham and publication of Graham's photograph in the *National Tattler* for Dolarhyde to see. Paradoxically, as Graham forsakes his consultant status and becomes more deeply involved in fieldwork, his uncanny ability to make intuitive leaps of insight into the murdering mind-set alienates him from the more orthodox members of law enforcement. Examples include the Atlanta patrolman whom, as a potential distraction, Graham refuses to let enter the crime scene at the Leeds house; and the Atlanta detective Springfield, who is initially puzzled by Graham's talk of idiosyncratic "fantasies" rather than easily understood financial motive, and then plainly disturbed by Graham's extraordinary discovery of fingerprints on the corneas of one of the Leeds family victims. While the FBI technocrats are more accepting of his gift (to the point where forensic psychologist Dr. Bloom is solicitous of Graham's mental health), Graham is still a lonely, distant figure. He is given to peering surreptitiously at photos of the Leeds family in ambivalent sympathy and objectification while the massive FBI investigative machinery dashes past him in all directions to very little tangible benefit. Graham, a workaholic away from his family, has found no surrogate home here.

The film makes clear that Graham's home in Florida with his wife, Molly, and his son, Kevin, is no refuge. Crawford's entry into Graham's comfortably isolated world is a clear violation, paralleling Crawford, in some metaphoric way, to Dolarhyde, the literal "home wrecker." Crawford's plea for

Graham's help begins as essentially whiny or self-pitying in tone: "Did you ever think about giving me a call?" Graham, visibly resenting Crawford's presence by turning his back to him, quickly sees through Crawford's attempts to manipulate him: "Don't try to run a game down on me, Jack." Molly, walking past the two men as they sit on the beach, completely ignores Jack's greeting—physically demonstrating her low opinion of Crawford and then later verbally expressing it to him after dinner: "You're supposed to be his friend, Jack. Why didn't you leave him alone?" The film's symbol for Graham's private family world surrounded by hostile forces is the turtle hatchery that he and Kevin build on their private beach to protect the fragile eggs from crabs—a project that Graham returns to while considering Crawford's request. That night, as he lies naked in bed with Molly overlooking the ocean, he informs her that he has made his decision to return to FBI work. She implores him to stay home with her and Kevin but admits her motives are selfish. Graham hollowly promises her he will keep at a physical and psychological distance from the investigation. His claim will prove to be true only in terms of his rapidly deteriorating relationship to his immediate family.

As the investigation proceeds, Graham, whenever realizing the extent to which he has been exploited and drawn away from his family deeper into a job that he had quit out of psychological necessity, lashes out at Crawford as a visible symbol of FBI paternal authority. For instance, when Graham's picture appears in the tabloid newspaper, Graham shouts: "Goddamn it, Jack! I promised Molly! I promised her!" His final verbal rebellion against Crawford's authority, as Graham nears his third and most revealing moment of epiphany into Dolarhyde's mind-set, neatly reverses their respective positions within the hierarchy of power. After a month of investigative red herrings and failures, Crawford is now resigned to the prospect of another family murder and ironically finds Graham's continued concentration on the first two cases foolish: "Admit we struck out this month. . . . for Christ's sake, it's a foregone conclusion. . . . Give it up. Forget this month. It's too damn late." Graham acidly responds: "I gave it up. Until you showed up with pictures of two dead families, knowing goddamn well that I'd imagine families three, four, five, and six, right?" Crawford defensively justifies his exploitation of Graham: "You're fuckin' right I did, and I'd do it again!" Graham then decisively seizes all power and responsibility for the investigation from Crawford by shouting: "Great! But don't talk to me about late, pal. I'll tell you when it's too fucking late. Until then, we go as late as I want to take it." Graham's assertion of independence and identity from Crawford immediately precedes his breakthrough insight into Dolarhyde's method of victim selection. The plot resolution demonstrates Graham's power over those who would choose to dominate him. It is only at this moment, the confrontation with not only a savage killer but the paternalist Crawford, that Graham can finally see a return to his threatened home in Florida.

The film's most direct threat to family sanctity comes from the narrative's twin killers, Lecter and Dolarhyde, who have entered into a small conspiracy to murder manhunter Graham's family. Dolarhyde has already established his chilling credentials as a slayer of entire families, right down to their pets, lending the threat immediacy. Reporter Freddy Lounds further aggravates the situation by giving Dolarhyde's rage against his FBI pursuers a tangible focus with his inflammatory stories about Graham as lead investigator. Dolarhyde's fixation on Graham as lead adversary is clear in his note to Lecter: "Investigator Graham interests me. Very purposeful looking." Lecter, who nearly gutted Graham once and vengefully wishes to harm further his captor, attempts to reverse the hierarchy of male power by killing Graham by proxy from his asylum cell. During their first interview, Lecter makes his agenda clear by asking Graham if he would "like to leave [his] home phone number," which Graham wisely refuses to do. Lecter quickly uses his phone privileges to reach an unsuspecting graduate assistant in Dr. Bloom's office, who provides Lecter with Graham's home address. This is all the information Lecter requires in order to exploit "avid fan" correspondent Dolarhyde as an instrument of personal vengeance. To heighten the gravity of the threat to Graham's family, Mann sets up a tense scene wherein Molly and Kevin are frightened by an outside prowler. In a dramatic reversal, the "prowler" ironically turns out to be the first of a police force sent by Crawford and Graham to spirit them away to a "safe house."

The safe house location, to which Graham goes in a momentary break from the investigation following the debacle of Lounds's death, is actually the site of the Graham family's dissolution. Though physically protected from Dolarhyde, the family is now threatened by Graham's deep personal identification with the serial murder case. Kevin is now literally scared of Graham, but demonstrates his budding male paternalism by refusing to leave Molly alone with his father. Graham, later sitting on a dock with Molly, informs her that he must leave again, but this time to go by himself back to the Atlanta crime scene: "I have to be alone." Remembering Graham's last solo effort, which ended in his confinement to a mental ward, Molly protests: "You're talking about doing exactly what you said you—" Graham interrupts: "This killing. It's got to stop!" Molly warns him: "William, you're going to make yourself sick. Or get yourself killed." Ignoring her, Graham makes clear the extent of his desire to abandon family obligations to dwell exclusively in the realm of mental isolation where he knows he will find the Red Dragon: "You and Kevin should go to Montana. See your dad. He hasn't seen Kevin in a long time. Then I'll come up and get you afterwards." Molly, injured by Graham's abruptness, leaves without a further word. Sitting in a coffee shop staring out at a rainy night, Graham talks to his quarry (his own reflection in the window): "Just you and me now, sport. I'm going to find you, goddamn it."

Only after he has found Dolarhyde and destroyed the killer's hold over self and family can Graham return to Florida. But he is still not ready for family existence. Alone on the beach, his face slowly healing from a slash inflicted by Dolarhyde and staring at the turtle hatchery, he is startled by Kevin's voice and sees Molly following behind him. Graham attempts to explain his silence even after the case has concluded: "I thought I had to work things out, call you after." Molly signals her forgiveness: "I thought I wouldn't wait." The film's concluding lines establish the coming together of the family unit again, as Kevin asks how many of "them" (the turtles, but also metaphorically the families at risk through Dolarhyde's murders) made it. Graham replies, in the most affirmative statement the film has to offer: "Most of them made it." Tony Williams best summarizes the film's final lonely but guardedly redemptive image of family: "The image freezes on a long shot of the vulnerable family looking at the ocean" (*Hearths* 259). A much more optimistic affirmation of "family values" than Harris's source novel, the image still emphasizes the ambiguous nature of family existence—its extreme isolation from other family units. Each family is exiled, of course, to the Gothic realm where murderers hatch their vengeful plots against an exclusionary social order they eye enviously.

In addition to family, gender is another key area of destabilization within the film, although masculinity receives the brunt of the film's critique. The act of looking, as a potentially objectifying force, is linked directly to the shared masculinity of Dolarhyde and Graham. A variation of the invasive male gaze, as Laura Mulvey has famously written of in *Screen* (1975), structures much of the narrative. Indeed, the film's first image is shot through the grainy lens of Dolarhyde's movie camera as he stalks through the darkened Leeds house, from the kitchen, up the stairway, past the children's room, and into the master bedroom, where Valerie Leeds awakens to her death in a spotlight mounted on Dolarhyde's camera. Very quickly, then, the murderous use of technology in combination with the predatory male gaze is demonstrated.

Further solidifying the connection between photography and murder,[24] Crawford doesn't truly convince Graham, prone to the killing mind-set himself, to return to FBI work until Crawford passes him photographs of the living Leeds family at play. Only upon possession and inspection of these photographs can Graham feel not only sympathy for the victims but also the urge to return to the thrill of the hunt. During his solitary tour of the Leeds house, Graham sees himself reflected in a mirror and is startled by Valerie Leeds' voice on the answering machine, establishing yet another link between male visual imagery (this time, mirror reflection) and the murdered woman. Dolarhyde eludes identification until his fingerprint is found on the cornea of a dead child's eye, demonstrating simultaneously his obsessive focus on the visual element as well as his resistance to a mutual return gaze. Lecter accurately diagnoses this component of Dolarhyde's fetishes during the first asylum interview with Graham: "This is a very shy boy, Will." Similarly, Graham is resistant to an appropriating gaze. He erupts into a rage and assaults Lounds on the basis that Lounds had taken pictures of Graham's injuries when he was lying sedated and symbolically emasculated in the hospital following Lecter's attack.

Lounds, of course, will pay the ultimate price for his irresponsible use of the weapons of visual technology. His insistence on publishing front-page photographs of the Tooth Fairy investigation, including his own part in it, will place him squarely at the focal point of Dolarhyde's murderous anger. As part of his torture of his captive Lounds, Dolarhyde shows him slides of the victims, the murders, and Lounds's own photograph from the newspaper. Photographer Lounds immediately recognizes this slide show as Dolarhyde's symbolic way of announcing he will murder Lounds. Lounds recognizes that "to see" is death, at least from Dolarhyde's perspective. For example, Lounds knows that he will die if Dolarhyde removes his panty-hose mask to reveal his features.

Graham, too, finally recognizes that Dolarhyde's secret power lies in his reliance on covert methods of seeing while at the same time remaining impervious to a return gaze. Fantasizing about murder as he comes ever closer to Dolarhyde's mind-set, Graham returns to the empty Leeds house. Standing in the master bedroom, he imagines Valerie Leeds's body, her eyes replaced by mirrors in a sanitized vision of what Dolarhyde actually did to her corpse, brought back to an eerie half-life: "I see me desired by you. Accepted, and loved, in the silver mirrors of your eyes." In reference to this same scene, Tony Williams writes that Graham has recognized that Dolarhyde's "condition pathologically reenacts Lacan's mirror stage." In other words, as a result of early childhood sexual abuse by a maternal figure, Dolarhyde has never psychologically separated from his mother's body to become a separate entity. So, he "recreates his desire for love by a maternal 'good object' while enacting rage against the 'bad object,' killing and blinding with fragments from a mirror" (*Hearths* 258). Williams's interpretation not only strengthens the film's focus on family and its dysfunctions but also its concern with the killing male gaze.

That Dolarhyde has never psychosexually matured is obvious, leading to another aspect of the film's critique of gender: embattled and "hysterical" masculinity. In his note to Lecter, Dolarhyde makes it very clear that he disapproves of the tabloid nickname for him: "I have a collection of your press clippings. I think they are absurd, as are mine. 'The Tooth Fairy.' What could be more inappropriate?" Dolarhyde is so concerned with the public perception that he might be homosexual that he places shorts on one of his victims, Charles Leeds, so that, as Dr. Bloom notes, no one will think that the "Tooth Fairy" is gay. Dolarhyde reacts with fury to the print allegations, formulated to be intentionally provocative by Dr. Bloom and Graham and then disseminated by Lounds, that he has "molested all his male victims. He may be impotent with members of the opposite sex. Our forensic psychologists have projected, though are not sure, that he may have had sexual relations with his mother." Dolarhyde is so angered by what he sees as a direct challenge to his masculine omnipotence in his murderous identity that he abducts Lounds not only to kill him but to hear directly from Lounds that the references to the Tooth Fairy's homosexuality are deliberate lies. Dolarhyde furiously tells Lounds that "according to you, I'm a sexual pervert"— meaning that, from Dolarhyde's perspective, homosexuality is a perversion. He waits to hear Lounds's denial to the question "Do you imply that I'm queer" before killing him. In a bitter mockery of Lounds's writings about the killer's supposed homosexuality, Dolarhyde then dons the dentures he has used to bite the victims, tells Lounds that he will "seal your promise with a kiss," and bites off the reporter's lips.

Dolarhyde is aggressively heterosexual, as the narrative makes clear. Though he kills men and children, the focus of his attention is on the sexually desirable mother figures in each selected family. Perhaps this is so, as

Tony Williams argues in "Dark Mirror," because Dolarhyde has been the victim of maternal sexual abuse and thus reenacts his primal trauma again and again in an attempt to master his fear from his powerfully adult and male position. In direct contrast to Dolarhyde's height and bulk, his fear of grown women is manifested in the first scene that brings the Tooth Fairy as an offstage menace into the narrative foreground. In a shot visually reminiscent of the way in which Dolarhyde accosts Lounds from behind, a woman's hand reaches into the film frame and grabs Dolarhyde's shoulder. He jumps in fear and turns to face one of his coworkers, an attractive young woman named Eileen. Dolarhyde is frightened and inarticulate in her presence. He hides his scarred upper lip (the result of a surgically corrected cleft palate, readers of the novel would know) and nervously lowers and raises his impenetrable wraparound sunglasses. Overcome with fear by the brief encounter (a routine work order), Dolarhyde must retreat from Eileen's female gaze to a private room in the film lab where he can re-empower himself by gazing at the photograph of his next female victim.

The next female Dolarhyde encounters is Reba, the blind woman working in an adjacent lab whom he goes to in order to obtain infrared film for his next murder.[25] At first, Dolarhyde does not realize Reba is blind. As she turns on the lights in the darkroom, Dolarhyde goes into his customary shielding gestures against female surveillance but then, once confident she cannot see him, regains the kind of composure he has heretofore only felt with the sightless dead. Unlike a male coworker named Ralph, who briefly enters the lab to offer Reba a ride home, Dolarhyde does not condescend to her with his own offer of a ride, which makes him as attractive to her as she is to him. Lacking any real sense of the social courtesies expected of flirtation, Dolarhyde makes his sexual interest in Reba plain. As a fellow outsider, she reciprocates. Dolarhyde's one relationship with a living woman, however, is made possible only by her physical inability to return a threatening gaze at him. For once, the curiously vulnerable killer feels at ease, to the extent that he can accept her immediate notice of his painfully mastered speech impediment. As a result of his childhood problems with speech, he remains an inarticulate adult, as Reba candidly remarks: "You speak very well, although you avoid fricatives and sibilants." She wants to touch his face to see if he is "smiling or frowning"—whether he has taken her comments personally. Dolarhyde, threatened by her attempt to "see" him, physically prevents her hand from touching his face and says, deceitfully, "Take my word for it. I'm smiling." Later, at his house, Dolarhyde screens his films of the next family victims in front of her, suggesting that the only way he can achieve arousal is through this kind of solitary foreplay. Reba, sensing Dolarhyde's sexual excitement but not knowing its origins, willingly fellates and then engages in sexual intercourse with him. His ability to deceive her in such a way as to remain in masculine control and thus erase his insecurity with adult females enables him to enter into a marginally "normal" sexual relationship with her.

The liaison with Reba, though it makes obvious Dolarhyde's complete inability to form adult relationships, nevertheless has the effect of making the unseen monster that dominated the first two-thirds of the film suddenly human, and within the same parameters that have signified him as monstrous. Mann's sudden redrawing of the boundaries is a complex shift of audience sympathy toward the main narrative "monster" (and away from Graham, who is in simultaneous full withdrawal from human contact) that has no parallel in Jonathan Demme's cinematic rendition of Jame Gumb in *The Silence of the Lambs.* Yet any possibility of redemption for Dolarhyde is lost near the film's fairly routine conclusion. Dolarhyde, waiting eagerly outside Reba's home for her return, mistakenly interprets Ralph's caress of Reba's face as a romantic gesture and erupts into another killing frenzy. He fatally shoots Ralph and abducts Reba to his home. There, he prepares to subject her to his killing ritual with the mirrors so that he can render her a "safe" woman who will belong to only him. In a moment of female subjugation that negates Reba's former independence, Dolarhyde the phallic monster forces her into a helpless swoon. Only Graham's climactic, long-distance identification of Dolarhyde brings Graham and the FBI to the killing zone in the nick of time.

The psychological similarities between Graham and Dolarhyde are highlighted throughout the film's narrative arc in the most significant area of boundary destabilization. The doubling between murderer and detective betrays the presence of the haunted Gothic beneath the cool postmodernist surface of the film. Both men are troubled in the present by the memories of a traumatized past. In the film's opening scene on the beach, Crawford's words to Graham suggest an uneasy past history ready to erupt: "You look all right now." Graham, distinctly nettled by the observation, says too quickly: "I am—all right—now." His moment of conjugal affirmation with Molly is contrasted with the following scene. He enters the violated Leeds household and retraces the same path Dolarhyde took to the master bedroom as portrayed in the film's opening sequence. The ominous soundtrack score emphasizes Graham's doubling with the Gothic monster. As Graham speaks into his recorder for his crime-scene profile, he stands at the same vantage point from where Dolarhyde shot the sleeping couple. This is the same place he will stand toward the film's climax as he experiences the romantic vision of the eerily resurrected Valerie Leeds.

However, true psychological connection to Dolarhyde eludes Graham until he returns to his hotel room. Watching the slaughtered family's home movies, Graham sees Mrs. Leeds the same way Dolarhyde first saw her—as a moving image on a screen. Disturbed by the images and needing a break from their intensity, Graham makes a late-night phone call to Molly. He awakens his defenseless loved one from sleep in a manner the film pointedly suggests (the ominous soundtrack music again) is similar to Dolarhyde's "call" upon his "loved one." Only at this point has Graham established the first psychological link to Dolarhyde. Returning to the screen images of the Leeds family, he realizes how "lovely" Valerie Leeds was and how "maddening" it must have been to touch her with gloves on. Then he remembers the talcum powder on her body, realizes it just might have fallen from a glove as it was pulled off, and further extrapolates that Dolarhyde may have opened his victims' eyes so that "they could see you." This realization is the first of three major epiphanies Graham will have during the narrative. All are based on his intuitive, nonverbal awareness of Dolarhyde's voyeuristically based sexuality, extreme need for love, and paralyzing insecurity. Each epiphany places him closer to comprehension of Dolarhyde's distorted sexuality, but as the Gothic genre demands, the difference between perverted and normal sex is minimal.

After the first epiphany, Graham hurtles further into taboo territory by physically assaulting Lounds on the street. He flips the reporter onto a parked car and growls, "Stay the fuck away from me." His tendency toward violence is therefore dramatically illustrated, directly before he presents to Crawford his first profile of the murderer: "The Tooth Fairy's gonna go on until we get smart or we get lucky. He won't stop. . . . He's got a genuine taste for it." But he realizes he has not yet been retraumatized enough to empathize completely with the Tooth Fairy. So, he visits Lecter to, as Graham puts it, "recover the mind-set." As yet another double for Graham's dark side, Lecter is a pseudosupernatural denizen of that Gothic borderland. His past remains hidden from all sight—Graham's, the audience's. This opacity makes Lecter a truly monstrous enigma. He has, in the terms of the narrative, exiled himself completely from society through his "animalistic" and taboo-shattering behavior. He exists, in some levels, on the purely sensual level beyond and before language. For example, he identifies Graham only by the smell of his "atrocious" shaving lotion that he had worn to Lecter's trial three years previously. However, unwilling to completely dissociate himself from civilization, Lecter still delights in mocking social conventions beneath exquisite courtesy and manners. As a former psychiatrist, he plays the same profiling game in which Graham is engaged, flaying Graham's efforts to manipulate him into helping with the Tooth Fairy case: "You're very tan, Will. Your hands are rough. They don't look like a cop's hands anymore. And that shaving lotion is something a child would select. It has a ship on the bottle, doesn't it? Don't think you can persuade me with appeals to my intellectual vanity." Lecter takes a cursory glance through the crime-scene file but perceptively knows the real reason for Graham's visit: "You came here to look at me, to get the old scent back again, didn't you? . . . Do you know how you caught me, Will? . . . The reason you caught me, Will, is we're just alike. Do you understand? Smell yourself." Horrified by the truth in Lecter's words, Graham shuts down his intellect and perceptions to disengage from his "madness." He literally flees from the asylum, past the curious stares of guards and attendants, which we see from a subjective camera angle parallel to the other main subjective point-of-view in the film (Dolarhyde).

Graham's second epiphany occurs during his trip to Birmingham to visit the house of the first murdered family, the Jacobis. A *Tattler* headline in the airport has, by evoking the film's astrological subtext, set the proper mood for the scene: ASTRONOMERS SIGHT GOD! On the flight to Alabama, Graham falls asleep while studying the case file. He dreams of Molly in Florida. A medium, slow-motion shot of Molly juxtaposed with a close-up of Graham's impassive, staring face (with sea gulls flapping behind him) establishes a victim's-eye view of Graham's looming, godlike presence equivalent to Dolarhyde's self-image at moments of murder. Graham is jerked from this dream of male potency by female screams. A little girl in the neighboring seat has glimpsed the gory crime-scene photos of the mutilated Valerie Leeds and weeps in her mother's arms as a stewardess angrily attempts to conceal the photos. The scene cuts from Graham's social ostracism to Graham's stalking through the woods behind the Jacobi house in an effort to find more evidence or insight into the Tooth Fairy's mentality. Backing further into the woods to see the entirety of the house, Graham, talking to himself, finds a tree that the killer scaled to watch the house's inhabitants "all goddamn day long" before going in at night to kill them. From this godlike, distant vantage point, where his predatory gaze can encompass the house and all its residents, Graham realizes his second profound insight into the Tooth Fairy's methodology of victim selection: "That's why houses with big yards."

The discovery of Dolarhyde's note to Lecter shortly after Graham's second epiphany confirms the second killer's desire to achieve masculine potency in terms which he perceives as godlike. The note reads in part: "You [Lecter] alone can understand what I am becoming. You alone know the people I use to help me in these things are only elements undergoing change to fuel the radiance of what I am becoming. Just as the source of light is burning." Dolarhyde attempts to transcend his human weaknesses by imaginatively transforming into an omnipotent, transcendent being—quite literally, a cosmic force of nature manifested in the masculine sun devouring the feminine moon. Dolarhyde is fascinated by William Blake's painting, *The Great Red Dragon and the Woman Clothed in the Rays of the Sun*. His house is full of photographs and murals of planetscapes and stars. His potency challenged by Lounds, he rants to the helpless reporter before torturing and killing him: "Before me, you are a slug in the sun. You are privy to a great becoming and you recognize nothing. You're an ant in the afterbirth. It is your nature to do one thing correctly: tremble. But fear is not what you owe me. No, Lounds, you and the others, you owe me awe." Through the second epiphany at the Jacobi house, Graham intuitively recognizes that aspect of Dolarhyde's mind-set, based on voyeuristic appropriation of the human form, which aspires toward divine potency. But through this second connection to the Tooth Fairy, Graham has also moved himself even further into the Gothic borderland, as Dr. Bloom warns him: "You're getting deeper and deeper into this. Last time you did that, you did a real good job of pushing yourself all out of shape. You try it on again, or you go through some big trauma, you could relapse, my friend." Significantly, it is during this portion of the film that Dolarhyde literally enacts what Graham has fantasized about: killing Lounds.

The last third of the film brings Graham and Dolarhyde onto parallel psychological tracks. As Dolarhyde attempts a pathetic and doomed reconciliation with society, Graham distances himself from it. Graham sits in the FBI evidence room, fingering Mrs. Leeds's nightclothes and talking aloud to his invisible quarry/companion: "What is it you think you're becoming? The answer's in the way you use the mirrors. What do the mirrors make you think you're becoming?" His second interview with Lecter, by phone in an anonymous Atlanta hotel room, emphasizes how distant Graham has become from all human contact, even Lecter's. These two lonely figures discourse on the connection between human existence and metaphysics. Graham, at a conceptual impasse in his mental odyssey, vents his frustration: "Look, I'm sick of you crazy sons of bitches. You got something to say, say it." Lecter responds:

> I want to help you. You'd be more comfortable if you'd relax with yourself. We don't invent our natures. They're issued to us along with our lungs and pancreas . . . Why fight it? . . . Did you really feel so depressed after you shot Mr. Garrett Jacob Hobbs to death? . . . Didn't you really feel so bad because killing him felt so good? And why shouldn't it feel good? It must feel good to God. He does it all the time. . . . It feels good, Will, because God has power. And if one does what God does enough times, one will become as God is. God's the champ. He always stays ahead.

Lecter, an unlikely ally who has just attempted to have Graham murdered, provides Graham with the final puzzle piece he needs to construct a narrow enough profile of the killer's psyche. All that remains is to fix a name, an inescapable identity, to the construct. Now that he knows all of what he needs to know about the Tooth Fairy's fantasy life, Graham can begin the slow process of reintegrating himself back into civilized company.

Thus, Graham's third epiphany, in Crawford's presence, centers upon the last crucial remaining question of the investigation. The link between the Tooth Fairy's signature (his distinctive crimes) and his identity must be established. Graham asks rhetorically: "How does he find [the families]? When we find out how he found them, we'll find him." He refers to Lecter's profile of a powerless man who seeks ultimate power and then muses that the murder series originates in a former victim of child abuse turned into victimizer. In response to Crawford's indignant protest against Graham's sympathy for the Tooth Fairy, Graham demonstrates just how much insight he has gained into the act of murder through a quest into the Gothic borderland of paradox and destabilization:

> My heart bleeds for him as a child. Someone took a kid and manufactured a monster. At the same time, as an adult, he's irredeemable. He butchers whole families to pursue trivial fantasies. As an adult, someone should blow the sick fuck out of his socks. Do you think that's a contradiction, Jack? Does this kind of understanding make you uncomfortable?

The theme of doubling finds its textual resolution in the remainder of the scene. Graham, his empathy fully in tune with the victim/victimizer mindset, makes the intuitive leap that the killer, based on his knowledge of what he would find in the victims' houses, has seen the same home movies that Graham is viewing: "Because everything with you is seeing, isn't it? The primary sensory input that makes your dream live is seeing. Reflections, mirrors, images. You've seen these films! Haven't you, my man?" Graham, having provided Crawford the means to identify the man who would have been in a position to see two sets of home movies from the same photo lab, has now mastered his primal traumas of masculine victimization (Lecter/Dolarhyde and, more subtly, Crawford). Graham will shortly be free to return home. The detective, by becoming equivalent to the serial killer he pursues, preserves the domestic interests of the state, which gives the film its neoconservative happy ending and restoration of the nuclear family from the very jaws of hell. But Mann's film contains enough the source novel's ambiguity to make it clear that, the mutedly optimistic resolution aside, the Gothic territory into which the detective must venture contains its own subversions that are inseparable from its affirmations.

Detectives
Versus
Serial Killers

In this grouping of detective versus se-
rial killer texts—*From Potter's Field, Citizen X,* and *The Alienist*—one can
see the formula so firmly established by Thomas Harris still at work in varying
degrees of artistic complexity and ideological emphasis. Each work has been
selected for its applicability to one of each of three of the most ubiquitous
areas of concern raised by the tale of profiler versus murderer: gender in relation to serial murder, the ambiguities of working within a social system in
simultaneous need of condemnation and affirmation, and the efficacy of the
profiling method itself.

"I Knew the Victims Too Well": *From Potter's Field*

Given the serial killer tale's notorious misogynistic excesses and grotesque
violence, it is surprising, at least for those critics who have little knowledge
or appreciation of the Gothic influences at work, to learn that a substantial
number of female-authored texts feature male serial killers. These authors
include Joyce Carol Oates, Poppy Z. Brite, and A. M. Homes. In the detective fiction genre, undoubtedly the most recognizable female writer to dramatize serial murder is Patricia Cornwell, who debuted her fictional alter
ego Dr. Kay Scarpetta in 1990 with the novel *Postmortem.*[1] Over the past

eight years, Cornwell has gathered quite a devoted following, and her novels consistently reach the *New York Times* bestseller list. In the rarefied field
of genre writers who achieve mainstream A-list status, Cornwell is a genuine success story who has produced, at the time of this writing, fifteen novels.[2] She has also established a small sub-subgenre within serial killer fiction—the professional female pathologist/forensic psychiatrist/criminologist
tale of detection—that other writers are currently expanding.[3]

These Scarpetta novels and others like them constitute nothing less than
feminist appropriation of a disturbingly "gynocidal" (Jane Caputi's term)
subject in a sort of literary "take back the night" movement. In fact, Cornwell's novels are evidence that some writers have a vested interest in rewriting masculine-dominated genres, especially the detective story, for the purposes of de-escalating the levels of graphic violence or refocusing narrative
attention from identification with the murderer to identification with victims. A writer such as Cornwell approaching the daunting task of reconfiguring the serial killer subgenre in terms friendlier to female interests is faced
with several dilemmas, the least of which is appearing to endorse sexual murder merely by working within the subgenre. The primary dilemma is this:
how to elevate the female voice to a position of power within the male-domi-
nated text? One authorial solution, perhaps the most limiting because of its
rather masochistic acceptance of the sexist status quo where women are always victims and men are always the Other, is to accept the formula as a
given while working to restore the lost female voice, even if only from beyond the grave. In such works, men will continue to kill women but women
will move that action off center stage, so to speak, and now offer testimony
of their own suffering or their empathy for fellow victims.[4] This is the narrative choice largely dictating Cornwell's work.

The appeal of Cornwell's work can best be understood in terms of narrative sympathy not for the serial killer but for the murder victims and surviving family members. The point of audience identification in the novels
is Dr. Kay Scarpetta, the medical examiner of the state of Virginia and also
consulting forensic pathologist to the FBI's VICAP program. She is a female
law-enforcement professional (though not a "cop" in the strictest sense of
the word, making her yet another "amateur" detective in the subgenre) who
must not only directly work, or compete, with her often-hostile male counterparts (Tangorra 71) but also confront the serial killer as nightmarish embodiment of masculine backlash against female encroachment into the traditional male arenas of power. Owing a heavy conceptual debt to Thomas
Harris's Clarice Starling, Cornwell's Scarpetta as woman without a father

in a male professional world similarly positions herself in the interstices between masculine and feminine social constructions and transgresses those boundaries at will, though not without personal cost. Scarpetta's exposure to this outlaw realm shows her a Gothicized, fearsome, and paranoid world of lecherous and brutal men who, taking notice of her, threaten not only her physical safety but her psychic equilibrium as well. It is a world where she can be expected to identify not with the predatory males but rather the victimized females.

Almost any one of the Scarpetta novels would suffice for the purposes of this analysis, but her sixth novel, *From Potter's Field* (1995), shows her style in its mature form. (The novel is, at this writing, being adapted for the screen.) The novel also showcases Scarpetta's nemesis, serial killer Temple Gault, who is a returning character from Cornwell's fourth novel, *Cruel and Unusual.* Gault announces his return with the Christmas Eve murder of a derelict, brain-damaged, and unidentifiable woman in New York City's Central Park. As Kay Scarpetta struggles to identify the woman to give her a proper burial, Gault meanwhile begins slaughtering more victims, including a professional enemy of Scarpetta's, in an effort to compel her exclusive attention. (It is the same kind of murderous Gothic courtship that the NBC series *Profiler* will later establish between Jack-of-All-Trades and Dr. Samantha Waters.) Scarpetta must also juggle her professional obligations with the demands of family. Her mother is dying in the hospital in Florida, her older sister is given to irresponsibility, and her genius niece's status as FBI trainee is in consistent jeopardy because of her rebellious spirit and secret lesbian life. Finally, she must balance the competing attentions of the two men most important to her personal life. One of these men is Richmond police captain Pete Marino, a platonic friend of the "old-school" brand of hypermasculine, sexist, racist, and self-destructive cop. The other is FBI special agent Benton Wesley, another (married) friend with whom she has recently begun a secret love affair. Under all of this stress, Scarpetta becomes an emotional martyr to femininity's beleaguered place in the patriarchal world. Unable to shut herself off from her compassion like Marino or Wesley, or redirect her anger and despair into the thrill of the chase of genius criminals, she suffers unbearable distress. Her quest is not so much to beat Gault as it is to identify the body of his Christmas-Eve victim so as to restore her identity to the savage world that obliterated it. The practical fact that her identification is irrelevant to the investigation actually becomes for Scarpetta the central justification—the moral imperative—for identifying her. Once Scarpetta makes this identification (Jayne Gault, Temple's sister), the novel ends.

The novel's central quest to identify Gault's female victim (the other victims are males whose identities are known) and save her from the anonymity of a cheap pine coffin bound for Potter's Field represents in microcosm Scarpetta's larger agenda. She wants to give a voice to the voiceless and, through so doing, establish her own identity as a "speaker for the dead." Going through the homeless victim's belongings with the other investigators, Scarpetta mentally tries to conjure her back into being: "We continued our excavation of this woman who seemed to be in the room with us. I felt her personality in her paltry possessions and believed she had left us clues" (116). In response to a male investigator who can't see the practicality of identifying "Jane" because her identification serves no purpose in finding Gault, Scarpetta looks at him: "[I] watched his interest in [Jane] fade. The light went out of his eyes, and I had seen this before in deaths where the victim was no one. Jane had gotten as much time as she was going to get. Ironically, she would have gotten even less had her killer not been so notorious" (117). In a meeting with Wesley, she insists that single-minded fixation on catching Gault has led the male investigators to neglect identification of "Jane":

> The cops, the Bureau, want to catch Gault, and identifying this homeless lady isn't a priority. She's just another poor, nameless person prisoners will bury in Potter's Field. . . . I think she has something yet to say to us . . . she's a priority because we are bound morally and professionally to do everything we can for her. She has a right to be buried with her name. . . . We really don't care . . . Not the cops, not the medical examiners, and not this unit. We already know who killed her, so who she is no longer matters. (136–37)

Scarpetta, who comes from an impoverished childhood, resents the inherent class biases of the FBI and other law enforcement agencies she collaborates with, and sees in "Jane" a symbol of her struggle to honor the dead of all classes. Her idealism on this matter is so strong that she refuses police protection from Gault because "most people don't get agents or cops assigned to them until they're already raped or dead" (175). She resents those who profit from the dead, as demonstrated by her spoken contempt for a local art dealer who has marketed silk-screened lab coats to capitalize on Scarpetta's media fame: "You're not disrespectful of me. . . . You're disrespectful of the dead. You will never be me, but you will someday be dead. Maybe you should think about that" (253). "Jane," homeless and poor and anonymous, summons all of Scarpetta's memories of her own identityless past, so Scarpetta struggles all the harder to give the woman a name. On the basis of rare gold-foil fillings in the victim's teeth, Scarpetta is able to track down the woman's former dentist and, when faced with his reluctance to check records, shames him into it: "Please. We're talking about a woman we're unable to identify. All human beings have a right to be buried with their name" (288). The New York City policemen want her to remain unidentified so that Gault will be tried for stronger murder cases in Virginia, where he can be executed. When "Jane" is buried in Potter's Field in spite of Scarpetta's efforts, Scarpetta is not fully satisfied with the closing of the Gault case until the body is exhumed and formally identified. The novel's final image, that of the pine box being pulled back out of its grave by the Rikers Island prisoners whose job it is to bury corpses in Potter's Field, is a redemptive promise that "Jane" will finally be identified and properly remembered as Jayne Gault. Thus, the obsessive quest to conquer Gault is softened by Scarpetta's presence in the world of masculine rivalries and jealousies.

Unlike her male colleagues, Scarpetta is not concerned with territories and jurisdictions. In place of male competition she elevates respect and concern for the victims of the crimes. She chides Richmond's new police chief, Paul Tucker, for his irritation with Marino's FBI affiliations: "When violence occurs anywhere, it is everybody's problem. . . . No matter where your precinct or department is" (15). She is furious with Wesley for honoring a military request to keep Gault's Medal of Honor–winning uncle out of the investigation: "I'm tired of boys and their codes of honor. I'm tired of male bonding and secrecy. We are not kids playing cowboys and Indians. We're not neighborhood children playing *war*. . . . I thought you were more highly evolved than that" (283). Scarpetta is a member of the same law enforcement apparatus as Tucker and Wesley, of course, but also apart from it. She focuses her considerable intellect and medical training on the lives of the victims and not their killers. Whereas Marino, for example, worries about witness testimony in court, Scarpetta knows that her work ultimately does not rely on the legal system: "I was accustomed to witnesses who did not speak to anyone but me" (36). Her gift at reading the clues on the bodies of the murdered, however, exacts an enormous psychological toll from her: "A day never went by when a memory wasn't triggered, when an image didn't flash. I would see a body bloated by injury and death, a body in bondage. I would see suffering and annihilation in unbearable detail, for nothing was hidden from me. I knew the victims too well" (41). Because she is still alive, her empathy for victims stops frustratingly just short of complete comprehension: "how does one measure the mental anguish of a woman made to strip in an isolated park on a bitterly cold night? How could any of us imagine what she felt when Gault marched her to that ice-filled fountain and cocked his gun?" (47).

Sometimes, this frustration borne of complete isolation overflows. She must then confront the first visible symbol of brutality so as to control, for once, the uncontrollable, as when she shouts at the carriage driver who beats an old mare for stumbling on the ice and threatens him with the loss of his livelihood. She laments to Wesley: "I'm so tired of cruelty. I'm so tired of people beating horses and killing little boys and head-injured women" (63). This degree of empathy ironically shuts her off from most human contact, as she tells her outlaw-lover Wesley: "I don't think I could be intimate with someone who does not understand what it's like for me" (41–42). Her sister Dorothy, from whom she has been estranged, lectures Scarpetta: "you've spent most of your life worrying about dead people. . . . I think all your relationships are with the dead" (64). Through a brief and awkward exchange between Scarpetta and New York City Transit Police Commander Frances Penn (wherein Penn says: "Your story is my story. There are many women like us. Yet we never seem to get together"), the novel implies that professional women, or at least those entrusted with insuring national security, are so burdened with empathy for all around them, and a contradictory desire to out-man the men in terms of commitment to career, that they are incapable of forming the alliances and good-old-boy networks that men do to protect themselves professionally and personally. Cornwell thus advances a feminist critique of the patriarchal social structure by dramatizing the pathologies of the women who must work within it.

But in another fundamental way, Cornwell's novels also appeal to status-quo neoconservative ideologies, where law enforcement is the primary answer to social dysfunction. For all of her talk of empathy for victims, Scarpetta almost never considers the possibility of proactive measures against violent crime. Instead, her empathy is clearly designed to redeem the existing system by her very presence within it. The novel makes clear that the system of law enforcement is needed because the world is so dangerous. This reactionary element has been implicit in the first few Cornwell novels. However, as Sean French has noted, casual readers of the early novels might be tempted to mistake Cornwell for a "woolly liberal" because of her espousal of antiracism, rock music, and feminist notions of fair employment practices and professional courtesy (33). Beginning with the fifth novel, *Body Farm,* Cornwell through Scarpetta more clearly advocates a politics of fear.

In Scarpetta's world, women have no choice but to arm themselves heavily and turn their upper-middle-class homes into fortresses. In this aspect, her novels are the most Gothic among a Gothic-influenced subgenre. Gault's mystification dramatically works against Cornwell's trademark realistic portrayals of forensic procedure, as Elise O'Shaughnessy observes: "While Gault inspires satisfying shudders, his omniscient aspect keeps him from passing the ultimate terror test: Can you imagine this guy as one of the faceless encounters in your life?" (C10). Gault's first name, "Temple," connotes the degree of mystification Cornwell invests in his evil character. He is marked by unusual, striking physical features, specifically bright red hair and "eyes as pale blue as a malamute's" (207). He is a shape-shifter, with a murderous confederate who can take on his identity at will and vice versa. Scarpetta dreams about him "stealing" her reflection in the mirror as a superhuman, androgynous, blank-faced, and inscrutable monster in holy regalia: "A figure with a long dark robe and a face like a white balloon was smiling insipidly at me from an antique mirror. Every time I passed the mirror the figure in it was watching with its chilly smile. It was both dead and alive and seemed to have no gender" (174). She becomes so paranoid of Gault that she thinks him immortal: "I was to the point of thinking he was the living dead and no weapon known to us could stop him" (248).

Gault's monstrosity dominates the narrative throughout. In the opening "'Twas the Night Before Christmas" segment of *From Potter's Field*, Gault is immediately portrayed as an antichrist with extraordinary, nearly supernatural powers. He profanes Christmas Eve with the murder of a woman who is, as Scarpetta later discovers, his sister: "Temple Gault had always been magical, a god who wore a human body. He did not slip as he walked, for example, when he was quite certain others would, and he did not know fear" (1). Though this segment is related from Gault's point of view, and may at first seem only to reflect Gault's own religiously tinted monomania, Scarpetta and her law-enforcement allies also believe him to be more than human. Dr. Anna Zenner, who consoles Scarpetta after her collapse from stress, says she has avoided forensic psychiatry work because

> I cannot spend so much time with monsters. It is bad enough for people like you who take care of their victims. But I think to sit in the same room with the Gaults of the world would poison my soul. . . . You see, I have a terrible confession to make. . . . I don't give a damn why any of them do it . . . I think they should all be hanged. (221–22)

FBI profiler Benton Wesley is "incensed and bewildered by Gault's malignant genius" (22). This genius manifests itself in Gault's game-playing and
flirtations with capture. He poses victims' bodies as gruesome taunts. He
uses Scarpetta's stolen American Express card to signal his movements. He
sends a mocking police code to Scarpetta and her team through the pager
of a police officer he has just killed. He compromises FBI internal security
by sending a "secret agent," Carrie Grethen, to the academy. He leaves a note
on the body of a corrupt sheriff. Finally, he breaks into Scarpetta's office and
alters her screen saver to signal his presence. His diabolical genius resists human comprehension, as Scarpetta warns Frances Penn: "There is no description for what he is." Penn, having just witnessed Gault's murder signature
for the first time, shoots back: "Evil comes to mind, Dr. Scarpetta" (27). The
narrative, with no hint of irony, habitually refers to Gault as "evil" or a
"monster." Scarpetta reflects upon Gault's nature and concludes that he apparently has no recognizable human connection to ordinary criminals: "It
is not difficult to comprehend people being so enraged, drugged, frightened
or crazy that they kill. Even psychopaths have their own twisted logic. But
Temple Brooks Gault seemed beyond description or deciphering" (59).

Not that this stops Scarpetta from trying anyway. Her most consistent
"explanation" for Gault's behavior is that he is an animal. For example, finding that Gault had accompanied his female victim to a shark exhibit in the
Museum of Natural History, Scarpetta associates him with the inhumanly
smiling great white sharks she has just seen in the exhibit's film:

> I . . . [imagined] Gault watching monsters ripping flesh as blood
> spread darkly through water. I saw his cold stare and the twisted
> spirit behind his thin smile. In the most frightening reaches of my
> mind, I knew he smiled as he killed. He bared his cruelty in that
> strange smile I had seen on the several occasions I had been near
> him. (83–84)

During the final chase of Gault through the subway tunnels of New York
City, Scarpetta again calls him "a shark swimming through the blackness of
the tunnel" (346).

Gault's monstrosity defies limits and boundaries—even those of time,
space, and physics. The FBI's standard profiling techniques do not work with
the unquantifiable Gault. Little is known of his childhood on a plantation
in Georgia and his parents refuse to cooperate with the authorities. But profiling, in a twist on the standard media glorification of the technique, is

irrelevant to the pursuit of Gault anyway. Even though Gault's identity is known to the FBI, he still cannot be caught. He is ephemeral, insubstantial, and everywhere and nowhere. He can break into the FBI's Engineering Research Facility—where Scarpetta's niece and surrogate daughter Lucy, an FBI trainee, has been developing the Crime Artificial Intelligence Network (CAIN)—and introduce a "backdoor" into the system that allows him to tap by modem into the computer whenever he desires. His virtual presence, uncontainable and unstoppable, in the heart of the FBI's main crime-fighting (and public surveillance) system itself leads Scarpetta to further mystify him: "Gault moved freely through spaces most people could not see. He nimbly stepped over greasy steel, needles and the fetid nests of humans and rats. He was a virus. He had somehow gotten into our bodies and our buildings and our technology" (131). The "virus," Scarpetta makes clear during her contemplation of an old Civil War battlefield, is her metaphor for the corruptive influence of evil:

> That war seemed close when I thought of Virginia swamps and woods and missing dead. Not a year passed when I didn't examine old buttons and bones. . . . I had touched the fabrics and faces of old violence, too, and it felt different from what I had my hands on now. Evil, I believed, had mutated to a new extreme. (203)

Gault as virus justifies, of course, the most extreme law enforcement measures to stop him. And so, ironically, Cornwell's feminist hero becomes one of the strongest fictional spokespersons ever for patriarchy. But it should also be remembered that the Gothic elements of the narrative work to undermine simplistic conclusions about Cornwell's political agenda.

Perestroika and Profiling: *Citizen X*

In terms of melodrama, the serial killer's evil genius necessitates superhumanly intelligent opponents such as the profilers. The 1995 cable-television film *Citizen X,* directed by Chris Gerolmo, is representative of the subgenre's mystification of profiling as a nearly magical method of apprehending evil criminals, this time by uprooting the profiling methodology from its overwhelmingly American context and proving its efficacy in a distant, alien country. As a dramatization of actual events,[5] *Citizen X* is set in the province of Rostov in the Soviet Union during the 1980s and early 1990s, when the manhunt for a prolific serial killer of women and children in isolated rural areas took place against the dramatic backdrop of perestroika and the coming collapse of the Communist Party regime. The serial killer, Andrei Chikatilo, was eventually apprehended, convicted of fifty-two murders (making him one of the worst serial killers in documented history), and executed.[6] *Citizen X,* based on the book *The Killer Department* by Robert Cullen, dramatizes the search for Chikatilo by focusing on the decade-long labors of one forensics examiner and amateur detective, Victor Burakov, given sole responsibility (according to the film's dramatic license) for catching the killer. As portrayed in the film, Burakov is a grimly passionate pursuer. He alternates emotional bursts of weeping with dry-eyed clinical analysis. He is prone to self-righteousness, temper tantrums, and nervous breakdowns,[7] but he also manifests a rumpled nobility of purpose that wins over the admiration and loyalty of the initially pragmatic *militsia* (Soviet police) commander and bureaucrat Colonel Fetisov. Burakov is another outsider of the type so beloved of this subgenre. He is a newcomer to law enforcement, an empathic intellectual among soulless bureaucrats. His arrival at his new job, chief forensics examiner in the city of Rostov-on-Don, coincides exactly with the discovery of eight mutilated bodies at a nearby collective farm. Thus, the rise to public perception of "Citizen X," a psychiatrist's name for the unknown killer described in his profile, initiates Burakov's career as well.

What makes *Citizen X* a most revealing example of the serial killer narrative is its indictment of the Soviet system, the Reaganite "Evil Empire," as Burakov's primary nemesis, at least during the first two-thirds of the film. In the final third, the Berlin Wall crumbles, and Col. Fetisov in the nascent democracy becomes a general who is able through his renewed idealism to reform the backward communist social structure, at least at the local militsia level, into a form more amenable to the kind of unorthodox individualism beloved of American ideology. Burakov, at last, is able to practice the profiling techniques of his American peers without interference from the Communist Party. The Party is portrayed in *Citizen X* as the ultimate bureaucracy, the very antithesis to America's collective illusions of solo independence. Thus, the film emphasizes the subgenre's ambivalence toward institutional forces or collective social existence even more than usual, and mystifies the notion of an autonomous soul apart from socialization. The film's closing images, where a herd of grateful villagers applauds the three Americanized profilers following the capture of Chikatilo, neatly invert the horror movie cliché of peasants lynching a monstrous outsider. However, the larger foundational subtext is the same. The cult of the exceptional individual structures the narrative and themes of the serial killer narrative, whereas the social support system is as much of a threat as it is a help. For the American television audience, at least dimly aware of the political transformation of the Russian nation a few years before and certainly aware of the United States' self-congratulatory assumption of total political credit for that change, *Citizen X* centers on the former Soviet Union's communist bureaucracy as the ideal ethnocentric metaphor for man's hatred of his own need of organizational existence. The system is the enemy. The heroic profiler is its redeemer.

The discovery of the first murder victim's body in *Citizen X* takes place on a rural collective farm in Rostov province, as a decrepit tractor hauling a plow unearths the corpse. For the initially sinister and resentful rural policeman who brings the body to criminologist Burakov's laboratory on the first day of the latter's employment, the body is "fresh meat, straight off the farm." The remark creates an association between production of commodities and dehumanization and also establishes the slanted perspective through which the film will examine communism. Burakov, as site of audience empathy and identification, is a replacement for a previous forensics examiner who has left behind a sloppy and disorganized office. Consequently, Burakov is in a visibly bad mood as he is introduced to the audience. However, his irritation is acceptable to the audience because he is faced with incompetence on all sides. He signals his opposition to Party procedure right away by implying to the policeman that his new coworkers are as lazy as the former forensics examiner. He also insists, to much hostility, that the policeman return to the crime scene before quitting time to canvas for more clues no matter "how long it takes." Out at the scene, the sullen policemen go about their work, calling Burakov a "heartless son of a bitch" but secure in their institutional ability to conform individualism to mediocrity: "He's new. He'll come around." When seven more bodies are discovered, Burakov further demonstrates his circumvention of standard procedure by staying in the office all night until he has finished the autopsies. His dedication, the film makes clear, is exemplary. Nor is he as dehumanized as his more professional law enforcement colleagues. For example, he weeps as he inspects all of the savage mutilations on the children's bodies.[8]

That same morning, Burakov must next meet with his provincial governing committee, which wastes no time establishing itself as the film's primary villain. The various officials on the committee include the local head of the KGB, the secretary of ideology for the Communist Party, and the commander of the local militsia, Col. Fetisov. Fetisov sets the tone for the meeting by chiding Burakov for his sloppy appearance and poor hygiene.

Bondarchuk, the secretary of ideology, then reacts strongly to Burakov's mention of serial murder: "There are no serial killers in the Soviet state. . . . It is a decadent Western phenomenon." The crimes must be the result of gang activity or some such more "normal" crime, the committee believes. Burakov, sitting alone like a schoolboy on a small folding chair before the imposing panel of officials, is powerless before them—a dynamic that will continue for much of the film. His willingness to deviate from protocol, a natural character tendency in detectives in this type of story, meets insurmountable resistance. Only after the meeting has adjourned does Fetisov, canny bureaucrat and career opportunist, reveal his sympathetic positioning in the film's scale of morality and his potential for future redemption. He gives Burakov permission to investigate his serial murder theory and form his own "killer department" by leaving his criminologist title behind and becoming a detective. But Burakov, in spite of his unorthodoxy and commitment to justice, is so constricted by the political system that runs his life he must first make sure that the new job title will not lower his ranking on a seniority list and thus harm his chances of obtaining a two-bedroom apartment for his family—a wife and two children.

A second committee meeting worsens Burakov's status in the system. He first objects to the way in which the local detectives have coached a gypsy boy to confess to the murders so as to close the case with the first convenient scapegoat. He then compounds his errors of diplomacy by requesting money, publicity, computers, and consultations with the FBI Serial Killer Task Force in Quantico, Virginia. The Soviet Burakov's desire to talk to the American FBI, which the film later uncritically poses as the climactic answer to all of Burakov's problems, underscores the degree to which the FBI's theories of serial murder have been canonized by the popular media. Naturally, the committee rejects Burakov's requests. After the second meeting, Fetisov attempts to tutor Burakov, who complains that he wants "special treatment" to pursue the investigation his own way, in the fine art of collaboration with the bureaucratic enemy to gain advantages duplicitously:

> The strength of a bureaucracy is measured by its ability to resist giving anyone special treatment. . . . The reason they said no to your demands to ask for more men, or computers for that matter, is to admit to our superiors in Moscow that we are overwhelmed, which they will never do. To ask the FBI for help is to admit to the West that we are behind in both forensic techniques and at managing information, which they will never do. And to publicize the case is

to admit that such crimes exist in the Soviet Union, which is the thing that they would rather die than do, publicly admit that anything is wrong. The only way that I have ever been able to get anything done is behind closed doors. By hoarding favors, by bribing, by wheedling. . . . People will die. And it will take all our strength to suffer these outrages. But suffer them we must, because we are the people who have to catch this monster, Comrade Burakov. You and I. Because as you may have noticed, no one else is willing to even try.

(To which Burakov acidly objects: "That's why a beginner is the perfect choice. If I fail, I'll be dangling out there by myself!") Fetisov's long speech is instructive for the number of themes important to *Citizen X* it explicates. First is the moral outrage in the face of a "monster's" evil. Second is the self-satisfying insistence for the American audience that the Soviet system was inherently flawed and sowed the seeds of its own demise through secrecy and technological ignorance. Finally, there is the forming of a tentative alliance between two similarly independent temperaments who are only momentarily antagonists. Fetisov at the film's start is a degraded individualist. He is a political survivor and ideological sell-out willing to sacrifice Burakov's career in the very likely event that the latter fails. Nevertheless, the colonel is clearly drawn as a sympathetic figure in the film. He is fertile to a reconversion to the sacred cause of freedom when the bureaucratic shackles are finally released. By espousing a certain pragmatic (that is, cowardly) point of view, Fetisov first sets himself up for unfavorable comparisons to Burakov's "naïve" but courageous idealism, which will be therefore vindicated by Fetisov's future defense and paradoxical institutionalization of Burakov's idiosyncratic methods.

A few years into Burakov's fruitless investigation, the committee further demonstrates its systemic incompetence by bringing in a special prosecutor named Gorbunov. The special prosecutor's theory for solving the case involves mass arrests of known homosexuals and sexual deviants. Gorbunov quickly establishes his identity as the perfect communist Organization Man. He scoffs at Burakov's theories as "based on one man's intuition." The fact that Gorbunov's skepticism will be proven incorrect illustrates again the extent to which the irrational consciousness dominates the Gothic tale of serial murder. In this instance, the Communist Party in the former Soviet Union can now serve as the supreme embodiment of rationality and intellectualism gone amok. Fetisov again privately attempts to soothe Burakov's temper: "In a bureaucracy it is important to know which skirmishes to join and which to ignore." Fetisov next emphasizes his political pragmatism: "I don't fight for anything." Burakov characteristically paints Fetisov as a coward in his reply: "I know." But the scene also establishes the beginning of Fetisov's redemption from his craven servitude under a corrupt system. He hints, referring to the prosecutor and the committee's sudden interest in persecuting homosexuals, that he possesses compromising knowledge of Bondarchuk's private life—introducing the plot mechanism by which Fetisov, at a later meeting, will blackmail the secretary into utter defeat.[9]

The secretary, all glower and bluster, is every bit the villain that Chikatilo is, perhaps worse, and unwittingly in league with the killer's evil. When Burakov captures Chikatilo for the first time, the secretary demands the prisoner's release on the basis that Chikatilo is a member in good standing in the Communist Party. Bondarchuk, representing the Evil Empire, will be deposed with the collapse of communism. Fetisov will be the new, redeemed leader—still a Political Man, but now invested with Burakov's compassion and individualism. As the newly promoted general in charge of the investigation following the dissolution of the committee, Fetisov gives Burakov a gracious apology for his past "ignorance." Fetisov additionally grants every one of Burakov's earlier requests for money, computers, and most importantly, a telephone conference with the FBI to obtain their sacred knowledge. Burakov's ability to communicate with his better-educated American contemporaries is the turning point in the film. His again-weepy emotional reaction to this breakthrough is a validation of the superstar FBI profilers and the "universal" applicability of their methods. Burakov, who not only has his own moments of "profiler's" insight but has earlier solicited the surreptitious help of a Soviet psychiatrist named Bukhanovsky in creating an "intuitive, well-defended" (in Fetisov's words) profile of the killer he calls "Citizen X," is now free to follow the course of action suggested by the profile. Fetisov and Burakov use their newfound political authority to set up an elaborate and ultimately successful trap centered on Chikatilo's riding of the rural train system to target solitary victims of opportunity. None of this, of course, would have been possible with Bondarchuk running the show. The special prosecutor, another vestige of the corrupt system, must also be overthrown before democracy's victory is complete at the film's end. Gorbunov tries to steal back Burakov's authority by wringing a confession out of the captured (for the second time, this time for good) Chikatilo through old-fashioned confrontation. However, it is Bukhanovsky, whose mild-mannered and nonconfrontational reading of the "Citizen X" profile completely shatters Chikatilo's resistance and obtains the desired confession, who prevails in the war of ideologies.[10]

The overthrow of the secretary and the prosecutor, and by extension, the Communist Party, also signifies a change in Burakov. His unwillingness to play political games is transformed by Fetisov's sudden joining of the battle in much the same way that Burakov's passion changes Fetisov. Early in the film, Fetisov predicts that someday Burakov will learn to enjoy playing games with the system. Following a leave of absence in a psychiatric hospital and thus a kind of metaphoric death, Burakov is resurrected as a steely, iron-willed hunter. He now manipulates the system not only because that is what it takes to run the quarry down to earth but because he seems to enjoy it. Burakov tests his newfound strength of will by complimenting Fetisov and then asking to bring in a psychiatrist—an unheard of strategy in a Soviet criminal case—to create a profile of the killer. An amused Fetisov sees through the ruse but grants the request anyway: "Did you just come in here and go out of your way to make me feel good, then ask me for something? My God, are you learning how to manipulate people? I've created a monster." Fetisov's ability to ridicule the system, such as his aside to Burakov that he won't let them shoot Burakov "without a trial," proves a valuable asset to Burakov as well in his tutelage as a master manipulator of organizational men. For instance, after Fetisov mildly complains that Burakov has spoiled an upcoming surprise inspection for the soldiers in a train station by warning them, Burakov blithely states, "You have to give them a little sugar once in a while anyway." Burakov thus presumes to instruct his instructor. Both men redeem one another and the newly democratic system in Russia, to the extent that psychiatrist Bukhanovsky says to them at the film's end: "Together you make a wonderful person." And so profiling scores yet another miraculous success in the dozens of books and films devoted to its fabulation.

"A Reverse Investigative Procedure": *The Alienist*

If the FBI's profiling methodology can work so well in other countries, why not in other historical periods? This is exactly what Caleb Carr attempts to prove in his popular 1994 novel *The Alienist.* The novel is set in 1896 New York City and achieved enough financial and critical distinction to warrant a 1998 sequel, *The Angel of Darkness,* centered upon the same team of investigators. The lead investigator and title character of the novel is Laszlo Kreizler, a German immigrant and psychologist. Kreizler's theories about what we would now call dysfunctional family environments are scandalous at best to most of his contemporaries. When a murderer begins targeting boy prostitutes in New York's notorious Tenderloin district, the new and unorthodox president of the Board of Commissioners of the New York Police Department, Theodore Roosevelt, asks his old Harvard classmate Kreizler to enter the case to create a "profile" of the type of man capable of killing and mutilating young boys. Kreizler assembles an investigative squad of similar professional renegades: a carousing New York Times reporter, a female police department secretary who aspires to detective rank, and two Jewish detectives on the cutting edge of forensics science. They comprise, as James Baker puts it, a veritable "model of late-Victorian P.C." (76) to help Kreizler gather enough information to create a profile of the anonymous killer based on Kreizler's theory of "context." Carr's novel exemplifies the tendency of fiction writers to accept the basic formulations of the FBI profiling method, with its psychoanalytic bias toward childhood trauma as primary explanation for serial murder, more or less uncritically. The result is a novel that, for all its exquisite evocation of nineteenth-century mood and setting, maintains through its first-person narrator the tone of a distinctly twentieth-century moralistic crusader specifically tailored to complement our own time's conventional wisdom vis-à-vis serial murder.[11]

Carr endorses the most well-known features of the FBI definition of serial murder. These features originate from assessment interviews with a very small initial sample pool of thirty-six serial killers interviewed over a period of a few years during the 1970s and 1980s. The rather rigid set of conclusions about the "typical" serial killer that resulted are variations on two basic themes: "the dominance of a fantasy life and a history of personal abuse" (Ressler et al. 4). According to the FBI, the serial killer's psyche is that of a violent child's inhabiting the physically powerful body of a full-grown male. His development has been stalled because of some primal trauma or traumas that he cannot resolve. While the serial killer develops the intellectual powers of an adult, he also retains the volatile emotions of the unjustly wounded child. Both sensibilities are present in the same person. Of course, the same could be said about most if not all people, but the serial killer's behavioral patterns, formed and set in childhood, have turned to murderous aggression because of an "intense desire to be strong, powerful, and in control" (5). The more frustrated and rejected he feels by his perceived and actual failures during socialization, the stronger his compensating fantasies of domination become. At some point, the fantasies turn to murder.

The problem with the FBI's etiology of serial murder, however, is its reductiveness or deterministic simplicity. It focuses on a few clearly stated and understood factors that, quite frankly, could apply to almost anyone. Psychological explanations that focus solely on the individual's deviations from an implicitly absolutist notion of right and wrong, as Jon Stratton observes, fall short of accounting for serial murder because they are at once too reductive and too general. The writers that disseminate the FBI "wisdom" in bland imitation of Thomas Harris tend to replicate the system's simplicities with generally unflagging faith in their veracity. *The Alienist* is one of the better novels in the subgenre, in terms of its artistry and superb grasp of "historical immediacy" (McCay 87). However, it too suffers from a simplicity of cause and effect when it comes to developing its characters' motivations, as Henry Gonshak laments (13). Rather than mystifying the killer, Carr moves radically toward the other end of the spectrum. The result is a clockwork or mechanical killer who is all too easily comprehensible.[12] This reductiveness is endemic to the detective/serial killer subgenre because the idea of "profiling" itself, in its attempt to reason backward from a general set of characteristics into one specific identity, is so mechanical and deterministic.

In reference to Carr's novel, Gonshak states that its "clear theme is that the sole factor in the creation of a serial killer is childhood trauma. Explaining away this evil with such a psychological trauma seems rather simplistic" (13). Though Gonshak's use of the word "evil" is suspect, implying he wishes to replace one set of deterministic assumptions with another one about metaphysics, the basic core of his critique is valid. The novel, in spite of its insistence on complex web theories of etiology, always comes back to child abuse as the determining factor in the production of the criminal mind-set. John Beecham/Japheth Dury, the childish child-killer, is only the most extreme example of a bevy of very traumatized adult-former-victims-of-child-abuse found in the novel.[13] The sheer number of victims of subtle or blatant childhood abuse in the novel gives credence to Philip Jenkins's thesis that advocates of a cause, be it the elimination of child abuse or misogyny or liberalism or conservatism or rock music, find it nigh near irresistible to portray a serial killer as the logical end product of the social evil the individual author wishes to excoriate.

Almost every major character in *The Alienist* is a survivor of, at least, childhood neglect, and usually more. Kreizler, the title's "alienist," has physical scars—a badly broken arm—from an abusive father. The novel's semidisreputable narrator, journalist John Moore, comes from a family that strongly discouraged emotional displays of love and affection and disowned him when he dared to express anger about his childhood at the funeral of a younger brother. Street urchin and juvenile criminal Stevie Taggert, Kriezler's ward, driver, and errand boy, was abandoned by a mother with an opium habit. Cyrus Montrose, Kriezler's black valet, driver, and bodyguard, is an orphan who, as a boy piano player in a brothel, killed a drunken policeman who was assaulting a prostitute. Mary Palmer, Kreizler's maid, housekeeper, and potential lover (before she is killed), was sexually violated by her father; when she reached the age of seventeen, she burned him alive. Jesse Pomeroy, another serial killer whom Kreizler interviews in Sing Sing for potential insight into the unknown killer's mind, suffered maternal neglect and public ridicule because of a cleft palate and a disfiguring disease. All of Beecham's victims, from the Zweig children to Georgio Santorelli to Ali ibn-Ghazi, have been physically abused—in the case of ibn-Ghazi, sold into sexual slavery by his father. As the novel's most complex survivor of child abuse, Kreizler has structured his personal and professional life into a crusade against domestic violence. He has done so to the extent that he alienates the nineteenth-century bourgeois. They would rather not hear unpleasant truths about the horrors of family life and in fact see Kreizler as a threat to the social order. Kreizler also brings legally jeopardized victims, in spite of their atrocious acts, into his house and his institute in an effort to recontextualize their wretched lives with sympathy and understanding of their passions. His sympathy, then, for Beecham is a foregone conclusion.

Beecham is, if not the most wounded, certainly the most dangerous survivor-of-child-abuse-turned-criminal in the novel. As Kreizler's investigation slowly uncovers, Beecham is actually Japheth Dury. Dury is the unwanted and loathed son of marital rape whose childhood with his missionary parents was marked by harsh discipline and cold indifference. His only relief, it turns out, was fantasy. Unfortunately, his fantasies were morbidly twisted by his father's photographic collection, obtained through missionary work in South Dakota, of Indian atrocities inflicted upon white settlers. His older brother caught him skinning a live squirrel, indicating his imagination had been irreparably harmed by contact with those hideous photographs. As a young boy, he was raped by an older man and ostensible friend named George Beecham, whose identity Japheth will imaginatively assume during his murders. In so doing, he becomes representative of the rage felt by every such survivor in the novel, even if he or she doesn't directly manifest it. Japheth remakes himself as an essentially conservative social crusader against injustice, as Kreizler eulogizes:

> He was—perversely, perhaps, but utterly—tied to that society. He
> was its offspring, its sick conscience—a living reminder of all the

hidden crimes we commit when we close ranks to live among each other. He craved human society, craved the chance to show people what their "society" had done to him. And the odd thing is, society craved him, too. (489)

Kreizler, who expresses similar outrage against society at several points in the novel but ultimately serves its interests, can speak authoritatively to Beecham's psyche because of Kreizler's ability to construct profiles of child-abuse victims.

Moore utters the novel's best definition of "profiling," which Moore in turn has learned from experience with Kreizler:

We've adopted what you might call a reverse investigative procedure. . . . [W]e start with the prominent features of the killings themselves, as well as the personality traits of the victims, and from those we determine what kind of a man *might* be at work. Then, using evidence that would otherwise have seemed meaningless, we begin to close in. (308)

From that "meaningless" evidence left behind at the crime scenes—the nature of the bodily mutilations, the religiously significant dates of the crimes, the locations of the crimes near water, and a vicious note sent to the mother of one of the victims—Kreizler and his squad of profilers, after a few false starts and perceptual red herrings, laboriously extrapolate an "imaginary man" constructed largely on a meeting-room chalkboard. This individual is about thirty, had a childhood marked by trauma originating from an emotionally abusive mother, was exposed to terrifying and gruesome stories during childhood, has some decent schooling, acts alone, loves sport, can climb or rappel down buildings, has military experience, displays a religious sensibility, has been to the frontier, works at a job that allows him freedom of movement and unquestioned access to the city's rooftops, and suffers from a physical deformity of some sort. As it turns out, every one of these features fits Beecham. In the terms established by the book, Beecham has no choice except to act out a script predetermined by his childhood torment:

What [Beecham] saw when he looked at those dead children was only a representation of what he felt had been done to him—even if only psychically—at some point deep in his past. Certainly, when *we* looked at the bodies our first thoughts were of vengeance for the dead and protection of future victims. Yet the profound irony was that our killer believed he was providing himself with just those things: vengeance for the child he had been, protection for the tortured soul he had become. (158)

Beecham's past, when uncovered, validates more than the profile which led to his capture. It also validates Kreizler's methodology and, by extension, the twentieth-century FBI theory that guides the "nineteenth-century" novel.

Kreizler's "context" theory is the foundation of the profile he will construct. His philosophical perspective seems constructed in deliberate opposition to that of his former Harvard teacher, the famous William James, and yet relies on it as a conceptual starting point. The ghost or memory of James, the intellectual Dark Father who must be both honored and slain in a manner not dissimilar to the murder campaign of the novel's killer against memories of bad parenting, haunts Kreizler and his profilers throughout the intellectual progression of the case. As narrator John Moore recalls, he and Roosevelt and Kreizler all took the same psychology course from James in the fall term of 1887. The only student immune to James's considerable classroom charm was Kreizler. Kreizler was "unable to accept James's famous theories on free will, which were the cornerstone of our teacher's philosophy" (47). Instead, Kreizler, under the intellectual influence of Schopenhauer, Spencer, and Darwin, began to develop a philosophy of context. This philosophy is defined as "the theory that every man's actions are to a very decisive extent influenced by his early experiences, and that no man's behavior can be analyzed or affected without knowledge of those experiences" (48).

In his professional career, then, Kreizler frames his experiences in terms of this self-confessed system of psychological determinism. He interprets German psychologist Emil Kraepelin's recent classification of "psychopathic personalities" to mean that "psychopaths were produced by extreme childhood environments and experiences and were unafflicted by any true pathology. Judged in context, the actions of such patients could be understood and even predicted (unlike those of the truly mad)" (52). After agreeing to undertake the profiling assignment for Roosevelt, Kreizler indoctrinates his "students" into the literature of determinism, even though disingenuously warning them to abandon any preconceptions about human behavior. Kreizler's creed as Moore understands it is:

> We must try not to see the world through our own eyes, nor to judge it by our own values, but through and by those of our killer. *His*

experience, the context of *his* life, was all that mattered. Any aspect of his behavior that puzzled us, from the most trivial to the most horrendous, we must try to explain by postulating childhood events that could lead to such eventualities. This process of cause and effect—what we would soon learn was called "psychological determinism"—might not always seem logical to us, but it would be consistent. . . . It was pointless to talk about evil and barbarity and madness; none of these concepts would lead us any closer to him. But if we could capture the human child in our imaginations—then we could capture the man in fact. (130)

Neophyte profiler John Moore quickly adopts Kreizler's theory with the same eager vacuity he embraced James's romantic notions of free will. Moore rhetorically asks team member Sara Howard: "Is the mind a blank slate at birth, or do we have innate knowledge of certain things? My money's on the blank slate" (133). Yet James's theories underlie the entire framework of this "contextual" case and occasionally erupt to the surface, like a repressed Gothic memory. During one consultation with the team's forensic detectives, Moore paraphrases his and Kreizler's deposed mentor James: "The law of habit and interest, just like Professor James says—our minds work on the basis of self-interest, the survival of the organism, and our habitual ways of pursuing that interest become defined when we're children and adolescents." In response, Detective Lucius Isaacson directly quotes from James: "'Habit dooms us all to fight out the battle of life upon the lines of our nurture or our early choice, and to make the best of a pursuit that disagrees, because there is no other for which we are fitted, and it is too late to begin again'" (130). Though the quoted passages seem to suggest that James shares at least in part Kreizler's view of psychological determinism, Kreizler later denies—metaphorically killing the father once more—that James applies deterministic thinking to the dynamic field of emotional development. Instead, Kreizler insists that James confined his discussions only to "functions, such as taste and touch" (245). Ironically, the free-willed determinist Kreizler is accusing the free-will advocate James of being unable to rise beyond a limited concept of determinism. By implication, Kreizler chides his mentor for intellectual cowardice.

Kreizler, then, sees himself as a bold pioneer into forbidden intellectual areas that James could or would not go in spite of theories that suggested the direction. However, Kreizler is as deterministically bound to his traumatic past as the killer he profiles. This is Carr's way of suggesting that the tyranny of the past determines the flow of the future regardless of all romantic but self-deceiving attempts at transcendence or liberation from trauma. In any event, in Carr's novel, determinism is the privileged perspective, even if the characters are unable to accept completely its harsh realities. The characters instead prefer the somehow more reassuring notion that destructive or deviant human behavior can be unlearned on the basis that there is a preformed original pattern, presumably benign, to revert to. Moore himself, though powerfully attracted to Kreizler's method, resists its implications from time to time. Kreizler warns him: "Be careful, Moore. . . . You're about to suggest that we're born with specific a priori concepts of need and desire—an understandable thought, perhaps, were there any evidence to support it" (246). Yet ironically, Kreizler's entire methodology is subject to criticism based on one of James's own principles, the psychologist's fallacy. Moore paraphrases the fallacy as "a psychologist getting his own point of view mixed up with his subject's" (250).

The concept is applicable to Kreizler's own perceptual blindness regarding the investigation. As Sara and Moore discover from old police records, Kreizler was himself the victim of early childhood abuse from a drunken father, leaving the six-year-old Laszlo with a shattered and permanently withered left arm. Moore then realizes that Laszlo's resistance to Sara's alternate theory of the case (that a neglectful mother contributed more to their murderer's mental history than an abusive father) has been based on Laszlo's own personal experiences with abuse and not on a shedding of personal preconceptions. The foremost determinist is unable to escape determinism. For a romantic like Moore, determinism is an uncomfortable mental conundrum. However, for the mechanistic profiler, faith in determinism is the one hope for catching a preprogrammed killer.

4

Serial Killers
and Deviant
American Individualism

Moving away from the Gothic origins of serial killer fiction, it is useful to examine some representative recent works in relation to the specific American culture that produced them. It is, of course, generally true that the fictional serial killer evolves out of Gothic or neo-Gothic conventions that in some mythopoetic ways attempt to divorce "eternal" human character from temporal context. Serial killers' murder of strangers and the killers' oft-cited ability to seduce victims into their own deaths while simultaneously avoiding police detection render these criminals compellingly supernatural, mythic, and indeed almost godlike in effect. But it is also true that any given depiction of the Gothic killer will be inextricably linked to the historical context in which the author composes his or her work. In his individual assertion of violent control, the fictionalized serial killer remains recognizably American in ideologies both subversive and conservative. Thus, the serial killer is a socialized (even over-socialized) individual. For a multiplicity of reasons both accessible and inaccessible to others, the serial killer chooses to write an identity on the body politic through what came to be known to sociologists and laymen alike in the 1980s as "wilding." Wilding is defined as brutal, apparently motiveless attacks committed by malefactors on luckless strangers.

Initially considered to be an urban crime with racial overtones, "wilding" is now identified by writers such as Charles Derber as a much more generalized and politicized expression of American individualism run rampant in the economic, political, and social arenas and thus culturally sanctioned to some degree (17). The serial killer as "wilder" achieved iconic status during the late 1980s, according to Robert Conrath, precisely because the serial killer's extreme egocentrism parallels to the "money-grubbing . . . megalomaniacal likes of Donald Trump and Michael Milken" ("Serial Heroes" 150). Because the serial killer conceives of and carries out actions in a manner not dissimilar to the violent methodology of the larger social structure, the killer stands a good chance of remaining unremarkable, indeed largely undetectable or invisible. Hence, the serial killer is nearly unstoppable amid the generalized tapestry of institutional violence. In some ways, this "invisible killer" suits New Right rhetoric, which emphasizes the need for strong law-and-order social institutions to constrain man's fundamentally corrupt soul. But as earlier leftist and feminist critics discovered first, the same "invisible killer" concept is ambiguous enough that it can be used to level devastating critiques of the violence underlying traditional American values.

Many serial killer narratives of the past two decades make exactly that point by depicting murderers in full wilding mode and either conspicuously omitting any significant presentation of law-enforcement efforts to impede their invisible killing spree or irrevocably subverting the profiler-as-hero status conditionally endorsed by most detective/serial killer works. In the "psycho profile" work of fiction, few of these remorseless killers come to any true moral reckoning with their consciences. Even if captured, they ultimately manage to escape justice. The killers escape personal accountability in such a way as to spread the blame for murder among the society that helps create "monstrous" serial killers. This type of plot probably contributed to the high degree of bourgeois public and critical anger directed at least two of these narratives and their authors. One is the 1986 film *Henry: Portrait of a Serial Killer,* directed by John McNaughton. The other is the infamous 1991 novel *American Psycho,* by Bret Easton Ellis. A lesser-known but no less disturbing work, Joyce Carol Oates's *Zombie* (1995), both promulgates and subverts certain assumptions about the psyche of the serial killer as most popularly defined by his FBI adversaries. Oates's novel attempts the same kind of murdering-stream-of-consciousness monologue as Ellis's novel to greater success, and certainly to more critical approval, perhaps because Oates as a well-respected writer evokes more sympathy for her project. Oates's novel also provides a means by which to address the critical controversy over violence and misogyny in the serial killer subgenre.

"Gotta Keep Movin'": *Henry: Portrait of a Serial Killer*

Henry: Portrait of a Serial Killer is specifically based on McNaughton's study of serial killer Henry Lee Lucas. Lucas came to McNaughton's attention in 1985 on an episode of the television news program *20/20*. Some of Lucas's biography appears in slightly fictionalized form in McNaughton's film. For example, Lucas's oedipal hatred of his "prostitute" mother, and the specific story of her dressing him up as a little girl the first day of school, finds its way into Henry's explanation to Becky as to why he killed his mother. The character of Otis, an implied homosexual child molester, and his murderous alliance with Henry is loosely based on Ottis Toole's teaming up with Lucas on a cross-country murder spree that may or may not have happened, depending on whether one believes their numerous confessions. The ill-fated Becky is the fictional analogue of Freida, Lucas's teenage wife, whom he later killed.

However, more important to McNaughton's project is not slavish recreation of the sordid details of the actual Lucas's life. Rather, the film is a psychological study of a man who can repeatedly kill strangers and intimates alike without remorse and an examination of a culture in which that can so easily happen. Waleed Ali, McNaughton's video-distributor associate, explains: "[McNaughton] didn't want to shoot the usual blood-and-gore film. . . . He wanted to take the audience inside the mind of a man who had absolutely no conscience or empathy and could kill as easily as most people go out to buy a pair of shoes" (qtd. in McDonough 44). Therefore, McNaughton chooses to shift his focus away from the kind of police procedural story such as those written by Thomas Harris and onto a cross-genre mix of true-crime case study, film noir, and horror film. One of his most important decisions in the film is to respond specifically to the mid-1980s law enforcement definition of the serial killer and the resultant media deluge of serial killer stories about men like Lucas. A prominent feature of this coverage was an implied need for stronger, more centralized law enforcement capabilities to combat the lower-class drifters preying upon decent society. (See Jenkins, "Myth and Murder.") McNaughton both echoes and subverts this concern by acknowledging the existence of a Henry Lee Lucas but also admitting the impossibility of ever stopping those rare few like him, no matter what kinds of law-enforcement procedures are implemented. Whereas the most skillful of Thomas Harris's FBI profilers achieve success, McNaughton questions the basic enterprise of profiling itself, especially its optimistic insistence that the intuitive, artistic reading of signs, or "clues," can scientifically point to the malefactor.

For example, one of the most important scenes in the film involves Henry's tutelage of Otis on the finer points of evading police detection. While Otis (concealed behind bushes) videotapes the beating of a homeless man by two others (a prime example of wilding behavior), Henry tells him:

> If you shoot somebody in the head with a .45 every time you kill somebody, it becomes like your fingerprint, see? But if you strangle one, stab another, one you cut up and one you don't, then the police don't know what to do. They think you're four different people. What they really like, what makes their job so much easier, is a pattern. What they call a *modus operandi.* . . . It's like a trail of shit, Otis. It's like the blood droppings from a deer you've shot. All they gotta do is follow those droppings and pretty soon they're gonna find their deer. . . . You can use a gun. I'm not sayin' you can't use a gun. Just don't use the same gun twice.

Henry's insistence on avoiding pattern through studied randomness and unpredictability of modus operandi indicates a degree of amateur insight into what criminologist Steven Egger in a nonfictional context has called the "linkage blindness" (164–65) of police when confronted with a series of what may or may not be unconnected homicides. Henry's ability to vary his modus operandi to evade outside reading identifies him as not so much a criminal genius but rather an "everyman" serial killer. His lower-class bluntness contrasts directly with the elitist, manipulative Hannibal Lecter. Henry as killer is not interested in outwitting the authorities in a highly public, teasing game of "catch me if you can." Rather, Henry wishes to remain undetected and hence invisible. FBI profiling, if indeed it could ever discern the shadowy existence of Henry, would be helpless to identify him. In fact, law enforcement is conspicuously absent in McNaughton's film. The audience never sees any police reaction to, or even recognition of, Henry's murders.

He is aided in this invisibility by a casually brutal and itinerant society of wilders and potential wilders, as implied by the pointless beating of the homeless man that goes unnoticed by all except Henry and Otis. In Henry's America, scores of homicides do not arouse any official reaction and go unnoticed by the media-reliant public. The serial killer who wishes to "go public" with his murders must be unusually inventive in his (paradoxically) easily identifiable pattern (the serial killers of Thomas Harris or the biblically influenced killer of David Fincher's *Seven*). Alternately, he must compile an enormous victim toll so as to attract the simultaneous attention of the police and media.

Henry, on the other hand, disguises himself behind the enormous violence level and corresponding desensitization inherent in American society. The means of violence are also readily available, Henry knows. As he tells Otis, it is easy to obtain different guns for different murders: "Anyone can get a gun. A phone call can get you a gun." The last cultural component crucial to Henry's success is American pride in its own mobility. Henry's vagabond lifestyle of the road mirrors the larger nomadic wanderings of the average American. His drifting dimly echoes not only the specific fictional genre of the road movie but the larger issue of American pride in its very rootlessness. Mobility in America has always meant freedom to escape one's past and the consequences of that past. For Henry, that mobility allows him to escape punishment for murder. Again, in his extended tutorial with Otis, Henry knows that "the most important thing is to keep movin'. That way they might never catch up to ya."

But none of this interaction with Henry and Otis is ever enlarged upon or given any real direction. One of the key metaphors in the serial killer narrative is aimless circling toward specific moments of murderous clarity, then more circling. *Henry* as narrative never really "gets" anywhere either. Undeniably, Henry's portrait as sketched by McNaughton remains vaguely outlined. It approaches simplicity in the most negative sense at times. We never do get a true sense of the how or why of a Henry Lucas, as promised by McNaughton's deliberately misleading title. We are expecting not only a description, as the FBI attempts to do in its 1980s serial killer pronouncements, but an explanation and a meaning, as we often optimistically expect our fiction to do. Instead, McNaughton presents a narrative that prevents closure. Richard Dyer says of the film that "it realises, in macabre and terrible form, the quintessence of seriality, the soap opera, the story with no beginning and no end. . . . it opens up the spectre of endlessness, forever trapped by the compulsions of serial watching, engulfed in repetition without end or point" (16).

Henry undeniably possesses deeply unsettling power as cinema, in spite of (and maybe because of) its obviously low budget and use of then-unknown actors. The tone of the film is uniformly disturbing throughout, not simply because of the escalating numbers of victims (most of whom die offscreen) but because of the mundane dreariness of the protagonists' lives juxtaposed with the casual violence endemic to their socioeconomic positioning. Henry, Otis, and Becky are utterly without education, job skills, or hope of economic advancement. Becky is suited only to shampooing the hair of the well-off patrons of a downtown Chicago beauty salon. Otis is a parolee who can only find employment pumping gas at one of the few remaining full-service gas stations. Henry is an illiterate ex-con (he cannot read the "I Love Chicago" slogan on Becky's new T-shirt) who drifts from part-time job to job with about as much frequency as he murders.

That most of Henry's murders are based on a non- or preliterate rage against class distinctions is undeniable. In fact, one of Henry's most horrifying and protracted murderous episodes takes place in an upper-middle-class suburban home, directed against a hapless nuclear-family husband, wife, and teenage son reminiscent of the families murdered by Francis Dolarhyde in Harris's *Red Dragon.* Henry's savagery is also infectious among those who have as little to lose as Henry does. Otis quickly overcomes his initial resistance to killing and surpasses his mentor Henry in sheer *lustmord.* Even the sweetly vulnerable Becky becomes complicit in Henry's murder and disposal of Otis and thus joins Henry in outlaw status. Whether the film is in essence an indictment of social disparity or a neoconservative polemic against the animalistic lower classes remains ambiguous. This open-endedness liberates the film from any easy conclusions about its political agenda.

The film resists easy reading precisely because it refuses to pass its own judgment on Henry's character. Consequently, *Henry* found itself castigated for its "disturbing moral tone" by the MPAA and was given one of the few "X" ratings assigned on the basis of content other than sexually explicit material. The ratings controversy over *Henry's* tone predated the much more intense flap over the novel *American Psycho* but shared many of the latter's central assumptions. The film was supposedly misogynistic, gratuitously violent, morally objectionable, and so on. John McDonough summarizes what seems to be the main objection the MPAA had toward *Henry:*

> In movies, bad seeds must still suffer, at least through a final reckoning with their conscience. Because Henry the killer cannot feel compassion, he cannot suffer. He is beyond the reach of moral self-awareness. When he kills his girlfriend at the end as coolly as he's dispatched a slew of strangers, the audience is denied its catharsis. The issue, in the eyes of the rating board, wasn't breasts, genitals or

even violence. Most of Henry's killings are offscreen anyway. The issue was the film's attitude of neutrality toward Henry. (44)

While the film does not entirely resist the temptation to pass didactic judgment on Henry—after all, his dissociation from his fellows is obviously coded as the most extreme kind of dehumanizing alienation and thus something to be avoided—McDonough's point is, for the most part, valid. The film disturbs precisely because Henry never comes to an ethical reckoning with his own savagery. Henry does not fritter away his time wringing his hands in ersatz remorse and regretting the waste of his own life, let alone the lives of others. In short, he never visibly repents, even for a moment.

His climactic murder of the sympathetic character Becky finishes any lingering expectations the audience may harbor about Henry's spiritual redemption or damnation. While exhibiting a surprisingly old-fashioned, even prudish gallantry toward Becky throughout the film, he does not hesitate to kill her when she threatens to become a personal hindrance. He completes the insult to audience expectation as he expressionlessly disposes of her dismembered corpse in a bloody suitcase by the side of the road. This may well be, as Peter Bates claims, "one of the bleakest endings in film history, more downbeat than *Detour,* Edgar Ulmer's classic film noir" (57). Unlike the audience reaction to Chilton's imminent death at the hands of Hannibal Lecter, no viewer is primed to cheer for the pathetic Becky's murder by Henry. But neither is it much of a surprise. It simply happens.

Given that Henry doesn't "learn" anything about his condition other than that he must keep moving, what is the value of watching his fictional non-progress? Because we are not given the in-depth psychological study impishly promised by McNaughton's title, we must look toward an examination of the genres from which the film draws its inspirations. On that basis, *Henry* suddenly becomes much more accessible, and its psychological case study overtones largely irrelevant. Henry is representative of the nihilistic outsider who defies external exegesis. Unlike his mad-scientist genre forebears, as Andrew Tudor has identified them, Henry claims no mission, no obvious vendetta, and no search for godhood or sacrament. From a metatextual vantage point, *Henry*'s audience is purposefully not given the customary "signature" murders. Such murders, according to Jeffrey Pence, "function . . . as internal allegories, supplemental texts of commentary to the primary text of the serial killer's actions" (531). They also optimistically imply a pattern killer can be caught if a skillful enough reader, or detective, is available. The film's decaying landscape is unbearably bleak and violent. It offers little hope and no redemption for its characters, who are not as psychologically analyzed as the film's title might suggest. Rather, as Dave Kehr notes, Henry and his two doomed companions, Becky and Otis, are better understood as proletarian failures. Their lack of intelligence, job skills, or money consign them to marginal, squalid existences that terminate as gracelessly as they do quickly:

> Henry . . . carries little psychological resonance; his coding is more cultural or social, marking him as a product of a dying rural underclass, uneducated, desperately poor, precivilized. Henry, Otis, and Becky seem the last survivors of a condemned tribe, whose final migration has led them into a hostile urban landscape. . . . It's as if McNaughton had discovered a new kind of monster in *Henry*: no longer supernatural, no longer psychotic, but somehow sociological—the specter of an extinguished class. As such, there is no resisting him, no talismans to wave or Freudian phrases to invoke. Henry is as inevitable as history, and indeed the film does away with any notion of suspense. (62)

Just as history is susceptible to a multiplicity of interpretations, so is Henry's personal history. As viewers, we are granted little insight into the personal history that contributes to Henry's present-day savagery, although we do learn from Otis that Henry spent time in prison for killing his mother. Thus, we are primed by genre knowledge (based primarily on Hitchcock's *Psycho*) to expect a traditional blame-the-mother tirade from Henry. He doesn't disappoint us. In a moment lifted directly from the real Henry Lee Lucas's confessions to police, fictional Henry tells Otis's sister Becky that his mother was a whore. While this in and of itself wasn't so bad, he says, she did make him and his father watch her liaisons and made Henry wear dresses. These are his stated reasons for killing her. Immediately, the film coerces the gullible viewer into seeing Henry as yet another patriarchal avenger, out to re-empower himself in opposition to a castrating bitch-mother-goddess, such as the one whose desiccated, preserved corpse presides over the cannibalistic family in *Texas Chainsaw Massacre 2*. But Henry himself complicates this simple reading of his own pathology. Over time, he gives two or three different explanations of how he killed his mother: with a baseball bat, a knife, a gun. Becky calls one of these discrepancies to Henry's attention. Henry shrugs it off and changes his story about the instrumentality he used to kill his mother. Why? Is he lying about killing her at all? Is he lying about the manner in which he killed her? The efficacy of the "my momma was a whore" reason for Henry's behavior is ruined by Henry's own narrative inconsistencies. Those in the audience influenced by genre convention to expect a standard psychoanalytic explication of Henry's motives are deliberately left puzzled and floundering, such as the indignant reviewer who claims *Henry* is a failed dark comedy because it does not provide "a clear commentary on the character's actions" (Grant 367).

Henry does seem to have a lethal aversion to sexual contact, as his ultimately murderous discomfort with Becky's romantic interest in him makes clear. However, the viewer is unable to fathom why this sexual prudery on Henry's part exists. Henry also disapproves of Otis's uncontrolled sexual desires, particularly his incestuous designs on his sister Becky. One is tempted to trace Henry's sexual conservatism back to the prostitute-mother explanation again, as at least three of Henry's murders involve prostitutes. But a closer reading of the film reveals a more free-floating emotional anxiety only tangentially related to sexual intercourse. Henry's emotional withdrawal from Becky's sexual advances, to the point where he is able to kill her and then cut apart her body to hide it in a suitcase, betokens an inability to connect (to say the very least) in any empathetic way to the needs of another.

This is not to say Henry routinely treats Becky badly like Otis does. Henry even saves her from Otis's rape by killing Otis. Becky has a hand in this murder when she stabs a comb into her brother's eye. She also voluntarily accedes to Henry's grisly plan to cut up Otis's body and dump the remains in the river. These actions render her even more complicit in Henry's crimes. Of course, she does not know that Henry is a serial killer. To her, Henry has saved her from Otis and now will rescue her from the despair of her life. Peter Travers summarizes Becky's feelings for Henry: "Sensing nothing of [his] current murderous proclivities, she sees him as a lifeline" (69). The supreme irony in all this, of course, is that Henry is a perfect gentleman, whom Kim Newman calls "the most normal, well-balanced person in the film" ("*Henry*" 44), right up until the point he kills Becky. His murder of his potential lover thus illustrates the dangers inherent in romantic notions that a man can save a woman from the grimness of daily existence. The deconstruction of gender myth is central to the kind of American neo-Gothicism exemplified by writers such as Tennessee Williams, whom McNaughton cites as a key influence (McDonough 45).

Another irony is that Henry as neo-Gothic seducer is dangerously attractive but sexless. He resists Becky's physical overtures. He also seems more relieved than embarrassed when Otis drunkenly catches them and thus ends the threatening encounter. During none of this does Henry express any hostility toward Becky. Henry's sexual reticence has the effect of skewing audience sympathy toward Henry and away from the loutish, incestuous Otis. Henry seems to appreciate Becky's gentleness and love for him. He even mouths the ambiguous words "I guess I love you too" to her. But when the potential bond to her threatens to arrest his downward spiraling momentum, he kills her and moves on without betraying any reaction to this most personal of his murders.

Henry is indeed inscrutable, as Peter Bates notes: "Henry . . . appears to take no pleasure in killing. There are no shots of his face after any of the murders, thus no clues to what he feels afterwards" (57). If any meaning or pattern can be assigned to his murder series, the audience cannot rely on Henry, or even the creators of the film for that matter. This is why *Henry* does not structure its subject matter in terms of detective or police procedural conventions. The detective or police officer's basically optimistic insistence on sign-reading in order to infer pattern simply will not work with Henry. As he proudly advises his protégé Otis to emulate, he consciously varies his weapons, victim selection, and modus operandi from murder to murder so that police sign-reading will not be able to track him. Only bad luck or self-destruction can stop him. No outside moral agency is capable of saving his victims. In fact, society isn't even aware of Henry's predations. The only representative of the criminal justice system in the film, Otis's probation officer, is a disinterested bureaucrat whose heavy caseload and general indifference to his clients allow Otis, and by extension his friend Henry, to circumvent supervision at will. Henry moves in silent anonymity and with impunity. The film appears (superficially, anyway, though the ominous soundtrack music paired with Henry on the prowl reeks of standard horror-film narrative coaching) to impose no judgment or sanction upon him, a quality that led to its "X" rating. Henry simply *is,* going nowhere and everywhere at once. In this quality, *Henry* is more unsettling than its big-budget, glossy Hollywood counterparts like *The Silence of the Lambs,* as Martin Rubin argues in his analysis of psycho-profile films, including *The Honeymoon Killers* and *Badlands* as well as *Henry.* Rather than provide cathartic resolution, as *Silence* does, and at least some qualified restoration of a reassuring status quo, *Henry* simply departs from its still-free subject at the film's conclusion. The serial continues offscreen. Rubin elaborates on the uniquely disturbing qualities of films like *Henry:*

The characters just seem to wind down, overcome by exhaustion and inertia. . . . The films end with the main characters left in a limbo of disconnection and suspension. . . . [T]hese films are [also] centered on a position with which it is difficult to sympathize but which we cannot get outside. Their inaccessible protagonists stand in contrast to the ambivalently sympathetic outlaws and psychopaths of *Gun Crazy, Peeping Tom, Psycho, Bonnie and Clyde,* etc. On the other hand, the films are not centered on the side of normality, with the inscrutable killer positioned as an external threat, as in *Cape Fear, Experiment in Terror, Sleeping with the Enemy,* and the most characteristic stalker/slasher movies. We remain at nearly all times on the killers' side of the narrative. The realm of "normal values" is not only distant but is often regarded by the criminal protagonists with a kind of sneering disdain which the films make it difficult to discredit entirely. (56)

A film like *Henry* stands at an ironic distance not only from mainstream values but the conventions of genre itself while never truly departing from any of them. Contempt for traditional systems is present, but neither is the killer's agenda validated. Devin McKinney, though finally critical of the film, lauds its overall tone: "It stands at just the right distance from its subject, never enforcing a sociologically judgmental thesis" (19). Terrence Rafferty, clearly frustrated by this same ambiguity, concludes that the film, "both hip and deeply conservative, is consistent only its bad faith" (91). As the latter comment illustrates, the film is deliberately hard to read, though its landscape remains enigmatically cluttered with portents suggestive of disaster (again, however, not clearly so).

For example, early on in *Henry,* the camera pulls back from a close-up shot of Becky gutting a fish in the kitchen sink and discussing the absent Henry with Otis. It is an uncomfortable scene to watch, not only because of its narrative foreshadowing of Becky's complicity in her own fate but because of the sight of the knife slicing through the fish's entrails. In the doggedly realistic landscape of *Henry,* a look enhanced by the film's painfully obvious low budget and use of unknown actors, the casual levels of dismembering violence associated even with the actions of doomed Becky, a cinematic "natural-born victim" if ever there was one, suggest the omnipresence of brutality rumbling underneath even the most prosaic of encounters. Otis leers at Becky, taunts her about her husband Leroy when she asks him not to, orders her to wait on him, and eventually rapes her. Becky herself guts a fish as competently as Henry dismembers his dead friend Otis or would-be lover Becky later in the film. Henry and Otis calmly discuss the do's and dont's of serial killing while videotaping a mugging of one homeless man by two others that no one interferes with. No one notices that Henry and Otis are killing a string of people: two prostitutes, an obnoxious fencer of stolen goods, a Good-Samaritan motorist, and a suburban nuclear family (probably the scene that threatened to give *Henry* its X rating). The fact that violence is so pervasive and unquestioned—just part of the scenery—lends *Henry* an oddly muted tone in spite of its gorier moments. The subdued tone is pivotal to contemporary horror, according to Pete Boss:

> The bodily destruction of the modern horror film is . . . often casual to the point of randomness; devoid of metaphysical import, it is frequently squalid, incidental to the main action, mechanically routine in its execution and lonely but for the unwavering scrutiny of the lens as it seeks out details of broken bodies. (16)

Though speaking of 1970s "splatter" like *Catch-22* and *Jaws,* Boss could also be referring to McNaughton's dispassionate inspection of Henry's murder victims. They have been variously shot, stabbed, strangled, clubbed, or punctured with broken bottles and then left in seedy hotel rooms, ditches, and rivers. Their savaged bodies seem intrinsic to the generally deteriorated lower-middle-class suburbs of Chicago. McNaughton achieves this effect by keeping the victims' deaths offstage and then casually panning over what's left. His camera does not flinch from the brutalized flesh, but he does not titillate as many directors of lesser ability might decide to do. Even the surrealist touches—distant background screams and Henry's echo-chamber "killing" voice yelling things like "Die, bitch!"—aurally superimposed over these unflinching views of murder victims do not lead the audience in the same heavy-handed way they have come to expect from the "slasher" genre. The audience cannot root for the forces of decency. There are no heroic FBI profilers chasing through the Gothic landscape to save the endangered American family in *Henry.* Instead, Henry and Otis make their own snuff movie of the proceedings wherein they murder an entire family. It is this secondhand, grainy, in-and-out-of-focus representation of the murder scene that the audience actually sees.

As another key postmodern concern, the technology of representation comes in for a subtly devastating critique in *Henry.* Even Henry himself isn't comfortable being in front of the video camera, which they have taken from the dead stolen-goods dealer. Otis, whose limited mentality cannot fill up his leisure time without a television set anyway ("Shit, I's gots to have a TV"), takes an immediate liking to the camera. He tapes his sister and Henry danc- ing, much to Henry's discomfort, which is obvious even filtered through the unsteady video image. Otis's art direction to his actors consists entirely of shouts of "More!" He insists they keep dancing even when both sit down on the couch to escape his camera gaze, which metaphorically violates his sister long before he does so in actuality. Otis as an auteur leaves much to be desired. His dance set piece is deliberately paralleled to the tape that Henry makes of his and Otis's invasion of the suburban house. The "home movie" that Otis and Henry compose, in spite of its undisputed status as "probably the scariest home-movie footage ever to make it to the big screen" (Wilkinson 75), is another moronically directed piece of work that continually and, even worse, unintentionally violates its own boundaries. Henry shouts another set of offstage directions to his eager but hammishly amateurish "star" Otis and has to drop the camera in midscene and enter the picture frame to chase down the murdered couple's teenage son and break his neck.[1] But Henry and Otis's subject matter is so inherently sensational that one is forced to pay attention to it.

One supposes this snuff movie within a movie to be John McNaughton's self-reflexive commentary on the lurid nature of his own movie. McNaugh- ton's film may at times resemble the unintentional monochrome drabness of Henry's movie but does not partake of its dehumanizing, misogynistic, egocentric point of view, in spite of Amy Taubin's assertion that the film becomes all of these things at precisely this point ("Allure" 17).[2] *Henry* as a film may disturb, but it does not exploit.

Rather, it critiques audience expectations of genre and finds them nearly as disturbing as Henry's acts of wilding against his fellow humans. Most of the standard touchstones of genre narrative are present in this film. There is the foreboding horror-film music, the doomed girlfriend, the drifter on the road, the male-bonding subplot, and so on. Knowledgeable genre viewers recognize these moments and anticipate certain plot developments as a re- sult. When normally that anticipated plot develops according to expecta- tions, viewers are content with its rote familiarity. However, *Henry* continu- ally disappoints (or rewards, depending on one's point of view) in this regard. The horror-film music builds to a crescendo where nothing happens. (Note, for example, the disjunctively long scene where a prowling Henry drives a car down a highway off-ramp to ominous soundtrack accompaniment.)

Becky's offscreen death is frustratingly neutral in tone. Henry's road journey is not a flight to or from anything. Otis and Henry's alliance is brief and
undeveloped. Watching this film presents the genre-conscious viewer with
a number of false starts and red herrings, creating an uncertainty that is crucial to McNaughton's insistence that signs cannot be reliably read. Just as
Henry evades detection, the film eludes easy analysis or categorization. One
thing is clear, however. The film painstakingly, even conscientiously, presents
to its audience a (post)modern American murderer in full wilding mode.

Wilding on Wall Street: *American Psycho*

In the traditional sense, *American Psycho* contains no plot or characters of
any substance. Instead, the novel presents one epic catalogue of designer
brand-names and products after another. This textual strategy not only illustrates its title character's obsessive nature but also sets up a self-aware
distance between the reader and the narrative, as Leigh Brock observes. Brock
further argues that Ellis's distancing strategy may be the method by which
he thought he could honestly present the gruesome details of a violent killer's
crimes and still keep an audience (6–8). If so, Ellis miscalculated. His ex-
hausting prose style alienated most reviewers of the novel long before the
violence begins (approximately a third of the way into the seemingly endless narrative). The passages that describe the murders of women are likely
the most graphic in the subgenre of serial killer fiction. Yet they are presented
in the same passionless and detail-obsessed voice as narrates the rest of the
novel. The central character's lack of emotional affect rings true to any student of real-life serial murder. However, it is this same graphic violence against
women that led to the novel's troubled publication history. Most reviewers
were not predisposed to be kind to Ellis.[3]

However, beyond the controversy and distracting surface clutter of Ellis's
writing style, what the novel really offers is a startlingly "liberal" reaction to
the ideological excesses of the triumph of capitalism in the 1980s. Most of
these excesses are given corporeal form in the narrative's serial-killing protagonist (Patrick Bateman), as Ellis explains:

> I already had the idea to write about a serial killer before I moved
> to New York in 1987. . . . That summer, before the Crash, I was
> hanging out with a lot of Wall Street guys. What fascinated me was
> that they didn't talk about their jobs at all—only about how much

money they made, the clubs and restaurants they went to, how beautiful their girlfriends were. It was all about status, about surface. So I thought about juxtaposing this absurd triviality with extreme violence. . . . If people are disgusted or bored, then they're finding out something about their own limits as readers. I want to challenge *their* complacency, to provoke them. . . . *American Psycho* is partly about excess—just when readers think they can't take any more violence, or another description of superficial behavior, more is presented—and their response toward this is what intrigues me. (qtd. in Hoban, "Psycho" 36)

While it is generally a critical fallacy to take an author's statements about his own narrative agenda at face value, it seems likely that Ellis has summed up as well as anyone can the overriding theme of *American Psycho*: the self-cannibalizing aspects of 1980s capitalism. As Juchartz and Hunter observe: "Ellis uses violence and greed, in their most extreme forms, as metaphors to reflect the real-life corruption in the world of his readers" (67). His novel is only a more extreme example of similarly themed polemical works of the same time period, such as Tom Wolfe's novel *The Bonfire of the Vanities* and Oliver Stone's film *Wall Street*.

These narratives contend that a society based largely on the manipulation of stocks and credit is abandoning its last connections to tangible economic foundations and thus, by implication, its sense of shared community. Money, in and of itself always more of a concept than a solid medium of barter, becomes even more ephemeral in a world financed by stock manipulation and purchased by individuals with Platinum American Express cards. One is left only with Gordon Gekko's assertion of capitalist human values in the film *Wall Street*: "Greed . . . is good." In an environment where ruthless hoarding at the expense of others' literal survival is not only tolerated but rewarded, it is axiomatic that violence will accompany avarice. Ellis sets out to prove this axiom ad nauseum. Michelle Warner concludes: "[*American Psycho*] depicts the end project of a society that teaches its members only to consume others. [It] takes psychological cannibalism to its physical extreme" (144).

The cannibalism metaphor extends even to Ellis's use of previous texts. *American Psycho,* like other serial killer narratives, is heavily influenced by, and pays obvious textual homage to, the popular horror/Gothic narratives of genres past, if one can overlook the exhaustive lists of clothing labels.

Patrick Bateman is obviously named after Norman Bates and less obviously Batman. These two genre shape-shifters, uneasily positioned between the poles of "hero" and "villain" in a destabilizing tactic recognizably Gothic, are ideal referents for protagonist Bateman. Bateman, whose identity is constructed solely from whatever pieces of 1980s consumer society he can integrate into his public persona, naturally gravitates toward those horror narratives, fact and fictional, with which his audience and potential victims should be familiar. As he tells an acquaintance in a sushi restaurant: "I'm into, oh, murders and executions mostly" (206). He is an example of "serial killer chic," which can be further defined as a sensibility that depends on a culturewide voyeuristic interest in notorious murderers to simultaneously dwell upon (in deceptively casual conversation) and mask its own obsession with the subject. Bateman talks about notorious real-life serial killers and fictional ones with no apparent discernment between them. He becomes quite agitated when his listeners express disinterest or confuse the names, as evidenced in the following exchange between Bateman and his Wall Street "friend" McDermott on the subject of Leatherface, the chain-saw killer from Tobe Hooper's film *The Texas Chainsaw Massacre*:

> "Don't tell me he was another serial killer, Bateman. *Not* another serial killer. . . . you *always* bring them up, . . . And always in this casual, educational sort of way. I mean, I don't want to know anything about Son of Sam or the fucking Hillside Strangler or Ted Bundy or Featherhead, for god's sake." . . . I say . . . "*Featherhead*? How in the hell did you get Featherhead from Leatherface?" (153, 155)

Bateman's annoyance with McDermott's contemptuous dismissal of serial killer popular lore reveals the former's deep investment in such narratives as structuring frameworks for his own identity. But it is a socially framed identity that is paradoxically insular and Gothic. This identity is visible to no one except Bateman's victims in spite of his public flaunting of and explicit confessions to outrageous acts of murder.

For instance, Bateman attends an office Halloween party wearing a suit covered with real human blood, a sign on his back that reads "MASS MURDERER," and a fingerbone from one of his victims attached to his lapel. Of course, everyone treats this as just one more harmless manifestation of Bateman's quirky obsession with serial murderers (330). Bateman becomes

increasingly agitated that no one seems to remark on his behavior as anything to be alarmed about, so much so that he feels compelled to confess his
crimes to people who still do not listen to or believe him. At a dinner with
his former lover Evelyn, in response to her comment that he's "being a lunatic," he angrily insists, "Goddamnit, Evelyn. What do you mean, *being*?
. . . I fucking *am* one" (333). He then agonizingly admits his "*need* to engage
in . . . homicidal behavior on a massive scale cannot be, um, corrected, . . .
but I . . . have no other way to express my blocked . . . needs" (338). Com-
pleting missing the point, Evelyn thinks he is nagging her again to have breast
implants. He confesses two murders to Harold Carnes's answering machine
only to find later, during a barroom confrontation in which Carnes drunkenly mistakes Bateman for somebody else, that Carnes considered the message a joke (387). Bateman is so frustrated by this that he shouts, "You don't
seem to understand. You're not really comprehending any of this. *I* killed
him. *I* did it, Carnes. *I* chopped Owen's fucking head off. *I* tortured dozens
of girls. That whole message I left on your machine was *true*" (388).

In the world of *American Psycho,* superficially slick but hollow characters such as Carnes are too self-absorbed to listen to another's words and too
vapid to realize their content. Their narcissism, expressed in their fitness
quests for "hardbodies," provides the climate of social indifference in which
the homeless and the helpless can be victimized (or "wilded") with impunity by a Patrick Bateman. Bateman and his peers are also "hardbodies" in
the sense that they seem literally hollow, mechanical, inorganic: clockwork
yuppies. Through Bateman, urban society mouths platitudes about a "return to traditional moral values" and a curbing of "graphic sex and violence
on TV, in movies, in popular music, everywhere" (16) while never acting
upon these principles. Their inability to empathize is perfectly expressed by
Bateman. He is the spokesman for the commodities brokers, the corporate
raiders, the account executives, the stock traders, the financial manipula-
tors, and all the other upper-class wilders who try to touch meaning through
purchased sensation:

> There wasn't a clear, identifiable emotion within me, except for
> greed and, possibly, total disgust. I had all the characteristics of a
> human being—flesh, blood, skin, hair—but my depersonalization
> was so intense, had gone so deep, that the normal ability to feel
> compassion had been eradicated, the victim of a slow, purposeful
> erasure. I was simply imitating reality, a rough resemblance of a

human being, with only a dim corner of my mind functioning. Something horrible was happening and yet I couldn't figure out why—I couldn't put my finger on it. (282)

Here is a clear evocation of Baudrillard's theory of simulacra as it applies to an individual's construction of his or her social identity. Bateman usually cannot feel. Hence, he can only watch his increasing alienation from humanity. But in spite of his psychic emptiness and the physical ferocity of his murders, Bateman's insistence on immediately graspable truths, along with his sporadic recognition that real human beings surround him (Warner 145), renders him the most intellectually compelling character in the narrative.

Which isn't saying much. Intellectualism is only a distant memory—a loss not even mourned—in the novel's indictment of Donald Trump's postmodern New York. There are few larger truths to be grasped in Bateman's world. There are only material goods to be consumed and discarded for the next shiny bauble or new line of designer clothing. Bateman and his peers have artistic pretensions, but only in the self-flattering sense that "art" somehow stands at a critical distance from common culture and thus can only be appreciated by those such as themselves, possessed of sensitivity and refined intellect. However, the traditional modernist distinction between high and low art (with high art occupying the privileged position once held by religion) has been effaced in the signature fashion of the postmodern murder narratives. The songs of Huey Lewis and the News and Phil Collins equate to high culture for Bateman. He spends many pages laboriously critiquing these 1980s musical icons in a parody of academic textual analysis while simultaneously welcoming their ease of accessibility. One such passage begins:

I've been a big Genesis fan ever since the release of their 1980 album, *Duke*. Before that I didn't really understand any of their work. . . . It was *Duke* (Atlantic, 1980), where Phil Collins' presence became more apparent, and the music got more modern, the drum machine became more prevalent and the lyrics started getting less mystical and more specific (maybe because of Peter Gabriel's departure), and complex, ambiguous studies of loss became, instead, smashing first-rate pop songs that I gratefully embraced. (133)

Bateman then proceeds to explicate the meaning of each song on the album in a confused ramble that extends for four pages in excruciatingly minute detail. Sadly, he is the only character in the novel to attempt an intellectual process, even as ludicrous as his analysis of Genesis becomes.[4] Bateman's world is bereft of meaning or beauty, so analysis of its contents produces only mockery.

Not even Bateman's mythically influenced attempts to end the cultural absurdity through enacting a local apocalypse count for much. No one realizes a yuppie serial murderer is at work. Any Armageddons are merely the imagination reflecting back on itself its own pathologies. Bateman sees portents of cosmic disaster everywhere, but they exist only within his head: "When we look up at the clouds . . . I see . . . a Gucci money clip, an ax, a woman cut in two, a large puffy white puddle of blood that spreads across the sky, dripping over the city, onto Manhattan" (371). In a longer passage, Bateman conceives of absolute, unmediated reality as a "desert landscape" denuded of "life and water" and

> resembling some sort of crater, so devoid of reason and light and spirit that the mind could not grasp it on any sort of conscious level and if you came close the mind would reel backward, unable to take it in. . . . This was the geography around which my reality revolved; it did not occur to me, *ever,* that people were good or that a man was capable of change or that the world could be a better place through one's taking pleasure in a feeling or a look or a gesture. . . . Fear, recrimination, innocence, sympathy, guilt, waste, failure, grief, were things, emotions, that no one really felt anymore. Reflection is useless, the world is senseless. Evil is its only permanence. God is not alive. Love cannot be trusted. Surface, surface, surface was all that anyone found meaning in . . . this was civilization as I saw it, colossal and jagged. . . . (374–75)

Indeed, this is a bleak landscape of apocalypse, but it is an abstract, purely personal concept of Bateman's. As such, it has no warrant in reality. The evil that he refers to exists only as lingering metaphysical nostalgia. There is no one-to-one correspondence between sign and signed (another Gothic resonance), which is why Bateman is always seeing people that *look* like so-and-so. This disconnect also explains why his conversations always involve people who are never talking about the same thing, except for random fragments of linguistic connection that break apart as quickly as they form.

In such a dissociated world, nothing is verifiable. Even Bateman's murders may not have occurred in actuality. He may be lying about them, or hallucinating about them, or remembering them incorrectly. There is some textual evidence to indicate that none of these murders are happening. The aforementioned Carnes tells Bateman that he couldn't have killed Paul Owen, as Carnes claims to have had lunch with Owen in London well after Bateman's confession to the answering machine (388).[5] At a moment when Bateman feels tempted to abrogate his coldness and form a connection with a woman named Jean, he hints that all of his murders may have been fantasies: "Sometimes, Jean, . . . the lines separating appearance—what you see—and reality—what you don't—become, well, blurred. . . . I think it's . . . time for me to . . . take a good look . . . at the world I've created" (378–79). At the very end of the novel, Bateman responds to an isolated word "Why?" that he hears in a bar and directs a pointed, contemptuous aside at his audience that hints this entire chronicle of waste and murder may have been a deranged joke on a voyeuristic readership:

> Just opening my mouth, words coming out, summarizing for the idiots: "Well, though I know I should have done that instead of not doing it, I'm twenty-seven for Christ sakes and this is, uh, how life presents itself in a bar or in a club in New York, maybe *anywhere,* at the end of the century and how people, you know, me, behave, and this is what being Patrick means to me, I guess, so, well, yup, uh . . ." and this is followed by a sigh, . . . and above one of the doors covered by red velvet drapes in Harry's is a sign and on the sign in letters that match the drapes' color are the words THIS IS NOT AN EXIT. (399)

Bateman's (Ellis's) last joke on the reader, then, is to plant the suggestion that this rambling confession may be an admission to crimes that did not even happen. Instead, Bateman's/Ellis's story may simply be a metaphoric indictment of the masturbatory narcissism of the New York upper-middle-class nightclub circuit from which there is no exit. Whether Bateman actually committed these murders, then, remains ambiguous. The reader who attempts to find textual confirmation one way or the other will suddenly be halted by the realization that the novel, as fictional construct, can finally provide no reliable key to deciphering its contents. To have ever thought that it or any other novel *could* is to become disturbingly aware of one's own susceptibility to imaginative absorption by the tricks of narrative. To search for clues as to whether Bateman's story as written by Ellis is "true" is a patent absurdity. Yet this search is exactly what fiction readers, or at least the more reflective ones, attempt to do with and to their secondhand narratives. Fiction is read as reality—particularly if a strong emotional engagement is willed by the spectator toward an identifiable character, event, or theme within the text—and reality constructed in terms of fiction.

This boundary dissolving is what the serial killer narrative does best. It destabilizes assumptions about not only the nature of good and evil but the distinction between reality and appearance and fact and fiction. One would be hard pressed to find a clearer example of a boundary-undermining novel than *American Psycho*. The end result is a Gothic implosion of sign/signifier confusion and complexity. Bateman's attempt to murder not only people but imagination itself proves itself an ontological dead end ("THIS IS NOT AN EXIT"), a valuable enough insight. However, by the time one forces a reading of Ellis's turgid, detail-obsessed prose interspersed with unflinching but relatively infrequent accounts of grisly excess, one begins to appreciate the wisdom of avoidance of the imitative fallacy in fiction.

Then again, that may be the point. Readers may be so weary and disgusted of Bateman, Ellis, and themselves by novel's end that it will likely be a long time before they want to read another serial killer novel or see a film on the subject. Perhaps Ellis has rendered a public service to those who worry about fiction glamorizing criminals. It is difficult to decide if Ellis has written the most conscientious, demystifying, demythologizing novel about serial murder possible, and thus one of the best, or the most pretentious, nauseating, nihilistic, and generally despicable one yet. Ellis possesses undeniable stylistic skill, but to see it used on a project such as *American Psycho* is quite troubling. Again, however, reader frustration may be the point. Seldom has individual violence been presented in as deglamorizing and demystifying a light as in this novel.

Through the Eyes of the American Psycho: *Zombie*

Of course, one of the most frightening aspects of Patrick Bateman's character is his channeling of the sexual drive into murder. Whether Bret Ellis himself is a misogynist is debatable, but certainly his main character is a woman-hater—a convention of character that often subjects serial killer fiction to withering attacks from some critics. As a social commodity, one of the most troubling components of the serial killer narrative is its frequent misogyny. Many critics are inclined to see this misogyny as representative of Western culture's approval of violence directed against women. Jane Caputi best summarizes this view:

The murders of women and children by serial killers are not the result of inexplicably deviant men. On the contrary, sexual murder is a product of the dominant culture. It is the ultimate expression of a sexuality that defines sex as a form of domination/power; it, like rape, is a form of terror that constructs and maintains male supremacy. ("Fathers" 2)

Without disputing Caputi's basic thesis, the most comprehensive way in which to understand the serial killer narrative is to scale back momentarily the prominence of gender theory in critical debate and realize that gender is merely *one* of the boundaries being violated here. The serial murderer's amorphous identity crosses not only gender lines but also socioeconomic hierarchies and the very limits of the flesh itself at will. None of this is to deny the patriarchal violence encoded into the social structure so much as to say that the immediate effect of violence—its not-to-be-ignored razoring through of representation and complexity and difference—seems to be the primitivist killer's main objective. John Fraser writes that the artistic range of violence is "vastly greater than that of sex" and that the narratological functions of art are many: "violence as release, violence as communication, violence as play, violence as self-affirmation, or self-defense, or self-discovery, or self-destruction, violence as a flight from reality, violence as the truest sanity in a particular situation, and so on" (9). Of course, in a patriarchal society such as our own, violence as an expression of the will to power is generally coded as a male prerogative. So it will be males who typically resort to physical violence as a culturally sanctioned method of nonverbal communication.[6]

Joyce Carol Oates's novel *Zombie* won the 1996 Bram Stoker Award for Best Horror Novel and the Boston Book Review's 1995 Lilla Fisk Rand fiction prize.[7] Considering the literary revulsion that greeted *American Psycho,* the general critical respect accorded to Oates's character study of a male sex killer—obviously modeled after real-life serial murderer Jeffrey Dahmer and drawing heavily on father Lionel Dahmer's moving account of his painful attempt to comprehend the magnitude of his son's deeds—is initially puzzling. Perhaps the main reason for the critical praise is the attempt by a famous *female* writer to demystify the cultural obsession with brutal serial murders by making the killer's motivation and acts, however reprehensible, at least explainable in terms other than inhuman evil.[8]

The book's killer is named Quentin P__, after Quentin Compson in William Faulkner's *The Sound and the Fury* (Malin, "Letter" 572). He targets primarily homosexual black men—perhaps Oates's way of removing the female portion of her readership from the metaphoric killing ground to allow them some psychological distance and perspective.[9] Like the real-life Dahmer, the otherwise nonassertive Quentin is motivated by a desire to control absolutely the strong young men whose physical presence he covets but has no way of compelling short of brute force (Tompkins 693). Quentin's desire compels him to experiment with a variety of crude and ultimately fatal methods to turn his objects of desire into "zombies." Quentin is predisposed to murder anyway, largely as a result of his emotionally barren relationship with his cold and distant father, a university professor of physics and philosophy. The relationship is a fictional parallel to Dahmer's stiff relationship with his own educated father and an intriguing if simplistic reversal of the usual blame-the-mother narrative agenda of most psycho-thrillers, most famously Alfred Hitchcock's. Also like Dahmer, Quentin is an alcoholic and drug abuser with a previous conviction for child molestation.

The number of parallels between Dahmer and Quentin establishes that Oates, like most other writers in this subgenre, is relying on a shared cultural narrative of murder—in this case, the enormous publicity given to the Dahmer case through television, newspapers, and popular magazines—to create a more complex and insightful "Dahmer" than the one available in most other media forums. In a review of "true crime" serial killer books, which ends with a short critique of Lionel Dahmer's self-lacerating memoir focused on his relationship with his infamous son, Oates announces the thesis of her soon-to-be-published fictionalization of Jeffrey Dahmer's life:

> How does one confront a zombie son with no interest in educating or training himself, no friends, no future? Is it a defective gene? Or simply bad luck? The blunt fact of Jeffrey Dahmer, as it would appear to be the defining fact for male serial killers in their adolescence, is that . . . the serial killer-to-be is fantasizing violent sadistic acts that empower him sexually and yearning for the day when he has the opportunity to make them real. ("I Had" 59)

In *Zombie,* Oates will take the reader from the external vantage point found in Lionel Dahmer's anguished nonfiction into the fictional inner life of an aimless, semieducated, and completely nondescript young man whose sexual fantasies turned private reality indeed empower him in a way he cannot achieve in everyday interactions.

Part one of the novel is entitled "Suspended Sentence." The title is an apt description of Quentin's stasis-in-life as he paradoxically rewinds and replays the memories of his past while denying their hold upon him. He is the "Zombie" of the title at this point. Only in part two of the novel, entitled "How Things Play Out," does he come alive through the stalking, abduction, and murder of SQUIRREL, a teenaged busboy. SQUIRREL seems to Quentin to be the resurrection of Barry, a childhood friend who drowned. The mystical connection between SQUIRREL and Barry compels Quentin to articulate his philosophy of the cosmic chain of being: "For everything that happens, has happened. & will happen again" (149). The statement is also an apt description of the structuring principle of the serial killer subgenre. To the extent that *Zombie* has a semblance of a linear plot, part two is it. Most of the novel, however, is recursive and diffuse, as are most of the "psycho profile" entries in this genre, to reflect the circular meandering of the human consciousness and its primary structuring not through rationality but fantasy.

Quentin's fantasy life is so powerful because his reality is so bleak—not because of any physical abuse he must endure but because he suffers from a variety of mental disorders. For one thing, he is hampered in his social interactions with a fast-paced world by a certain mental torpidity: "Because sometimes things happen to me I can't comprehend. Too fast & confused for me to comprehend" (46–47). An incapacitating self-consciousness and a certain rigidity of manner in the presence of others, even his family, also contributes to his dullness. His father, mother, older sister, and grandmother are solicitous of Quentin and attempt in their own flawed ways to be understanding of his troubled life. However, Quentin simply lacks the psychological capacity to return their exasperated affection. In turn, they are awkward in relation to Quentin. For example, following his suspended sentence for child molestation, Quentin can barely return the embrace of his relieved but equally rigid family members: "It is so fucking hard for me to hug them! Especially Dad. There is a stiffness in all our bones. But I do it & I believe I am doing it O.K." (21). Quentin's relationship with his family is characterized by a surface cordiality disguising a subterranean mutual incomprehension.

The women in Quentin's family are the least threatening to Quentin, though he demonstrates little enough empathy for them, as the following typical remark makes clear: "There has always been a special feeling between Big Sis & me. On her side at least" (89). He completely dissociates himself from the concern of his mother. In one instance, he tunes her out during a phone call when she, knowing his disregard for personal health and hygiene, reminds him to make a dentist's appointment and then asks if she can make the appointment for him. Quentin does not understand the emotions and interactions of his female relatives: "with females & their feelings about one another you can't tell" (107). To the extent that he has any insight into the female psyche, he uses what he sees as their emotional generosity for personal gain: "They want somebody to love & live for—women. It doesn't matter who like it would with a man" (139). He treats his grandmother with courtesy, runs little errands for her, and does her yardwork, but all for the purpose of obtaining money from her. Quentin knows that women respond with all the generosity at their command to his apparent helplessness. His sister Junie, whose academic and athletic successes and her high-status job as a school principal mark her as the pride of the P__ family, regards Quentin as not so much a troubled little brother as "a challenge to her . . . one of her problem students only needing to be redeemed by some adult" (177). At another point, she lectures Quentin about his drug habits and the kind of company he keeps because of his lifestyle:

> You know what I'm afraid of, Quentin?—one of your *secret associates,* some druggie will injure you one of these days, that's what I'm afraid of. For Mom & Dad's sake. Because you're too naïve & you're too trusting like it's the Sixties or something & you're too plain God-damned *stupid* to know your own best interests. (137)

In spite of Junie's harsh words, however, Quentin is not threatened by her. He knows that she, like his other female relatives, is not passing judgment upon him. Women as a general class are not that threatening to him, not only because his sexual interest lies elsewhere but because "[women] believe you, they are not always watching you" (4). Quentin lives in terror of the judgment of others.

　　In fact, one of the most important keys to understanding Quentin's psyche is his fear of disapproval from his intellectually intimidating father, referred to in the text as Professor P__. In relationship to his father, the adult Quentin typically visualizes himself as a small boy squirming beneath Dad's disapproving gaze, as happens when Professor P__ interrogates Quentin about a small, foul-smelling metal locker that, unbeknownst to the elder P__, contains rotting body parts:

> Distinguished Professor, Mt. Vernon State University. . . . DAD'S EYES behind his shiny glasses. Looking at me like when I was two years old & squatting on the bathroom floor shitting & when I was

five years old playing with my baby dick & when I was seven years old & my T-shirt splotched with another kid's nosebleed & when I was eleven home from the pool where my friend Barry drowned & most fierce DAD'S EYES when I was twelve years old that time Dad charged upstairs with the Body Builder magazines shaking in his hand. (33–34)

The passage reveals that, whenever confronted with his father's knowledge or potential discovery of embarrassing secrets, which is how Quentin views his adult secret murders, Quentin mentally reviews past humiliations suffered under his father's omnipotent gaze. Quentin remembers another such shameful moment following a childhood incident when Quentin, attracted to a schoolmate named Bruce, hurt Bruce by nearly strangling him with swing chains and then stole his glasses as a totem of the encounter:

[Bruce's] parents came over to talk to Dad & Mom. I hid away hearing their terrible voices. Dad finally came to get me—*Quentin! Quen-tin!*—flush-faced & his glasses damp against his nose & his goatee quivering when he discovered me hiding curled up like a big slug behind the trash pail in the cupboard beneath the sink. *What do you mean hiding from me, son? Do you think you can hide from me?* (62–63)

The dynamic of the P__ father/son relationship is thus established early on. Quentin will act out his sexually based fantasies only to be exposed to the paternal gaze later. He will either hide from Professor P__ or refuse to discuss the latest embarrassments to the family name. Professor P__ will consistently drop the uncomfortable subject entirely and attempt to resurrect the façade of normal family life. As Quentin summarizes after Professor P__ accepts Quentin's unconvincing explanation of the metal locker's presence in his squalid apartment: "For finally Dad gives up for *he does not want to know* and he wipes his face with a handkerchief & says, 'Quentin, the main reason I dropped by is—how would you like to come home with me for dinner tonight? Your mom has made banana-custard pie'" (36–37). As Quentin sees it, the effort to maintain social appearances is all important to Professor P__. Once Quentin is arrested and convicted of child molestation, Professor P__ uses his status and connections to the legal community to minimize Quentin's punishment not so much to help Quentin but as to preserve whatever is left of the good family name:

> Since the trouble last year—the arrest & the hearing & the sus-
> pended sentence etc.—Dad looks at me differently I think, I'm not
> 100% sure because I am shy to raise my eyes to his but I think it's
> like he is fearful of me as in the past he was impatient and always
> finding fault. Like Q__ his only son was a student failing a course
> of his. Yet I believe he is thinking we are all pretty lucky like my
> lawyer said. No matter the shame to the P__ family that Q__ is an
> *"admitted" sex offender* at least Q__ is not incarcerated at Jackson
> State Prison. (74)

Quentin recognizes how difficult it is for his father to not pass judgment
on him: "Of all of them, of Mom & Dad & Grandma & my sister Junie it
has been hardest on Dad. I know. For women, it is their nature to forgive.
For men, it is harder" (20). In contrast to the unconditional love of his female relatives, Professor P__'s love, given a body blow by Quentin's con-
victed-sex-offender social status, always seems contingent upon Quentin's
willingness to conform his life to Professor P__'s expectations. When hearing of Quentin's indecision about continuing his classes at the local technical college, for instance, Professor P__ expresses his contempt for Quentin's
lack of professional ambition: "Dad got excited saying *What of your future,
son?—you are over thirty years old, you can't be a caretaker all your life can you
& the word 'caretaker' on his tongue like a turd*" (98). Professor P__ is thus
the first, and severest, judge in Quentin's life. The professor is a man who
can reduce his grown son to infantilism because of the latter's fear of disap-
pointing the paternal expectations.

    With terror of the Dark Father's disapproval providing the script,
Quentin's life is determined in large part by his avoidance of the judgments
of others, symbolized in the narrative by his consistent refusal to make eye
contact with others. His terror of disapproval increases exponentially with
the onset of adolescence, when Quentin realizes he is homosexual. He consciously avoids the gaze of his male classmates during communal showers at
the gym:

> Their eyes sliding onto me & even the teachers & in gym class I re-
> fused to go through the shower refused to go naked moving through
> them & their cocks glistening & scratching their chest, bellies &
> some of them so muscular, so good-looking & laughing like apes
> not guessing except if seeing me & my eyes I couldn't keep still
> darting & swimming among them like minnows if seeing me they

knew & their faces would harden with disgust QUEER QUEER QUENTIN'S QUEER. (38)

In group therapy sessions (part of Quentin's terms of probation), "eyes are avoided" in spite of Dr. B__'s insistence that "*nobody's judging anybody else*" (43). Another of Quentin's therapists, Dr. E__, asks that Quentin reveal his fantasies. The demand evokes unpleasant memories of Quentin's classroom silences: "I am blank & silent blushing like in school when I could not answer a teacher's question nor even (everybody staring at me) comprehend it" (54). With the tenants of the family-owned rooming house that Quentin lives in as caretaker, Quentin scrupulously avoids eye contact when they come to him with requests for routine maintenance. Even when Quentin wants people like SQUIRREL (his name for a teenage boy he stalks as the "perfect victim") to take visual notice him, he is thwarted: "*If you would look at me. If you would smile. Just once!* But . . . he does not see *me*" (125). When Quentin finally abducts SQUIRREL on his way home from his busboy job and kills him, Quentin is enraged by the boy's past inability or refusal to notice him: "Looking through me in the [restaurant] like there was nobody where I sat. & provoking me, that sidelong dimple-smile & green eyes" (150). Quentin's fearful refusal to expose his feelings through the symbolic gesture of eye contact, combined with his anger over not having his covetous gaze returned by SQUIRREL, demonstrates the degree to which Quentin's sense of self has been crippled by any number of factors, both genetic and environmental, during his development.

His fear of the judgmental gaze of others, in fact, forms the basis for his homicidal desire to create "zombies." These zombies are living beings whose mental faculties have been debased to the extent where rational thought, and thus judgment, has been rendered literally impossible. Though Quentin's zombies invariably die, he does not set out with the specifically formulated desire to kill them. Rather, he wishes to incapacitate his victims to the point where they will never be able to implicitly "judge" him by the act of leaving him. Quentin's fear of the negative judgment of others paralyzes him, literally, into impotence: "I was having trouble keeping my dick hard with guys' AWAKE EYES observing me at intimate quarters" (29). His physical inability to maintain an erection under the watchful eyes of his lovers parallels his psychological inability to withstand close scrutiny in other, less intimate, but no less threatening social situations, such as the classroom, the therapist's or probationer's office, and the courtroom. As Quentin self-diagnoses: "EYE

CONTACT HAS BEEN MY DOWNFALL" (4). To compensate for this psychologically debilitating malady, Quentin transforms men into "zombies" whose eyes, while open, hold no glitter of human intelligence.

Quentin declares his need for a zombie lover in a fashion indicative of his social inadequacy and personal will to power:

> A true ZOMBIE would be mine forever. He would obey every command & whim. Saying "Yes, Master" & "No, Master." He would kneel before me lifting his eyes to me saying, "I love you, Master. There is no one but you, Master."
>
> & so it would come to pass, & so it would be. For a true ZOMBIE could not say a thing that was *not,* only a thing that *was.* His eyes would be open & clear but there would be nothing inside them *seeing.* & nothing behind them *thinking.* Nothing *passing judgment.*
>
> Like you who observe me (you think I don't know you are observing Q__ P__? making reports of Q__ P__? conferring with one another about Q__ P__?) & think your secret thoughts—ALWAYS & FOREVER PASSING JUDGMENT.
>
> A ZOMBIE would pass no judgment. A ZOMBIE would say, "God bless you, Master." He would say, "You are good, Master. You are kind & merciful." He would say, "Fuck me in the ass, Master, until I bleed blue guts." He would beg for his food & he would beg for oxygen to breathe. . . . We would lie beneath the covers in my bed in the CARETAKER's room listening to the March wind & the bells of the Music College tower chiming & WE WOULD COUNT THE CHIMES UNTIL WE FELL ASLEEP AT EXACTLY THE SAME MOMENT. (49–50)

This long passage simultaneously reveals Quentin's fear of isolation and abandonment, his solipsistic need for an adoring lover, and his extreme and dehumanizing sexual brutality toward the unfortunate objects of his affection. Indeed, one of the most obvious aspects of Quentin's psyche is his blanket dehumanization of other people. He manifests it in little ways, such as reducing the identities of men he meets (and kills) to idiosyncratically significant nicknames such as Frogsnout, Velvet Tongue, the Tease, BUNNYGLOVES, RAISINEYES, BIG GUY, SQUIRREL, and even NO-NAME.[10] And he manifests dehumanization in hideous ways. He performs amateur lobotomies on his drugged victims by ramming an ice pick through their eyes to puncture their brains. When these home lobotomies inevitably fail and end in death, Quentin carves souvenirs from and disposes of the bodies in landfills or rivers. In a final act of objectification, he calls the corpses he transports in his van "*contraband cargo*" (83).

The ice-pick lobotomies give him further satisfaction in that they allow him to mimic (and mock) privately the scientific method of his famous father.[11] Quentin both shares his father's mathematical mind-set and reacts against it. On the one hand, Quentin performs rapid and intuitively algebraic equations and geometric problems to pass the time in jail. On the other hand, he resents the intrusion of "fucking clocks & calendars" (6) on his inner self. On the rare occasions when he thinks of career or school, he leans toward engineering. In fact, at times, he conceives of himself and his organic functions in terms of biomechanics: "you can feel the electrically charged neurons of the prefrontal brain realigning themselves like iron filings drawn by a magnet" (26). Throughout the narrative, Oates clearly places primary blame for Quentin's harmful external influences on the kind of patriarchal science represented by Professor P__ and his Nobel Laureate mentor Dr. K__. The text views science's narrow focus on systems and numbers as reductive or constrictive, inhuman, and potentially lethal. Quentin does not have the intellectual range or educational training of his father, much to his parents' disappointment, but he shares his father's predisposition toward objectification. Quentin crudely inflicts his brand of objectification on his victims with the help of stolen library textbooks such as Freeman and Watts's 1942 clinical how-to manual *Psychosurgery*. In this way, through envy and imitation, the intellectual sins of the fathers are generationally transferred. "*Quentin has a natural love of numbers,*" Professor P__ says, "*A gift for numbers. Inherited from me. I should have realized*" (4). In fact, Quentin P. decides on the idea of murder one day as he attends one of his father's lectures on astrophysics and sees the robotic students copying down, without reflection or true understanding, every word his father says:

> There was a hum & a drone & a vibrating in the room. That sense you have that the floor is tilting or the Earth shifting & settling beneath your feet. Professor R__ P__'s students were busy taking notes & I observed their bent heads & shoulders & it came to me that almost any one of them would be a suitable specimen for a ZOMBIE. (27–28)

His father's lecture about the mind-boggling immensities of black holes and quantum physics, combined with a more personal conflict regarding his trouble with intimacy, has a truly life-altering effect on Quentin. The following passage demonstrates this effect:

> Seeing the Universe like that . . . you see how fucking futile it is to believe that any galaxy matters let alone any star of any galaxy or any planet the size of not even a grain of sand in all that inky void. Let alone any continent or any nation or any state or any county or any city or any individual. (29)

Paradoxically, Quentin—from his self-absorbed private universe—finds solace in the long view provided by contemplation of cosmic immensity even as he fears individual obliteration. Given to long, semimystical reveries in the attic of his parents' house, he is naturally drawn to moonlight but fears the harmful effects of cosmic rays:

> This space in the attic is like certain dreams I used to have where shapes meant to be solid start to melt. & there is no protection. & there is no control. Unlike the cellar which is safe UNDER GROUND, the attic is far ABOVE GROUND. The concentration of COSMIC RAYS is higher at higher elevations on Earth than at lower elevations. (19)

He at times conceives of a macrocosmic merging of self with universe. But he then shakenly retreats from the brink of what he sees as self-annihilation: "Parked the van overlooking the ice-jammed shore & the lake & the sky steely gray & a glare so you can't tell where one ends & the other begins so you could climb up from Earth into Heaven if you believe in that kind of shit WHICH Q__ P__ DOES NOT!" (52).

Quentin's self-induced trances, or moments of dissociation from his environment, provide more understanding of why he murders. His flirtations with transcendence invigorate him. He feels alive only when in proximity to the cosmic void. One of the strongest attractions of murder for Quentin is that it allows him, through personally controlled extinction of another consciousness such as NO-NAME, to come to the brink of nothingness and then pull back alive and empowered:

> NO TURNING BACK! which is the point that must be reached.
> The threshold of the black hole that sucks you in. A fraction of a
> second before & you are still free but a fraction of a second later &
> you are sucked into the black hole & are lost. & my dick hard as a
> club. & as big as a club. & the sparks of my eyes. (80)

Even as the light of life dies in NO-NAME's eyes, then, Quentin's dull eyes
glitter. His phallus, literalization of his male will to power, engorges. Another strong attraction of the cosmic point of view for Quentin is that it
allows him to rationalize his narcissistic murders. For one thing, individual
lives compared to eternity are meaningless, he believes: "How many hundreds, thousands in a single year. Like sparrows of the air they rise on their
wings & soar & falter & fall & disappear & not a trace. & God is himself
the DARK MATTER swallows them up" (30–31). Also, his particular form
of homicidal illness allows him to ignore the past because in the cosmic
scheme of things history means absolutely nothing. If time belongs only to
him, he muses, then "you can do what *you* want. Whatever. You create your
own time" (6). Quentin's sanctification of individual desire at the expense
of other concerns is given symbolic expression through Quentin's appropriation of a watch from RAISINEYES, one of his victims. Any time the traumas of his past intrude too uncomfortably on his present, Quentin resolutely
determines: "Fuck the PAST, it's NOT NOW. Nothing NOT NOW is real"
(18). Simultaneously, he does not want to forget his murders because their
memory is so personally empowering to him, but neither does he want to
be haunted by remorse or regret. So, he keeps tokens or totems of murder,
such as teeth wrenched from screaming mouths, while denying the past any
legitimacy: "I keep mementos but no records. My clock face has no hands
& Q__ P__ has never been one to have hang-ups over personalities or the
past, THE PAST *IS* PAST & you learn to move on. I could be a REBORN
CHRISTIAN is what I sometimes think, & maybe I am waiting for that
call" (85). It is the cosmic perspective that allows him this moral freedom to
enact murderous desires:

> For the first time driving that day I believed I could feel the mo-
> tion of the Earth. The Earth rushing through the emptiness of
> space. Spinning on its axis but they say you don't feel it, you can't
> experience it. But to feel it is to be scared & happy at once & to
> know that nothing matters but that you do what you want to do

& what you do you *are*. & I knew I was moving into the future. There is no PAST anybody can get to, to alter things or even to know what those things were but there is definitely a future, we are already in it. (90)

From this perspective, any actions are acceptable, including the type of dehumanizing murder he needs to perform for sexual satiation.

Quentin does pay enough attention to the reality principle, however, to know that he must become socially invisible to carry out the desires formulated in his fantasies. He becomes a law-abiding, absolutely unnoticeable citizen. He maintains this strategy even when confronted with legal inquiries into his more undisciplined actions, such as during his sentencing for child molestation or his police interrogation following the disappearance of SQUIRREL. Like most serial killers in the subgenre, Quentin is a social chameleon dependent on further obscuring or transforming his unstable identity. Such short-term sacrifice is needed in order to maintain the long-term liberty needed to murder again and again. As part of his disguise, Quentin is agreeable to the point of sycophancy with others: "I never contradict. I am in agreement with you as you utter your words of wisdom. Moving your asshole-mouth & YES SIR I am saying NO MA'AM I am saying" (3). He drives a drab-colored 1987 Ford van (with an American flag decal and bumper stickers) at the speed limit: "[The van] passes through your vision like passing through a solid wall invisible" (4). He covertly observes others, such as the students at the technical college he attends, to learn the social graces and to enlist individuals as possible allies should he ever be arrested:

> But it is a shrewd idea to keep in practice speaking with them. Though mainly I listen. To learn their words, their slang. . . . the words don't change that much, & there are not many of them. It's more the way they move their hands, mouths, eyes. . . . If I needed a character witness (for instance at a trial) you would remember Q__ P__ from Dale Tech & the fact that I was kind. (79)

He imitates the weepy confessions of the other members of his group therapy session to hoodwink Dr. B__ into thinking Quentin has achieved personal insight.

Part of his strategy to achieve practical invisibility is to repress his own sexual preferences for certain types of men and choose victims who are, literally and figuratively speaking, not a part of Quentin's middle-class world. To troll for lovers and victims in Detroit, Quentin affects an alternate, blatantly homosexual identity known as Todd Cutler. To ensure that he is not caught, he preys only on those who will not be missed by mainstream America, such as black and Asian homosexuals. While a white teenager like SQUIRREL is his preference, Quentin shares his culture's contempt for marginalized figures and calculates that only certain classes of victims are safe for him:

> You would want a healthy young person, male. Of a certain height, weight & body build etc. You would want somebody with "fight" & "vigor" in him. & well hung. . . . any University student (with the exception of the foreign students who are so far from home) would be immediately missed. Their families care about them. & they have families.
>
> A safer specimen for a ZOMBIE would be somebody from out of town. A hitch-hiker or a drifter or a junkie (if in good condition not skinny & strung out or sick with AIDS). Or from the black projects downtown. Somebody nobody gives a shit for. Somebody should never have been born. (28)

Quentin to some extent thus transforms himself sexually and culturally to ensure his continued freedom. He best summarizes the importance of his ability to change the surface parameters of his identity following a mugging in Detroit where his face has been literally beaten and distorted into another shape: "& I understood then that I could habit a FACE NOT KNOWN. Not known ANYWHERE IN THE WORLD. I could move in the world LIKE ANOTHER PERSON. I could arouse PITY, TRUST, SYMPATHY, WONDERMENT & AWE with such a face. I could EAT YOUR HEART & asshole you'd never know it" (60).

Quentin's task of self-concealment is made far easier by the indifferent society he inhabits. Like McNaughton's Henry, Quentin encounters little significant social and legal obstacles to his murders. The disappearance of ethnic homosexuals goes unnoticed by the bourgeois police. Only the disappearance of SQUIRREL, a white teenager from a good middle-class home, incites public outrage, media coverage, and police interest in Quentin as a murder suspect.[12] Quentin banks on institutional indifference to commit murders that, in technique and victim selection, are paralleled to the mass

lobotomies of thousands of "unwanted" Americans during irreversible psy-
chosurgical procedures performed during the 1940s and 1950s (Marcus 13).
His probation officer, Mr. T__, makes only cursory twice-monthly inquiries into Quentin's personal life and employment. His court-appointed therapists, Dr. E__ and Dr. B__, are acting only in their official capacities as part
of the bureaucratic hoops Quentin must jump through as part of his suspended sentence. Professor P__'s professional status within the Mt. Vernon
community renders his son Quentin relatively immune from judicial vin-
dictiveness: "Judge L__ . . . is known to Dad & Dad is known to him" (21).
Quentin's light sentence, on the basis of his middle-class social positioning
and race, is a foregone conclusion in spite of his obvious guilt:

> People were saying where money changes hands & it is the word of
> an inexperienced white man, unmarried, thirty years old, against
> the charge of a black boy from the projects, & this black boy, twelve
> years old, from a "single-mother welfare" family, there is not much
> mystery guessing what probably occurred. Nor what kind of "jus-
> tice" would be extracted. (87)

The family lawyer advises Quentin on how to handle the police investigation and search of his house following SQUIRREL's disappearance. When
confronted by such adversarial authority, Quentin resorts to silent self-ef-
facement as a defensive tactic. During his sentencing, for example, Quentin
wears a new suit, cuts his hair, and otherwise adjusts his appearance and manner so as to disarm his judge as much as possible: "I was not wearing my sexy
aviator-style glasses but the clear plastic frames & I was not crying now but
smiling & hugging my family the way you would do at such a time" (88).
Quentin's inoffensive demeanor, then, is perfectly crafted to allay the sus-
picions of a society already predisposed to overlook all but the grossest of
crimes against its disenfranchised classes.

Quentin of course disavows any political ramifications of his crimes.
The politics of the moment, such as the television coverage compressing
famine in Africa and ethnic cleansing in Bosnia and gubernatorial races and
Dodge Ram commercials that he watches shortly before his abduction of
SQUIRREL, mean little more than background noise to Quentin in his hal-
lucinatory half-life. Yet Oates allows the reader from the metatextual position to make the ideological connection between Quentin's murderous asocial self and the culture in which he exists. He often denies larger agendas;

for example, he claims not to be a racist in spite of the skin color of his typical victim. But as an unreliable narrator, he fails to realize that his "asocial" point of view is constructed in part from specific ideological positions. One of those positions is the privileged status of patriarchal science and consumer culture in the United States, which itself routinely fails to realize or acknowledge its manipulation or destruction of others. Quentin's sadistic coupling of sexual deviance with patriarchal science illustrates a worst-case scenario of a common male character type (such as Mr. Ramsey in Woolf's *To the Lighthouse*) in literature: the clockwork male whose desire to break things down into their components to see how they work proves destructive and inhuman. From this perspective, Oates's read on male serial murder is not terribly innovative or original, but it does perhaps explain why some readers are kinder to Oates than, say, Bret Easton Ellis.

However, as a mark of her refusal to provide simplistic solutions, Oates also implicates women in the cultural milieu that contributes to the perpetuation of serial murder. Junie, Quentin's overachiever sister, is a more politically aware character but in some ways as imperceptive as Quentin. She and her academic friends debate ubiquitous 1990s issues such as corporate degradation of the environment, the lack of adequate national health care, the spread of crime and subsequent electorate vulnerability to right-wing politics, gun control, and abortion. Meanwhile, Quentin, the silent killer sitting next to the socially concerned but completely unaware activist, thinks about his cellar slaughterhouse being clean enough to pass police inspection. The next-to-last scene in the novel, in fact, depicts Junie and her friend Lucille inspecting with admiration Quentin's wristband, made of Quentin's hair braided together with the dead SQUIRREL's ponytail. Playing to his 1990s "progressive" audience, Quentin informs them the wristband is from a Chippewa reservation, leading Junie to make her standard condescending remark about Quentin's social naïveté: "Quen is some kind of hippie, you know? Born thirty years too late" (180). Junie and Lucille are not only completely blind to the danger Quentin poses to others, but their interpretive reading of him as a post-hippie also indicates the degree to which the serial killer's mirrored face can reflect back a number of conflicting interpretations.[13]

To sum up, Quentin is an extreme narcissist—so withdrawn and private into his own concerns that he creates a void or zone of negative space around him, into which others have little choice but to project their own presences to interact. Quentin, for his part, can only feel like a strong, self-determining being when he projects his will onto others in the most literally possessing fashion possible. In this way, he is immune from others' attempts to read, or possess, him. Within the text, this destabilization of identity through the null-character of Quentin is a legacy of Gothic border-crossing, of course. But it is also indicative of the bipolar degree to which American individualism both privileges itself as a hermetic construction and fears/covets the Other for what untapped depths it may harbor.

The Serial Killer,
Myth, and Apocalypse
in 1990s Cinema

More mythic, and hence apolitical, interpretations of multiple murder dominated the next major wave of American serial killer narrative, specifically located within the Hollywood cinema of the mid-1990s. The overt engagement with ideological criticism that shaped many 1980s serial killer narratives is subordinate to the spectacular aesthetics of catastrophe characteristic of many recent films in the subgenre. Politics does play a part in the structuring of these recent texts but only insofar that the serial killers within attempt to divorce themselves from context and live in the eternal present of fascistic myth.

Mickey Knox attempts to transcend the image pollution of his native culture in Oliver Stone's *Natural Born Killers.* Early Grayce wants to ascend from dead-end menial jobs through the "doors of perception" in Dominic Sena's *Kalifornia.* John Doe tries to achieve lasting notoriety through literally inscribing his culture's sacred texts on the tortured bodies of those who represent the seven deadly sins of Christianity in David Fincher's *Seven.* These characters' murderous acts are performed not as coherent political manifestos but as idiosyncratic expressions of American individualism paradoxically reliant on scraps of inherited, easily graspable narratives of primal simplicity and violence. This supposedly apolitical stance is in and of itself a recognizably American political statement—a sort of politics of apocalypse wherein all class boundaries are leveled through acts of violence directed at the symbolic object of one's frustration, hatred, bigotry, or class envy. Such actions are socially destructive, not constructive (except in the most limited individual sense—for the killer).

Perhaps the primary concern all of these diverse works scrutinized up to now share is the neo-Gothic anxiety over boundary, wherein representation impacts reality and vice versa. In the some of the most recent and high-profile films of this subgenre, the dissolution of boundary constitutes a "virtual" apocalypse of imagistic flux that the serial killers have no choice but to embrace—but against which they struggle to pierce with actions of extremely brutal physicality. The goal is to establish a stable core identity. This identity can only be reached through a mythic existence that transcends the destabilizing change inherent in temporality. In these works, ritualized repeat murder is the strategy by which the besieged individual grasps eternity. For the identity-obsessed serial killer, the inescapable immediacy of extreme physical violence erases intermediary thought, modes of interpretation, conflicting ideologies, and so forth. Metatextually, the narrative strategies of these texts are specifically tailored to implicate the reader/consumer into the writer/producer's violent project of slashing through taboos and barriers in an attempt to achieve moments of pure insight.

Thus, in many of the mid-1990s popular serial killer films, the political overtones that shape earlier entries in the subgenre are subordinate to the aesthetics of apocalypse. The narratives these killers populate likewise enact a kind of literary apocalypse wherein aesthetics and genre melt down and recoalesce into intriguing, if extreme, new forms. Politics does play a part in the structuring of these texts but only insofar that the characters within attempt to divorce themselves from social context and live in the eternal present of myth. In the 1990s American mainstream cinema of serial murder, the deliberate critique of American ideology integral to earlier, lower-profile serial murder treatments, such as John McNaughton's *Henry: Portrait of a Serial Killer,* becomes subsumed by the Hollywood showman's desire to craft the most visually striking murder spectacle possible. As part of this sensationalistic agenda, the cinematic narratives work very hard to depict their serial killers as monstrous beings. The killers are human, to be sure, but unmistakably signified in terms of a demonic Other that justifies the most violent and reactionary impulses in the American character. The threat, while capable of corrupting the fragile social fabric, arises primarily from outside the culture or foreign invaders within the culture, rather than from within its most precious policies and ideologies.

The cinema of serial murder's current emphasis on expressionistic demonizing of the external Other, solidified by the 1991 mainstream breakthrough of Jonathan Demme's neo-Gothic spectacle *The Silence of the Lambs,* complements the larger 1990s cultural movement toward millennialism. The apocalyptic leitmotif also implies that the American cult of barbarism is far too deeply ingrained in the national character for cathartic expurgation and redemption. Whereas earlier violent films such as Terence Malick's *Badlands* typically adopted extreme violence as the last-resort methodological tool of overthrow of an irredeemable culture, the pessimistic cinema of murder of the 1990s routinely depicts protagonists who have been so dehumanized by a combination of lived and media experience with violence that they are incapable of accepting, or even recognizing, more constructive options.[1] Robert Conrath, isolating a specific type of media-zombified antihero, puts it this way:

> The serial killer is a product of the pervasive penetration of media technology and televised representations into our daily lives. . . .
> At the same time, violence has lost its cathartic value; it no longer exists as a mediating apparatus for filtering out and deciphering the message. ("Serial Heroes" 153)

The more popular 1990s films that mythologize serial murderers' exploits generally subordinate or dispense with social critique in favor of depictions of apocalyptic (as opposed to cathartic) levels of violence. Sociological explanations, to the extent that the films even bother with intellectual or academic discipline as a legitimate force for social change, tend to focus on individual deviancy—a demonic Other—rather than mass ideological culpability or reform.

Part of the demonization strategy of these films requires not only that the serial killers are more intelligent and insightful than their middle-class contemporaries but that they also are sublimely brutal in a way that shocks increasingly jaded filmgoers. This narrative need to shock does not necessarily translate into mindlessly graphic or cartoonish depictions of gratuitous bloodletting, as is the case with many of the big-budget Hollywood epics. All but one of the murders in *Seven,* for example, happen offstage. Even *Natural Born Killers,* the subject of congressional denunciations and legal targeting because of its supposed extreme violence, contains nowhere near the number of on-screen murders of the typical PG-rated summer action flick.[2]

Rather, the serial killer spectaculars invest horror in the dehumanizingly brutal techniques of the killers. The crimes are rendered even more horrifying to the imagination by the mere suggestion of the broad outlines of the individual killer's modus operandi. This narrative focus on the killer's ritualistic technique or pattern-making accounts for the frequent textual analogies between serial murder, artistic creation, and religious sacrament.

Through such symbolic associations, serial murder becomes regenerative for its fictional practitioners. They seek to recover a mythic existence that transcends the destabilizing change inherent in a complex postmodern existence. Thus, they have no interest in true social reform, unlike many other violent "action heroes." In fact, the texts imply that the serial killer's success depends on American culture staying exactly the way it is. While this stagnation *can* be presented as a scathing indictment of the culture, in most cases it is not. The texts portray ritual, repeat murder as the apolitical strategy that these primitives choose in order to transcend the excesses of materiality in the postmodern moment.

If multiple murder derives its undeniable impact from its postindustrial or postmodern character, as Mark Seltzer argues, it is first of all necessary to comment on one of the most paradoxical aspects of postmodernism—its relation to primitivism, or neoprimitivism. Michael Arnzen remarks that "most postmodern texts are rife with allusions to primitivism" (184). The serial killer, typically portrayed in fiction as a contemporary practitioner of magical thinking, is a manifestation of a general cultural turn to primitivism. This primitivism is not necessarily romanticism, with its implications of idealized individual insularity as negotiated between the poles of innocence and experience. Rather, it is a Gothic primitivism that implies an antidiscursive, eternalized individual communion. This brand of neoprimitivism is the egocentric's natural response to a complex modern existence that, by compartmentalizing knowledge into specialized and exclusive branches of expertise, according to Jürgen Habermas (9), threatens to overwhelm the ego. Drastic, dramatic measures are required to preserve the ego and restore one's sense of empowerment in the contemporary environment. The real-life phenomenon of serial killing, surely one of the most melodramatic expressions of the will to power, serves such a purpose for a limited minority whose mindset otherwise differs little from the majority. The fictional serial killers dramatize this murderous, egocentric mysticism.

That serial murder serves as a method of personal transcendence is not so incomprehensible when analyzed in the context of myth and ritual. According to Mircea Eliade, the mechanism by which one accesses pre-existing outer reality is participation in repetitive, ritualistic liturgical drama intended to imitate or repeat an archetype. Thus, "he who reproduces the exemplary gesture finds himself transported into the mythical epoch in which its revelation took place" (35). The serial killer in fiction often longs for the spiritual surety of apocalypse, and attempts to will it into being through constructing a grammar of murder. Murder or sacrifice is essential to the project because, as our modern conceptions of entropic exhaustion dimly echo, the energy of the godhead requires regeneration through mediated exchange of life energies (Eliade 109). The serial killer's apocalyptic performance attempts to recycle or loop, through rote performance of a murderous ritual the origins of which lie in antiquity, a lost link between language and underlying warrant of meaning. The repetitive performance becomes a method of creating being and meaning, not just a substitution for it. Ideally, the artificiality of the performance could be lost and its eternal veracity invoked through the mimesis of the ritual. As René Girard has concluded in his work *Violence and the Sacred,* mimesis is an attempt to call forth the atemporality of apocalypse.

But from the ironic postmodernist perspective, the absence of an eternal center (not the elusiveness of it, as in modernism) taunts the metadiscursive performance, no matter how convincing in its destructiveness. One begins to weary of an unrelenting battle to shore up the besieged ego and wishes to end the war decisively through a divine intercession that rewards the faithful and damns the unjust. What happens in a culture based at least in part on such an individualistic mythos is a desire for that society's own end, as that would be the culmination, and the fulfillment, of all spiritual impulse. It is not really a wish for cultural suicide so much as a longing for meaningful (and extrahuman) resolution of what seem to be presently insurmountable problems inextricably woven into the corrupt social fabric. America particularly resorts to eschatological thinking in times of crisis because of what Christopher Sharrett describes as a national "ideology preferring total annihilation (including self-annihilation) over radical change or even reform" ("Horror Film" 108). The eschatological desire permeates most American cultural modes of expression, including diverse literary genres.

According to Lois Zamora, there are two distinct brands of American apocalyptic thinking: the more optimistic millennial tradition and the bleak cataclysmic tradition. The cataclysmic tradition is what Americans now tend to associate with the word "apocalypse."[3] Whereas the divine Christian millennium of previous generations was essentially a promise of hope and ultimate redemption for an elected few of the Puritan believers, the more secularized millennium some now dread augurs only catastrophe and extinction without the distant guarantee of restoration. Zamora explains:

> Our modern sense of apocalypse is less religious than historical, the cataclysm resulting from the events of recent history and man's own capacities for self-destruction. The current pessimism about our collective future has its basis in the cataclysmic side of apocalypse as surely as our earlier national optimism proceeded from its millennial vision. (1)

Zamora further contends that our latter-day concept of apocalypse ignores the word's original Greek root (*apokalypsis*), meaning "to reveal," and instead treats it as a synonym for "disaster."

It is no accident that in the contemporary horror genre in particular, we frequently find a motif that John May, on a parallel track to Zamora, has labeled the "secular apocalypse" (33). The secular apocalypse borrows the Christian pattern for works of a nonreligious and decidedly bleaker nature. The symbolic language of this kind of apocalypse often borrows the trappings of its religious forebear, including secularized images of Satan as wandering instigator of deceit and destruction, essentially protean in nature. Additionally, indications of general moral decline are present. Despair, not religious faith in renewal and salvation, characterizes the secular apocalypse. Destruction is the primary result, not rebirth in any redemptive sense. The threat of widespread, nihilistic devastation looms in the near distance. May's description fits perfectly the mythscape of the mainstream serial killer movies of the 1990s, in which the murderer, while human, "channels" a demonic outside force antithetical to civilized existence. Narrative construction of the murderer as a "natural born killer," rather than a logical outgrowth of a culture's flawed ideologies and practices, conforms to deeply deterministic "bad seed" theories of criminality extant in the culture at large.

Thus, the level of extreme physical violence present in these narratives, combined with a metaphysical subtext of cataclysmic apocalypse, tends to erase thematically any alternative, socially minded ideologies. *Natural Born Killers, Kalifornia,* and *Seven* are three such apolitical political films, constituting a paradoxical brew of dialectical slipperiness typically called postmodern but, if one must apply a label to such an inchoate movement, might be more accurately called *neoprimitive*. As their most salient feature, however, these polemically toned texts paradoxically lack any coherent political agenda. Rather, they partake of a representational strategy that levels all political disputes into one primal scream of paranoid rage before the end of everything. They exemplify the politics of apocalypse.

"God Just Made It That Way": *Natural Born Killers*

Oliver Stone's apocalypse-in-progress film, *Natural Born Killers* (1994), is in many ways the most perplexing of the three films discussed here. The film is not problematic because of its violence, as some of its most vocal detractors insist, but rather because of what some of its more aesthetically attuned critics see as its overwrought assault on the contemporary age's image pollution.[4] However, it is difficult to doubt Stone's sincere desire to shatter audience complacency. Dispensing almost entirely with traditional Hollywood reliance on an emotionally gripping linear plot and engaging characters, Stone instead concentrates on giving his audience an aesthetic apocalypse wherein all genre boundaries are collapsed. Howard Hampton elaborates:

> Stone's kamikaze intent is to fuse all *NBK*'s antecedents in one big bang, an apotheosis that wipes the slate clean and then supersedes them, pushing every moment and gesture past its referents and finally itself, diving into the void like the Wild Bunch falling through a bullet-riddled looking glass. (4)

Similarly, Chris Chang argues that the film's stylistic "strategy has an overall destabilizing affect mimicking a schizoid hallucination experience that violates the filmic norms of how to view the world. No domain of imagery attains primacy—everything becomes suspect—as all plummet in missing-foundation freefall" (39). Striving toward this apocalypse of image and genre, Stone presents a dizzying blur of rapidly edited film stocks and video formats in both color and black-and-white. He also compresses multiple genres into the film's two-hour running time: the music video, the cross-country road movie, the superhero cartoon, the monster movie, the prison-riot movie, the outlaw couple movie, the police procedural, the "reality TV" re-enactments, the tabloid prison interview, and even the half-hour family sitcom complete with laugh track, applause on cue, commercials, and credits (the *I Love Mallory* sequence). Self-parodic references to other genre films (including *Scarface* and *Midnight Express,* both of which Stone scripted) fly by so fast that one is only aware that one has just missed something. Stephen Schiff, for one, says of all this visual disjunctiveness: "you feel as though you were seeing [Mickey and Mallory's] conscious and their unconscious lives and the forces that formed them, all at once" (46).

Through its kaleidoscopic fusion of genres and images, the first third of the film superficially argues that the formative force in Mickey and Mallory's lives is the modern media's conditioning of impressionable minds. Daniel Green summarizes this critical interpretation of the film: "Ultimately, *Natural Born Killers* strongly implies that its killers are not at all naturally born but are products of the media environment (including Hollywood movies) that has shaped them" (265). In this aspect, the film resembles Stanley Kubrick's surreal film *A Clockwork Orange,* where another young criminal, Alex, undergoes similar psychological distortion via the agency of a corrupt society. However, the final two-thirds of Stone's film insists that violence is more a function of individual human evil or deviancy than cultural conditioning. In one interview, Stone states that

> Mickey is a total predator. . . . He understands the universe only from a predatory standpoint and he justifies what he does that way. . . . [W]ithin our satire, we've surrounded Mickey and Mallory with such scumbags that predation seems like the natural, Darwinian thing for them to do in that world. (qtd. in D. Williams, "Overkill" 43)

In another interview, Stone makes the underlying philosophy even more explicit:

> The psychology of this film is Jungian—with a hint of Nietzsche. It's really about the idea of a superman and the need to control all life and attain true wisdom. At the same time, though, while Mickey and Mallory are pursuing this, they are cursed by a demon from the very beginning and they inherit the demon at the end.[5] So it's definitely closer to Nietzsche than Jung, but it doesn't have anything to do with Freud. He can't answer the problems here. It has to be an unconscious meditation of violence, it can't be conscious or *explained* violence, but so deeply ingrained in the psyche that the Jungian is the best approach to the material. (qtd. in D. Williams, "Analyzing" 54)

Stone makes clear that social or cultural factors are irrelevant to his mythologizing, Jungian-based project.[6] His screenwriters are in accord. Dave Veloz says: "Instead of being sick [Mickey and Mallory are] just plain evil. In another time, they might have become heroes worthy of attention, but in the mediocrity of our times, they just became serial killers" (qtd. in D. Williams, "Overkill" 43). Richard Rutowski adds, "I contributed . . . the demon concept, the realization that Mickey and Mallory are not simply driven by things we can understand, but ones we can't, and that they are just as real, just as physical" (44). All three contributors correctly note that causation is a complex web of factors. However, the writers reduce complexity to simplicity when they concur in their mystification of serial murder as a superhuman, incomprehensible evil that nevertheless draws their unspoken admiration.

The film finally suggests that given the presence of literal evil, especially its power to corrupt all it touches, there is very little we can do about it other than stamp out individual transgressors. To introduce his concept of human evil, Stone enlists a symbolic victim of American genocidal policies into serving as spokesperson for Stone's moral sensibility. The Native American visionary whom Mickey and Mallory inexplicably encounter in the wasteland occupies a privileged moral position in Stone's revision of Quentin Tarantino's far different, less mystically inclined original screenplay. Cynthia Fuchs notes, "the Indian is granted special insights into Mickey and Mallory's fiendish souls" (65). The visionary clearly "sees," without a hint of irony on Stone's part, that Mickey is an actual demon while Mallory, suffering from "sad sickness" and "lost in a world of ghosts," has just watched too much TV and is therefore of a lesser magnitude of evil than Mickey. The Native American is also a true prophet. While dying, he tells Mickey: "Twenty years ago I saw the demon in my dreams. I was waiting for you." The narrative clearly accepts the seer's reading as the one authentic reading in a plethora of misreadings, especially as Mickey's unintentional murder of the seer in a hallucinogenic panic leads not only to the killer couple's renunciation of meaningless murder but their immediate capture.

Just as the romanticized, "primitive" Native American is outside the scope of Stone's indictment of popular media, so too, it is implied, is the brutish Mickey. These are sublime characters, one light and one dark, and their sentimentalized portraiture does not sit well in the midst of Stone's otherwise accusatory tract. The Native American is absolved of all blame in the hyperreal proceedings. Oddly, so is Mickey, a point Stuart Klawans makes: "Mickey's evil isn't just a shadow of the media after all. His evil must be something absolute, something that escapes the media" (285). Nearly sub-liminal images of Mickey as a blood-soaked devil run throughout the film. The director's cut video release restores an excised scene that only strength-ens Mickey's association with the satanic. In the desert, he is purposefully guided to the Native American prophet by a mutated, three-horned goat of decidedly diabolical appearance and temperament. So, Mickey can be most accurately read as a demon of apocalypse. The demon is not necessarily Chris-tian (though Christian images of the Beast, the number 666, the horned devil, and so on are obviously present as a part of the continuum of the ico-nography of evil) so much as precivilization. Because he is outside human agency, he also manages to relieve us of culpability, and thus the need for self-correction, in some of the narrative goings-on.[7] The presence of these two extra-human and hypermasculine characters, the Native American and the demon, renders *Natural Born Killers* into an odyssey of Mickey's per-sonal quest to "kill the demon" within himself.

The reconstruction of a primal, premedia identity through violence dominates the film thematically, coloring its "outlaw-couple-on-the-run" narrative arc. Mickey and Mallory find a fulfilling joint identity in murder. Their demonic courtship and marriage, complete with a blasphemous ex-change of blood vows over a global vista that Mickey calls "my world," is the metaphoric culmination of their separate identities into one murderous hybrid.[8] Their spontaneous romance sets into motion what plot there is in the film: the stealing of the family car that lands Mickey in prison, his sub-sequent jailbreak through divine intervention in the dual forms of a con-cealing whirlwind and rattlesnakes that attack the pursuing guards, his Charles Starkweather–like liberation of Mallory through the killing of her parents, and the fifty-plus-victim killing rampage that follows. Their union thus unleashes a personal apocalypse upon the land, as Mallory envisions in response to Mickey's assertion that the end of the world is nigh: "I see angels, Mickey. They're comin' down to us from heaven. And I see you ridin' a big red horse. . . . And I see the future. There's no death, because you and I are angels." As Wayne Gale summarizes, they tear "up the country-side with a vengeance right out of the Bible." Spiritual identity is linked to violent sexuality.

The doubling between villain and observer in the film further destabi-lizes identity only to recreate it anew in the guise of the apocalyptic demon—a narrative strategy that again renders futile any notion of social reform ex-cept at the individual level. Of course, Mallory is the female mirror to Mickey, but others in the narrative also embrace his methods, destroy themselves, and in effect become Mickey.[9] For example, Jack Scagnetti, homicide detective, allows his spectator's hatred for killers (originating in his childhood witnessing of the shooting of his mother by tower-sniper Charles Whitman) to transform him into a psychopathic obsessive who sees no contradiction between his loathing of criminality and the pleasure he takes not only in his vigilante style of manhunting but in the near-strangling of prostitutes. When asked by Warden McClusky how he became an "expert" on psychopaths, Scagnetti explains what happened to his mother and concludes: "And ever since then I've had a strong opinion about the psychopathic fringe that thrives today in America's fast-food culture. I tend not to exhibit the self-discipline, y'know, becoming of a peace officer." This, of course, is a gross understatement of Scagnetti's willingness to transgress the law he is sworn to enforce. He is a willing conspirator in McClusky's equally extralegal plot to transport Mickey and Mallory from the prison to a psychiatric hospital for evaluation, at which time Scagnetti will manufacture an excuse to shoot them. Scagnetti's childhood trauma of witnessing his mother's murder has given him a reservoir of helpless rage, which like Mickey's agonizing memories of childhood disempowerment, expresses itself in adult overcompensation. Scagnetti's character is a double for the killer he pursues: three of the most obvious examples include the title of his shamelessly self-promotional book ("Scagnetti on Scagnetti"), which initiates the doppelgänger theme for the viewer; his abuse of the prostitute in a hotel room visually similar to the hotel room in which Mickey rapes and kills a female hostage; and his barely concealed sexual desire for Mallory, which ultimately leads him to place himself in a fatally vulnerable position quickly exploited by Mallory's lethal hands.[10]

The message conveyed by Scagnetti (and to a lesser extent, tabloid television reporter Wayne Gale, who willingly participates in the bloody prison riot that allows Mickey and Mallory to escape) is that all men are latent psychopaths and it takes but one inspired mentor to bring that latency roaring to life in the form of the apocalyptic demon.[11] Mickey Knox, in an interview with Wayne Gale that sparks a riot in the incendiary atmosphere of the tyrant McClusky's prison, summarizes this attitude:

Everybody's got the demon in here, okay [pointing to his breast]. The demon lives in here. It feeds on your hate. It cuts, kills, rapes. It gives you your weakness, your fear. Only the vicious survive. We're all told we're no good pieces of shit from the time we can breathe. After awhile, you kinda become bad.

The demon is Mickey's metaphor for the inborn human desire to kill, but he also posits it to be an essentially innocent instrument of survival. The culture represented by Wayne Gale twists the demon into an image of something evil and perverse, to be experienced vicariously by an audience that has repressed its murderous impulses but nevertheless retains the collective memory of the hunt. The hunt sanctifies Mickey's identity, whereas Gale's voyeurism demeans himself and his audience. It is up to Mickey, as demon, to bring down Gale's house in a final media Armageddon, but pointedly not as part of any reform agenda. Mickey as the image of the apocalyptic destroyer offers no compromises, no alternatives, and no solutions—other than the Final Solution. The Information Age culture cannot be redeemed or reformed but only destroyed by its own bad seeds.

In a media-saturated culture full of hypocrites, Gale is the biggest hypocrite of all. He feigns a moral outrage and a concern for audience he does not feel because the ratings demand it. After Gale "angrily" demands a reason for the Knoxes' killing spree, simply because this posture is expected of him, Mickey points out the contradictions in Gale's position:

> Y'mean was an instant of my purity worth a lifetime of your lies? . . . you and me, we're not even the same species. I used to be you, then I evolved. From where you're standing, you're a man. From where I'm standing, you're an ape. You're not even an ape. You're a media person. The media's like the weather, only it's man-made weather. Murder is pure. You're the one who made it impure. You're buying and selling fear. You say why? I say, why bother?

Gale himself gives lie to his stance of moral superiority during the ensuing prison riot.[12] The reporter initially covers the riot as a ratings bonanza but quickly embraces it as a liberation from his old life and becomes an active part of the story, as opposed to a recorder of it. He is so exhilarated by this anarchic release of primitive energy that he begins to ally himself with Mickey and Mallory's escape bid. Gale takes up arms against the law-enforcement representatives of the very society whose middle-class morality he has pandered to, and he also leaves his wife via cellular phone. Through these renunciations, he believes he is championing Mickey and Mallory's cause. Furthermore, Gale believes that the couple is grateful to him for helping them escape. He seems genuinely surprised as well as panicked when Mickey and Mallory inform him that they are going to kill him rather than take him with them to the fugitive underground network.

As with most of Mickey's murders, this last on-screen killing is not motivated by anger or hatred. Instead, Mickey wants to make a statement, although as he tells Gale: "I'm not one hundred percent exactly sure what it's saying." Mickey's uncertainty about his philosophy is not surprising. In spite of his rough-edged articulateness during the interview, where he spouts jailhouse Nietzsche or Jung, he is at his core a nonverbal primitive. He communicates primarily through his actions, as any other form of authenticity is virtually impossible in the image-polluted society he reluctantly inhabits and symbolically destroys by shooting Gale. Through so doing, Mickey reaffirms his primal identity.

Thus, in spite of the film's superficial insistence that the media environment is to blame for rampant murder, the title "natural born killers" suggests a different kind of determinism—a metaphysical one. Mickey is elected by God or destiny to be what he is, a human embodiment of the "natural" killing instinct symbolized by the rattlesnakes that litter the film's landscape. He is in fact helpless or unable to choose otherwise. There is some textual evidence for precisely this view, as already noted in Mickey's relationship with the mystic Native American. Mickey himself puts a lot of stock in the concept of fate, ascribing to it his meeting of Mallory on his meat delivery. He also tells interviewer Gale that he was a killer, or bad seed, from birth: "I was thrown into a flamin' pit of scum forgotten by God. . . . I came from violence. It was in my blood. My dad had it. His dad had it. It was all just my fate. My fate." In response to Gale's confident assertion that one must learn evil and is not born to it, Mickey questions the premise that murder is evil: "It's just murder, man. All God's creatures do it . . . the wolf don't know why he's a wolf. The deer don't know why he's a deer. God just made it that way." He also questions Gale's use of the phrase "innocent victims" by implying that these people have been preordained to die, through Original Sin, specifically at Mickey Knox's consecrated hands: "But I know a lot of people who deserve to die . . . everybody got somethin' in their past. Some sin. Some awful, secret thing. A lot of people walkin' around out there already dead, just need to be put out of their misery. That's where I come in. Fate's messenger." He finally concludes his interview with a tag line that drives ratings-conscious Gale into ecstasy: "Shit, man, I'm a natural born killer." The liberating riot that follows hard on the heels of this pronouncement vindicates for them the belief that fate has meant them to be together and free (after, of course, symbolically destroying the culture that attempted to keep them apart). But theirs is no social protest or call for reform—only an expression of individual fulfillment.

Stone's film, as controversial as it may be to those who decry its nasti-
ness and question its intentions, conforms to an apocalyptic variant of traditional American literary millennialism that simultaneously laments and
masochistically welcomes whatever spiritual ills the author chooses to blame
for the downfall of the United States.[13] As Mickey proclaims the "whole
world's comin' to an end" and Mallory fantasizes her and Mickey's trans-
mutation into angels in a future without death, they confirm Stone's thesis,
however fractured or obscured by intruding thematic tangents, that image
pollution may precipitate the apocalypse. However, Jungian *lustmord* itself
is a pure force for rejuvenation somehow transcendent of humanity's tendency to clutter its world with bloodless symbols. In keeping with America's
most anarchic impulses, total self-destruction is favored over self-reform.

The Highway to Heaven: *Kalifornia*

Dominic Sena's *Kalifornia* (1993), while on a much more modest and personal scale of apocalypse than Stone's film, also demonizes its murderous
antihero. It is quite tempting to claim that a film like this one is designed to
advocate ultimately reactionary political purposes. For example, as one reviewer puts it, *Kalifornia*'s "gruesome cross-country ride argues for capital
punishment" (Colby 44). As part of its apparently reactionary agenda, *Kalifornia* superimposes what reviewer Chris Darke calls "an Olympian moral
perspective on matters of Good and Evil" (46) in the form of cliché-ridden
voice-overs provided at frequent intervals by its writer protagonist, Brian
Kessler. But as the voice-overs themselves illustrate, *Kalifornia* does not sim-
plistically single out for scapegoating purposes any one or two social causes
of deviance. Instead, the film insists that modernist-style attempts at tidy
explanation are doomed to fail. The voice-overs seem designed to "coach"
the viewer into accepting *Kalifornia*'s primary narrative conceit that violence
is ultimately inexplicable, or at least far more complex than most social scientists would have us believe. Brian begins with a few pat, academic assumptions about the causes of serial murder and finds that real-life experience is
far more slippery.

For example, the first of Brian's voice-overs occurs in the opening credits
of the film, after killer Early Grayce has dropped a huge rock from a highway
overpass onto the windshield of a passing car and thus caused a fatal wreck:

I remember once going on a school trip to the top of the Empire
State Building. When I looked down at the crowds of people on

the street they looked like ants. I pulled out a penny and some of us started talking about what would happen if I dropped it from up there and it landed on somebody's head. Of course, I never crossed that line and actually dropped the penny. I don't think Early Grayce knew there was a line to cross.

The not-so-subtle implication is, of course, that Brian's childhood fantasy of randomly dispensing death-from-above has found literal expression in the actions of the child-man Grayce. The voice-over establishes the first of many thematic parallels between Brian's passive voyeurism and Grayce's active reality. Like most representatives of conventional decency in this subgenre, Brian has sympathy for the devil. He first chooses to emphasize his opinion that random killers like Grayce suffer not so much from evil intent as moral imbecility: not knowing "there was a line to cross." In Brian's initial apportionment of blame, Grayce's actions remain relatively pure, if not commendable. Society's abusive treatment of Grayce receives the lion's share of blame.

It is this fashionable "liberal" opinion that is put to the test in the course of *Kalifornia*'s narrative, exactly as in *Natural Born Killers*. *Kalifornia* is interested in complicating Brian's unidimensional worldview and restoring metaphysical evil to the American mythscape. The film's narrative arc clearly validates the early observation of one of Brian Kessler's friends that multiple murderers are not sick but "evil." The real question, then, is what does the film define as "evil"? Cosh Colby, for example, writes that " [Kessler] starts out as an apologist for murderers . . . but soon learns that evil is deeper than illness; it is a choice" (44). The film immediately establishes Brian's well-meaning but woefully inadequate experience with his pet subject. Discussing serial killers for what must be the *n*th time with some obviously long-suffering college friends at a party, Brian lectures:

> I'm talking about the mind of a serial killer as it relates to culpability. Someone who has no ability to distinguish between right and wrong is like a child. In the eyes of the law, he should be treated like a child. He should not be imprisoned, let alone executed. . . . Most of these poor people suffer from severe chemical brain imbalances. . . . The answer is research and treatment under hospital-supervised conditions. Not the electric chair.

One of Brian's friends quips, "Yeah, that's great, Brian. Unless it's your mother's head they find in the refrigerator." Brian responds: "True. But executing the killer would not bring my mother back, would it? . . . Actually, it wouldn't make me feel any better." Another of Brian's friends is having none of this "liberal" sentimentality: "Brian. The bottom line is, these people are evil, plain and simple."

The narrative thus initiates one of its primary arcs. As a sentimental humanist paradoxically intent on objective understanding, Brian must come to accept the reactionary, unapologetic beliefs of his friends. Indeed, he must learn to kill, under the tutelage of serial murderer Early Grayce. Brian's initial writer's empathy and pity for serial killers is the very engine that powers his flirtation with murder (represented by his homosocial attraction to Early Grayce) and corresponding near-downfall. His knowledge of murder, which he feels he needs to increase for fulfillment of a contract on a proposed book about serial killers, is frustratingly academic. He complains that "what little I knew about serial killers I'd learned in the university library, and the only thing I knew for certain was that people didn't kill each other in libraries." Inspiration strikes him after a drunken, stoned party one night. He takes his lover Carrie to a local abandoned warehouse where a woman, abused there some years ago by her father, committed a series of murders in her adulthood. Standing in the dark building, imaginatively reconstructing the crimes while Carrie takes photographs, Brian begins to formulate a plan for finishing his book. He expresses the plan to Carrie the next morning:

> For the first time I understood that woman as a human being. I was walking where she walked, where she killed. I was in her skin. I was looking through her eyes. I think we've got a book here. With your pictures and my writing it's a book. . . . A book on some of the most infamous murders in American history. I want to go where they lived and where they killed. And I want you to take the pictures and I'm going to write the text.

Under this pretense of honoring a book contract and simultaneously granting his lover Carrie's wish to travel to California for new career opportunities, he solicits for fellow riders on the ride board at his college to share expenses on this unusual cross-country road trip. Serendipitously, Early Grayce, looking for the personnel office on the direction of his parole officer, arrives as Brian is posting the notice. The stage is thus set for Brian's education in the fine art of murder.

It is only much later that Brian, after experiencing victimization at the hands of an actual serial killer, comes to realize that his earlier sympathetic stance was based largely on a self-rationalization of his own voyeuristic attraction to the subject. Early points out Brian's ignorance: "You ain't never killed no one, have you, Bri'? . . . Nope. Ain't seen nobody killed either, have you? . . . Nope. Tell me somethin', big time. How the hell you gonna write a book about somethin' you don't know nothin' about?" However, when later confronted with the option of finishing off a policeman wounded by Early, Brian discovers even on threat of his own death that he cannot murder in this fashion. At this crucial narrative moment, Brian breaks the sympathetic link he had been forging with Early. Brian is not so much like his "buddy" as he had thought.

However, Brian's renunciation of murder is not a personal triumph, but rather an inability to comprehend what *Kalifornia* calls evil. Early completely overturns Brian's proactive assumptions, which are simplistic and in need of expansion, about the roles child abuse and mental illness may play in the development of a serial killer. Instead, Brian learns to enact a typically reactionary strategy wherein brutality is answered with even greater brutality. To do so, he must first admit that his intellectualism is not capable of meeting the challenge posed to it by Early. For example, when Early finally reveals himself to be a murderer, Brian is compelled to admit his ignorance and the hollowness of his previous explanations: "You're right, Early. I don't know shit about killing. You gotta tell me. Does it make you feel good? Powerful? Superior? Who are you angry with? Your mother? Your father?" Brian runs through the standard progressive's litany of explanations for murder, but Early refuses to endorse any one explanation. He teases Brian by hinting that all this may stem from his father's abuse, leading Brian to assume that Early symbolically murders his father when he kills. But Early refutes this pat theory when he tells Brian, over the wounded policeman, that "I know that's not my father, you idjit. That there's a policeman in a world a' hurt." Though Brian refuses to kill the policeman as Early urges him to do, Brian is still well along the path to intellectual humility in the face of the unknowable.

Finally, after Early abducts and rapes Carrie, Brian surrenders to the urge to murder. During his climactic battle with Brian, Early mocks Brian's earlier attempts at comprehension: "Hey, Bri'. You wanna ask me some questions? . . . Do I feel powerful? Do I feel superior? No, I feel good." By killing Early in the film's climax, the initially anti–death penalty Brian ironically sanctions the very method he so criticized earlier in the narrative. He also gives up on his book as "an academic exercise in futility" (Bentley 64), and by extension, intellectualism, as he and Carrie hide from the world on a California beach. He confesses his inability to make sense of Early Grayce: "I'll never know why Early Grayce became a killer. I'll never know why any of them do. When I looked into his eyes I felt nothing. Nothing." Brian learns to kill a tormentor but doesn't learn much of anything else. In the tradition of Hollywood crime drama, *Kalifornia* concludes with Brian's solo act of vigilantism as the "proper" American response to a threat.

Early, obviously intended by the filmmakers to be an outsider to civilization, resists Brian's attempts to explain him in conventional humanistic terms. Like Mickey Knox, Early is a neoprimitive who fits right into the preliterate culture of the redneck bar where it is safe to assume that Brian's liberalism and yuppie appearance would not find a receptive audience.[14] Early Grayce, as his rather heavy-handed name implies, stands mostly apart from the complex linguistic structures encoded into law, sociology, politics, formal education, and good home training. To the extent that it is possible for a human being to eschew language and still function in the society of others, Early does so. He relies on nonverbal snorts and, when he has to, rural colloquialisms to convey his messages. Though he shares the murderous agenda of a similar "negative man," Hannibal Lecter, he stands in elemental opposition to Lecter's sophisticated mockery. Early does exhibit some rudimentary knowledge of a popular culture and mythology shared with others. For example, he quotes from a Lynyrd Skynrd song while beating Brian senseless at the film's conclusion and subscribes to the half-joking American stereotype that California is populated by "cuckooheads." He shares a rustic paranoia of cities and authority. He is suspicious of the government and corporate sectors, believing that covert missions to the moon are happening "all the time" and that the standard nutritional advice to "eat a good breakfast" is propaganda put forth by "the cereal people" (certainly a terrible pun in the context of a serial killer film). But, generally speaking, he lives a preverbal existence based largely on immediate appetites such as eating, beer-drinking, screwing, and impulsive killing. Brian says of him: "Early lived in the moment. He did whatever he wanted whenever he wanted. It was that simple. I didn't know if I was fascinated or frightened by him. Probably both." Brian also initially pities Early for his lack of social graces, saying, "He can't help the way he was raised. I kinda feel sorry for him." In one of his retrospective voice-overs, Brian remembers how he also thought Early was "harmless. Primitive but harmless. Of course, the fact of the matter was that he'd killed his landlord less than an hour before we'd met him." Early completely overturns Brian's ignorant abstractions about the roles child abuse and chemical brain imbalances may play in the creation of a serial killer. Early is an inscrutable and lethal enigma who cannot be read—a well-worn literary convention in America, from Puritan religious treatises through Hawthorne's scarlet letter and Melville's white whale to the present. Crudely put, Early is a caveman, or at least a marginally more socialized version of Leatherface from *The Texas Chainsaw Massacre,* in the postindustrial twentieth century. He is doomed to extinction but also deadly in his fall.

The urge to escape this kind of doomed temporal existence underlies the apocalyptic mode, which certainly informs the serial killer subgenre and gives an unattractive character like Early Grayce his transcendental resonance. Early embraces a mystical philosophy that aims for a transcendent "rapture" up through a "door." The door is his metaphor for the circuit or link between humanity and divinity. His impulsive behavior, including murder, is a self-medicating route toward the selflessness of eternity—a route designed to free him of the troubling intermediating force represented by rational thought. As Early begins to form a bond of friendship with Brian during the long road trip to the nirvana represented by California, the mystically inclined killer shares his philosophies with the interested (voyeuristic) writer. During their male-bonding side trip to a rural pool hall and bar, Early confides to Brian: "I'm bettin' we're going to find us some doors around here . . . openings to other dimensions. See, I read. I'm tellin' you if a man knows what he's doin', he can transport himself anywhere in this goddamn universe." Then, as the two men become even closer following their shared danger in the bar fight with the belligerent redneck, Early continues:

> You remember them doors, them doors I was talkin' about, Bri'? . . . I found me a couple of 'em in Kentucky. Hell, I wasn't even lookin' for the first one. I was on the side of the road swingin' my sickle, I turned around and there's this door, this big ol' door. And light's comin' out, blindin' me real good. And I'm thinkin' this can't be, this can't be. So I closed my eyes and I count one, I count two, I count three, four, five, and I open my eyes. It wasn't there.

In the standard FBI classification schema, Early would be classified as a "visionary" serial killer on the basis of statements like this. He sees a "higher calling" to his murderous quest—in his case, to find another door and this time to successfully enter it. As Early's secret sharer, Brian understands something of Early's perceptions:

When you dream, there are no rules. . . . Sometimes, there's a moment as you're waking when you become aware of the real world around you, but you're still dreaming. You may think you can fly, but you better not try. Serial killers live their whole lives in that place, somewhere between dreams and reality.

And just as Brian envisions California as "a place of hopes and dreams, a place to start over," Early hopes that his shared trip to California will show him a door. All the participants in this road quest have unfulfilled desires that they foolishly expect California to satisfy. Brian wants to find the knowledge he needs to finish his book. His lover Carrie wants to find a gallery that will show her "extreme" photographs. Adele, Early's girlfriend, wants to escape poverty and settle down with Early in idyllic surroundings. And Early wants to go up through that transcendental door.

Unfortunately, the traditional American westward journey to renewal and opportunity works about as well for three of these four inspired adventurers as it did for the Joads in Steinbeck's *The Grapes of Wrath*. Adele is murdered by her lover. Carrie is raped and brutalized by Early. Brian is not only savaged by Early but is unable to find the knowledge (even accompanied as he is by a real-life case study) that will allow him to finish the book satisfactorily. Brian and Carrie do make it a California beach house, but the house is haunted by the memory of what happened to them on the road as well as by the remnants of Brian's unfinished book. As fictional characters, they bear out Michael Atkinson's thesis that the nomadic heroes of the road movie (one of the genres to which *Kalifornia* generously helps itself) will not find whatever they envision as the American Dream: "Whatever might be found on the road, it won't resemble any universal truth, it will elude those explicitly searching for it, and it won't be easy to tie to the hood and bring home" (17).

That California-as-Heaven is a piece of philosophical hokum and self-delusion is suggested by the film's misspelling of the name in the title. Therefore, it is no real surprise that the protagonists fall short of their goal. Ironically, the only one who may have gotten what he wanted out of the doomed road trip is Early. Even though he is shot to death by Brian and never reaches California, the manner in which he dies suggests that at the moment of death he reaches his longed-for door. Paradoxically, he achieves transcendental heights at the exact moment he reaches the ebb of his humanity. At the remote desert locale where he takes Carrie to rape her, an old nuclear test site appropriately named Dreamland, Early degenerates into the most bestial form the audience sees him in. He becomes completely debased, nearly losing the power of speech beneath his thickening accent, resorting instead to snarling and slobbering. His swinging long hair hides his human features. In the course of this segment, he consummates the sexual desire he has felt for Carrie the entire trip (to the extent that he cut Adele's hair against her will into a fashion similar to Carrie's) by handcuffing her to a ratty bed in the abandoned target house and raping her. It is at this narrative moment, the low point of Early's socialized humanity, that Carrie stabs him with a broken shard of glass.

Though Early does not die right away, the loss of blood in combination with his sexual attack on Carrie weakens and disorients him to the point where his rationality is completely dispelled. He thinks he sees a "door" open up just outside the house, spilling intense white light over him. Gratefully, he walks toward the light, saying, "Door. Where ya been?" Just as he gets close enough for the audience to see that the light is merely the reflection of sunlight from broken glass in an broken doorframe lying in the yard (though whether Early knows this is uncertain), Brian appears from the halo of blinding light to bash Early in the face with a shovel. During the ensuing fight, Brian kills Early. But this death may have been a welcome one for the sufferer—implied by the visual equation of Brian the avenging killer with the light of divinity as it appeared to Early. Though the audience knows that the door and the light were a chimera, Early may have died believing he achieved his goal. Therefore, Early's murders have been primitive dress rehearsals for his own mystic transport. He privately appropriates the methodology of ritual sacrifice for essentially religious reasons. In doing so, he visits an apocalypse upon the American wasteland, given its most literal rendering in the nuclear test site.

As an apocalyptic free agent, Grayce roams a suitably bleak setting that cries out for the cleansing fire. From the opening of *Kalifornia,* Sena provides constant reminders that this is a debased world winding down into entropy. The camera begins tracking through a rainswept, uninhabited expanse of featureless concrete roadways and shadowy overpasses reminiscent of the desolate Philadelphia of Hitchcock's *Shadow of a Doubt:* the world as postmodern urban artifact. The only two people visible, a female hitchhiker and the married man who hopefully picks her up, are quickly killed by a hunk of crumbling concrete deliberately thrown onto the man's windshield. This is also the urban world of Brian and Carrie, two young sophisticates at a city college who will venture forth into another kind of wasteland: the rural wilderness that gives birth to mass murderers like Early Grayce. Grayce is an emissary from that American Third World, where farmhouses and trailer parks and abandoned mines in Tennessee and Texas and Nevada (all famous murder sites that Brian visits on his road trip) conceal the unquiet memories of terrible deeds. The memories themselves have the power to pollute or contaminate those who come after. For example, Brian notes of a slaughterhouse where a female survivor of child abuse killed a number of victims: "The victim returns to the scene of the crime and becomes the criminal." The moral decay is contagious, like vampirism.

Early Grayce may be a vampire-man who seduces Brian into murder, but Grayce is also a secularized satanic-type figure who brings down the apocalypse upon the heads of sinners, much like Mickey Knox does in Stone's film. This theme is initiated when Early walks into a chili parlor in search of Adele and encounters an old man mumbling to himself at the lunch counter. The man says over and over, "The Antichrist would be a woman in a man's body, with seven heads and seven tails." Early leans in to hear him better, listens, and then affirms simply, "Yeah." The old man's ramblings are evocative of similar oracular pronouncements in other genre narratives (the *Omen* series, for example) where the "end" is foretold by apparently insane prophets. The main difference here is that the existence of the supernatural in *Kalifornia* is ambiguous. Early may believe in the occult, as implied by his enthusiastic endorsement of the old man's mantra. However, the narrative's slippery positioning on this issue gives no one else such assurance. The old man's words provide no foundation for belief even if taken at face value. He does not say that the Antichrist *is* a woman in a man's body, but *would* be (if he or she existed). Also, if we as audience accept that Early is the Antichrist (or at least a fellow traveler) spoken of by the old man, we must somehow reconcile the androgynous nature of the old man's Antichrist with the hypermasculine Early.

Such encounters, then, may be supernatural only in image, given bogus veracity by the trappings of the empty iconography of religion. Adele jokes that Early is fated to supernatural reincarnation because of all the bad luck coming to him from the numerous mirrors he broke at his factory job: "We came to 449 years it would take for him to work it all off, and after he'd died he's gonna have to keep comin' back to earth over and over and over again." But again in its narrative context this "prediction" lacks any warrant. Likewise, Early's repeated association with images of nuclear apocalypse—his climactic murder of a retired nuclear scientist living in the Nevada desert, his strapping of a nuclear-bomb casing to the hood of the convertible, his abduction of Carrie to an old nuclear test site named Dreamland[15] to "find us a door"—is not so much an indication that he is the Antichrist but rather an Antichrist-like figure. Hence, Grayce is only an image of Antichrist—a significant difference.

Grayce, then, as a replication of the image of evil is menacing but empty. He suffers from an internal emptiness that he seeks to fill with the glaring light of heavenly fire. In a deliberately antirational strategy, he attempts to erase the distance between himself and eternity through his unzipping of formerly seamless bodies and his reading of the released entrails. In this, he is metaphorically no different than millions of truth-seekers before him. Where he parts company from them and becomes an enemy of society is his willingness to sacrifice victims of his own choosing, as opposed to participating in what René Girard calls society's collective rituals of institutionalized murder (102). Such rituals are designed for the express purpose of preventing individual murders. Grayce finds his personal affirmation in a form of murder that is particularly threatening to the stability of his culture. While everyone around him, especially Brian, attempts to read his political agenda, Grayce has none beyond that most American of ideologies—what Richard Slotkin calls the cult of personal regeneration through violence. As with Mickey Knox, Grayce's *lustmord* elevates him to a higher plane of existence and identity. And another serial killer is given apotheosis in popular narrative.

"We Are Not What Was Intended": *Seven*

The serial killer "John Doe" in David Fincher's *Seven* (1995) is in many ways a polar opposite to Grayce. Whereas Grayce is apolitical, Doe is political; Grayce is illiterate, Doe is scholarly; Grayce rural, Doe urban; Grayce sloppy, Doe methodical; and so on. Yet both are visionaries preparing in their own spiritual ways for mystic transport, and both win their goals first through killing and then through dying. John Doe's project is inarguably successful for him, as the film's notorious "shocking" ending makes clear.[16] Perhaps on the strength of the word-of-mouth regarding several such grim but powerful sequences, *Seven* achieved unexpected box-office success and consequently drew the traditional round of recriminations from critics who could not understand why people wanted to see such a brutal, depressing film.[17] The offended critics refer again and again to the movie's brief but alarming glimpses of tortured bodies left behind by the killer, and it is certainly true that *Seven*'s villain is one of the most sadistic mainstream serial killers yet. A rundown of his deeds is chilling. He force-feeds an obese man spaghetti until one well-placed kick explodes the victim's stomach. He forces a lawyer to cut off one pound of his own flesh. He keeps a man tied to a bed until the man rots away into the bedsheets. He makes a whorehouse john literally rape a woman to death with a knife-edged dildo. He slices off a beautiful woman's nose "to spite her face." Finally, he kills a pregnant woman and decapitates her so he can have the head delivered to her husband. The audience does not see any of this as it happens, but the crime scenes and autopsies that follow more than convey the horror of the deeds. The killer's pattern, which is to punish ritually a given practitioner of one of the seven deadly Christian sins, is also one of the most sadistic and fetishistic yet in the mainstream serial killer film. The gruesome pattern illustrates nicely the escalating level of spectacle expected in such movies.[18] Yet, for all its violence and sadism, indeed because of it, the film's Christian framing device places it quite firmly in the millennial tradition and serves as a complex critique of the global fundamentalism of recent years. The killer is a Christlike antichrist. The film's intellectual protagonist, Detective Somerset, is a cloistered monk (never married) who must first understand the Beast and its world and then confront it on the desert battlefield of Armageddon.

John Doe does differ from his apocalyptic genre brethren in that he is more millennial—seeing a future for the world past revelation. No one would accuse Doe of being apolitical or socially disengaged. He is ferociously committed to the cause of reform. As a religious-minded killer he displays a fundamentalist's hatred of worldly sin, so much so that he is willing to forsake his ascetic, contemplative life. He gives himself over to action as God's warrior in a ferocious way that Somerset, in many ways a narrative reflection of Doe's alienation from most worldly passion, never has and that Somerset's partner, hot-headed David Mills, could never achieve. In a revealing verbal confrontation with Mills on the way to the desert, Doe justifies his murders in terms that explicitly blame the sinner:

> An obese man, a disgusting man who could barely stand up. A man who if you saw him on the street, you'd point him out to your friends so they could join you in mocking him. A man who if you saw him while you were eating, you wouldn't be able to finish your meal. After him, I picked the lawyer. And you both must have been secretly thanking me for that one. This is a man who dedicated his life to making money by lying with every breath that he could

muster to keeping murderers and rapists on the streets. . . . A woman so ugly on the inside that she couldn't bear to go on living if she couldn't be beautiful on the outside. A drug-dealer—a drug-dealing pederast, actually. And let's not forget the disease-spreading whore. Only in a world this shitty could you even try to say these were innocent people and keep a straight face. . . . We see a deadly sin on every street corner, in every home, and we tolerate it. We tolerate it because it's common. It's trivial. . . . Well, not any more. I am setting the example, and what I have done is going to be puzzled over, and studied, and followed forever.

Doe's diatribe reveals that he is so disillusioned with society's perceived moral decay that he is quite willing to be a martyr for the fundamentalist backlash movement. He believes that the remaining faithful will emulate his actions once they are shaken from their complacency; as he tells Mills: "If you want people to pay attention, Detective, you can't just tap them on the shoulder anymore. You have to hit them with a sledgehammer. Then you'll find you have their strict attention." In spite of his murder campaign, which conventional morality as represented by Mills dismisses as "insane," Doe views himself as the exemplar of the godly man living in an ungodly world, in a manner not unlike many more conventionally religious people. He is so devout that he is willing to kill those who fall short of his idealism. He tells Mills and Somerset that he feels no more pity for the murder victims than he does "for the thousands who died at Sodom and Gomorrah," the biblical equivalent to the nameless city Doe has targeted for his own small-scale apocalypse. When Somerset asks if Doe sees himself as an instrument of God's will, Doe replies smugly, "The Lord works in mysterious ways."

As a man who has decisively changed *his* ways and embraced a heartfelt course of action and recovering of meaning in a "shitty" world, Doe will no longer tolerate social apathy from the likes of Somerset. Somerset actually agrees with much of what Doe says, if not his actions. For example, in a barroom conversation with Mills, Somerset tries to explain his impending retirement:

I just can't live in a place where apathy is embraced and nurtured as if it were a virtue. I can't take that anymore. . . . [but] I sympathize completely. Apathy *is* a solution. It's easier to lose yourself in drugs than to cope with life. It's easier to steal something than to earn it. It's easier to beat a child than to raise it.

Somerset implies that the path of least resistance, the caving in to human weaknesses, is understandable but contemptible—a position shared by John Doe.

Significantly, Somerset, as the narrative's central character, is the first to begin to understand Doe's mind-set. This development quickly establishes the two as kindred spirits and prompts the audience to accept Doe's agenda as more than an expression of mere psychopathology.[19] In a voice not entirely unsympathetic, Somerset reads aloud some of Doe's journal entries: "'What sick, ridiculous puppets we are, and what a gross little stage we dance on. What fun we have, dancing and fucking, not a care in the world. Not knowing that we are nothing. We are not what was intended.'" While Mills consistently underestimates Doe as a "lunatic . . . dancing around his room in a pair of his mommy's panties, rubbing himself with peanut butter" and "reading *Guns and Ammo* and masturbating in [his] own feces," Somerset recognizes that Doe's crimes are rational, methodical, didactic, and mimetic of some higher organizing script or principle. Somerset tries his best to enlighten Mills, urging him to read Milton and Chaucer and telling him that Doe's murders "are his sermon to us."

All along, Somerset comprehends more of the sermon as it unfolds than his colleagues do. He is the first to discover the word "gluttony" written in the grease behind the murdered obese man's refrigerator. From this word he is able to link the seemingly isolated crime with the much higher-profile murder of Eli Gould, an expensive defense lawyer who was found murdered in his office, his self-mutilated body displayed next to the word "greed" written in blood on the carpet. A literate (and lonely) man who spends much leisure time in the vast city library bantering with the after-hours guards, Somerset immediately realizes that someone is committing a series of murders patterned on the Christian seven deadly sins. He attempts to explain their theological utility to Mills:

> The seven deadly sins were used in medieval sermons. There were the seven deadly sins and the seven cardinal virtues. They were used as a learning tool to show people how they can be distracted from true worship. . . . This is all about atonement for sin, and the murders are like forced contrition.

At another crime scene, Somerset finds a quote from Milton—"Long is the way, and hard, that out of hell leads up to light"—and perceives that the killer is referring to his own purgatorial journey. Mills, whose classical knowledge has been grudgingly acquired from hasty perusal of Cliff's Notes, quickly loses patience with Somerset's scholarly approach to crime-solving but does later provide Somerset with an inspiration when Mills gripes: "Just because [the killer's] got a library card doesn't make him fuckin' Yoda." In the hope of tracking down some addresses, Somerset decides to contact an FBI source who is in a position to run an illicit computer check on books that have been checked out by the city library's patrons. Rather implausibly, this extralegal shot in the dark brings Mills and Somerset right to Doe's apartment door.[20] But the plot contrivance does serve to illustrate that as a frequent library visitor, as well as someone who can justify breaking the law for a higher purpose, Somerset has been paralleling the killer in his daily movements all along.

The older detective and the killer share many similarities, all of which are designed to implicate the audience in the killer's millennial mind-set. Both characters are outsiders—the Other—and aware of it. The film opens with a scene that illustrates the degree of Somerset's alienation from his peers. A fellow detective at a crime scene tells him that everyone will sure "be real glad" when he's gone. Somerset himself admits to Tracy that others find him "disagreeable." Both Somerset and Doe live in a city they find morally irredeemable. Somerset loathes his urban environment so much that he pressured a former lover, many years ago, to have an abortion rather than bring a child into such a world. Doe also detests the "shitty world," and like Somerset, he is intimately involved in the destruction of an unborn child as a result.[21] Furthermore, both men fetishize the notion of time, though in different ways. Doe attempts to arrest time's progression—certainly an expression of the apocalyptic mind-set—with still photography and staged corpses. Somerset, alternatively, keeps a ticking metronome by the side of his bed to remind him of time's passage. He is also obsessively counting down the days (seven, naturally) to his retirement. But as he plunges deeper into Doe's atemporal mind-set, Somerset breaks his metronome, asks Mills to stay on as his partner indefinitely ("until this thing is over"), and begins to engage in ritualistic behavior, such as compulsively throwing an open switchblade into a dartboard on his apartment wall.

But most significantly to the film's narrative, Somerset and Doe share a contemptuous estimation of David Mills's professionalism (or lack thereof) and unsophisticated reformist zeal. Somerset suspects that Mills's unusual request to be transferred to urban duty reveals the younger man's dangerously egocentric desire to clean up the city and make a name for himself. Also, Somerset immediately resents his neophyte replacement's incessant chatter and banishes him from the first crime scene to talk door-to-door with potential witnesses. He asks his supervisor to remove Mills from the case because Mills does not have enough experience to cope with the demands of a serial murder investigation. Somerset disdains Mills's bellicosity and tragic naïveté: the same two qualities Doe decides to exploit to make Mills his final victim. For Doe, fresh-from-the-country Mills is a literal godsend, enabling Doe to complete his series in unforgettable fashion.[22] Doe's climactic destruction of Mills and his family literalizes Somerset's earlier antipathy toward his hyperemotional partner and horribly inverts Somerset's tender regard for Tracy. Doe victimizes Mills and not Somerset because Somerset does not share Mills's self-blinding desire to take personal vengeance against the urban criminal class.

Thus, unlike Mills, who yearns to be an action hero and ends up a disgraced prisoner, the passive Somerset is the only qualified adversary against the Antichrist. The desert wasteland in which this combat takes place, just like the settings of *Natural Born Killers* and *Kalifornia,* is littered with derelict cars and hulking trailers. A dead dog rots by the side of the road, soon to be joined by Tracy's head and John Doe's body. All the principal players meet personal apocalypse in the desert. Mills loses his wife, unborn child, and career. Only Somerset, by virtue of his long years of solitary study, survives the battle by knowing when *not* to act. He throws his gun aside in a vain attempt to show Mills the proper course of action when faced with Doe's atrocities, but Mills characteristically ignores Somerset's wisdom and turns an already horrible situation into a complete defeat.[23] The desert as metaphoric hell serves as a fitting backdrop to Mills's damnation.

In the apocalyptic terms established by the narrative, the harshly brilliant, arid desert setting serves as the dramatic counterpoint to the gloomy, wet city. The parched landscape suggests that here decisive but terrible moral decisions are finally possible. Somerset faces and rejects his own misanthropy embodied in Doe; Mills gives in to wrath; Doe completes his earthly series of seven moral lessons. Of the "apocalyptic" films under consideration here, *Seven* is the most concerned with moral dilemmas and the one most definite in its resolutions of them. Mills and Doe destroy one another through their mutually entangled manifestations of wrath and envy. Somerset, distant by choice on the margins of the struggle, remains alive to carry on in the postapocalyptic world he must face on his return to the far more ambiguous moral battleground of the city. As Amy Taubin concludes, "Somerset knows he's no match for the evil that's taking over. All he can do is stand by, grave and powerless. A witness rather than an action hero, he's our point of identification" ("Allure" 23). All of Mills's swashbuckling and tough-guy posturings meet with defeat, including his frantic pursuit of Doe through a city maze of alleys. The frenetic, pulse-elevating SWAT raid on what is suspected to be the killer's home nets only a colossal red herring—another tortured victim set up by the killer. Law enforcement strategies fail to catch the killer, an observation Doe successfully uses to nettle Mills during the ride to the desert. Somerset's scholarly distance remains the film's favored vantage point. His unorthodox analysis of police work is borne out by the film's narrative trajectory:

> [We're] picking up the pieces. Taking all the evidence, all the pictures, all the samples. Writing everything down and noting what time things happen. . . . We put it all in nice neat piles, and we file it away on the slim chance that someday it'll be needed in the courtroom. . . . Even the most promising clues usually only lead to other clues, not convictions.

As such an insightful witness and relatively detached observer, Somerset finds that his perceptual distance from earthly passions allows him to survive the terrible confrontation in the desert. The local apocalypse so depicted, while damning Mills, seems to restore the flawed but virtuous Somerset. Mills's Hell is Somerset's Purgatory. Somerset, now cleansed of an earlier numbing apathy, decides to return to the city for more evidence collecting. In one sense, the narrative has suggested it is possible and worthwhile to confront the social problems of crime and dehumanizing violence. In another sense, the narrative postulates that the demonic Other still waits on the borders of a debased world crying out for external redemption.

By the film's climax, the viewer may well be ready for the redemptive apocalypse. Quite early on, *Seven* depicts a frustratingly indeterminate, decaying modern world slouching toward the much-needed clarity of Armageddon. This world is a rainy urbanscape quite similar to the one depicted in *Kalifornia*'s opening shot, an anonymous environment where grubby proles plod on through weary routine while waiting for the End of History. The city that serves as the film's setting remains nameless, featureless, and indistinguishable from any other. Its sharp edges are blurred by rain and gloom, a strategy employed by director Fincher to increase the film's claustrophobic effect.[24] This rainy city's trapped inhabitants engage in meaningless, sordid acts of mundane passion behind anonymous walls, as the film's opening shot establishes when Somerset investigates the bloody aftermath of yet another domestic shooting. ("Just look at the passion all over that wall," he says of the bloodstains.) The civil servants like Somerset who have to clean it all up, be they police officers or garbage collectors, approach their tasks with apathetic weariness. Media members slavishly convey gory images and empty official pronouncements to the voyeuristic public. Here, indeed, is a simulacrum of the Undead City.

However, as the film opens, this is a city on the verge of having its landscape transformed by the anachronistic presence of two mavericks, or Others. One is the identityless serial killer and the other is the young detective from the country. Both will eventually destroy themselves. But in the process, the one survivor of the murder campaign, Somerset, is vouchsafed a lesson on the nature of human destructiveness. Ironically, Somerset is restored to a semblance of his lost faith in police work by the serial murders. Like *Kalifornia*'s Brian, he too is educated by evil and thus in some sense profits from the murders just as the killer does. Unlike Brian, Somerset decides to continue his police work for a qualified romantic reason: the daily struggle for reform in and of itself provides meaning, but the world has no underlying divinity in it to be discovered. Somerset, alluding to another famous romantic existentialist, provides the moral of the story as the film's last line: "Ernest Hemingway once said, 'The world is a fine place and worth fighting for.' I agree with the last part." The irony here is that Somerset has learned to rely on his own internal resources by witnessing just how destructive the conflict between two outer-directed moral extremists, one of whom claims divine favor, can be.

The formerly apathetic Somerset's qualified rejuvenation through confrontation with the worst of human nature illustrates the fundamental and very American paradox of the serial murder narrative cycle. It deeply mistrusts individual outsiders while it reaffirms the cult of individuality. The survivors of the serial killer rampage are left with very little faith in collective human virtue and generally seek refuge from further victimization by withdrawal from society—Brian Kessler—or by return to law-enforcement measures of social control—William Somerset. Yet for all this, *Seven* in particular conveys a strange sense of lyrical exhilaration. Perhaps the film seems more "positive" because the ideological struggles outlined within are finally coming to some sort of moral resolution, as the blinding light of the apocalyptic images suggests.

An apocalypse as depicted in most American fiction, after all, signifies that spiritual salvation is still possible, provided a house-cleaning purge is initiated or a general enough level of devastation is visited upon the hapless evildoers who populate the narrative.[25] In David Ketterer's terminology, these kinds of texts emphasize the "positive charge" of apocalypse, wherein the narrative prophetic voice warns of destruction but simultaneously urges social reform (8). Unlike *Natural Born Killers* or *Kalifornia,* whose self-reflexive qualities pyrokinetically collapse in on themselves very quickly, *Seven* definitively restores a prophetic, revelatory voice to the 1990s cinema of serial murder. John Doe is much more interested in social reform than Mickey Knox or Early Grayce is. Fincher's film is every bit as self-reflexive and media-aware as these other three. Yet somehow, the film manages to turn genre conventions on their heads in a way the others do not. *Seven* is most likely the next stage in the evolution of the serial killer subgenre. The film represents a step back from the aesthetic nihilism courted so provocatively but futilely in, say, *Natural Born Killers.* *Seven* restores the traditional narrative structure and moralistic themes that are present in Stone's film but were lost on many of the latter's initial viewers, who mistook visual panache for thematic radicalism.

Whatever direction the popular cinema of serial murder takes next, however, the main problem remains. The eschatological voice common to the more recent films is essentially an ahistorical postmodern one because it so fears the modern historical. The primary actions affirmed are those that transcend the immediate physical and social context and grope, however blindly, back toward the light of revelation and primal assurances. It is not so much to ask, surely, that a subgenre as potentially radical as the serial murder film, which has produced reasonably complex films like *Manhunter* and *Henry: Portrait of a Serial Killer* and will undoubtedly generate other mainstream films hoping to be the next *Silence of the Lambs,* should now link its fashionable mysticism to a more balanced appraisal of the here-and-now American ideologies contributing to the national cult of individual violence—a foundational premise of which is the apocalyptic mind-set so central to these recent serial killer movies. Given the current political state of Hollywood cinema and the millennium rollover, however, it is more likely that the next American films hoping to replicate *Seven*'s financial success will only recycle its expressionistic shocks.

Conclusion

As this study has argued, many serial killers of popular fiction are portrayed as modernized Gothic villains—Shadow seducers who simultaneously live on the margins of society and within it. They stalk victims, mostly women, through a dark mythic landscape teeming with supernatural portents. The threatened women must fight back, with varying degrees of success. But more than any other element, the neo-Gothic serial killer narrative displays an astounding degree of indeterminacy, largely because the killer is such a polysemous entity. These serial killers defy easy reading as they impose their own reading upon an environment all too adaptable to their will. They invite subversive questions the consumers of ideology never before thought to ask. They destabilize pat assumptions about the world even as their threatening presence argues for the strongest possible restoration of protective social institutions. Almost every narrative in the serial killer canon of fiction exhibits this ambivalence toward stability and destability.

If the serial killer tale is one of the most popular contemporary subgenres, Thomas Harris is arguably its most influential writer. The American western, the detective story, and the horror tale all combine together into Harris's fiction. In the ambiguous imaginative world that Harris creates, politics loses some of its Manichean simplicity and we are invited to see the formidable Gothic villains as human beneath the masks. Yet the villains are horrific enough in their methodology to satisfy our unspoken desire to view the demonic. Harris's work is also traditional enough to allow reassuring narrative closure. The monsters are capable of being unmasked by the agents of the social norm, and therefore society is saved—until the next serial killer. For as Dr. Lecter's incredible escape and his continuing influence on his murderous pilgrims makes clear, there will always be more serial killers, and more need for profilers.

Narratives such as *From Potter's Field, Citizen X,* and *The Alienist* offer populist, fictional canonization of profilers as America's last best hope against an "epidemic" of serial murder. In the narratives, one can see a variety of genre influences at work, the most immediate of which is the foundation set down by Thomas Harris. Others include noir or pulp moral anxiety and the squalid realism of the police procedural (not to mention the appropriated FBI methodology). But the most important influence is the Gothic, especially the doubling between protagonist and antagonist wherein moral boundaries become indistinct, even nonexistent. This merging is not inherently negative. What makes it so is the pessimistic subtext that corruption or pollution is hidden within every soul. Further complicating matters, postmodern Gothic fiction, even when given a traditionally linear narrative form, typically refuses to grant the profiler/detective the rationalist and neutral objective point crucial to modernism and humanism. Just as the killer overidentifies with his victims, the profiler often overidentifies with either the killer or, less frequently, with the victims. In such an indeterminate world, hermeticism is impossible. The detective's traditional methods of ratiocination are no longer an adequate method of deciphering the coded text left behind by the killer. Irrationality and intuition, almost literally extrasensory in practice but still cloaked within the language of rationalism, are now the profiler's weapons in the metaphysical battle of wills with the killer. The narratives are pessimistic in that they warn that it is very easy for such traffickers in taboo psychology to get lost out in Lecter country. But they are reassuring to their consumers in one significant way. Genre convention and audience expectation demand that most of these contests go to the profiler as the representative of conventional decency and morality.

By contrast, John McNaughton, Bret Easton Ellis, and Joyce Carol Oates, observing the current fascination with and fear of serial murderers, decide to portray the killers in terms decidedly subversive of mainstream values. Instead of society's inexplicably evil outcasts, Henry, Patrick Bateman, and Quentin are instead its most logical products and indeed rely on American ideology for their murderous success. Though at divergent stations within the economic hierarchy, these three murderers share the American embrace of violence, or wilding, as an appropriate response to alienation and disempowerment. Bateman, more than the others, suffers from a crisis of not only identity but epistemology itself. So he literally strikes out in mechanical frustration against those disenfranchised people his peers victimize financially or sexually. Henry and Quentin, on the other hand, are not so "intellectual" or privileged. Rather, they kill anyone who threatens their identity and independence as they drift through Gothic America. Quentin, though not a literal drifter, brings victims into his private comfort zone for essentially the same purpose: to reaffirm an identity that in all other social interactions is in danger of complete extinction. In either case, these works illustrate clearly the political milieu in which the serial killer was defined. Thus, while Gothic elements remain in these four works, particularly the carnivalesque erasure of boundary, the primary emphasis falls on just what constitutes an American psycho.

The more apocalyptic works in this subgenre abandon the critique of ideology and focus on the serial killer not as a romantic rebel or a political terrorist but a debased transcendentalist concerned only with his egocentric immediate situation. Mickey Knox and Early Grayce seek violent satiation of their overriding carnal desires; even John Doe, the murderous reformer, confesses that he obtains personal pleasure from his quest for martyrdom.

These characters' anxieties for their personal identities betray a fundamental longing for the ultimate ego-trip of apocalypse.

So, given the high profile of the more sensational, end-of-the-millennium serial killer films, whither next this perplexing subgenre? It is quite possible that the serial killer tale, at least on the big-budget movie screen and within the mass-market paperback, has reached a representational crossroads of sorts, where the formative impact of Thomas Harris's approach to the subject matter has already been exhausted through shoddy imitation, overuse, and overexposure. However, given the enormous influence of Gothicism on American literary and cinematic history, it is hard to believe that a perfectly ambiguous character such as the serial killer will fade from sight. After the recent spate of apocalyptic films ceases, it is more likely that he will persist, as he has for two decades now, as a stock villain in contemporary police procedurals and woman-in-jeopardy melodramas—most of which will remain in obscurity. Parodies of the subgenre, such as *Serial Mom* or *So I Married an Axe Murderer,* will be hard for filmmakers to resist. But there are a few authors and filmmakers who, working at a slight remove either chronologically or artistically from the late 1980s and early 1990s explosion of interest in serial murder, have taken or are taking the genre in intriguing and complex new directions: Spike Lee and *Summer of Sam* (1999), Mary Harron's film adaptation of Bret Easton Ellis's *American Psycho* (2000), Poppy Z. Brite, Dennis Cooper, Bradley Denton, Carol DeChellis Hill, A. M. Homes, Thomas Keneally, Jay Russell. Though these authors are outside of the current study's focus on the "classics," it will be quite instructive indeed to revisit the subgenre in a few years' time, well past the beginning of the new millennium, and see the new serial killers of American fiction and cinema.

Notes
Works Cited
Index

Notes

INTRODUCTION: THE SERIAL KILLER IN FICTION

1. "Genre" is a notoriously slippery term to define. For the purposes of this study, Andrew Tudor's definition, while specifically relating to film, seems capable of including other media as well. He argues that genre can only be understood as a common cultural consensus as to what constitutes a certain type of story and distinguishes it from other types. An audience must generally agree on certain clearly delineated conventions or rules of a given genre; as Tudor says, "*genre* is what we collectively believe it to be" ("Genre" 122). Innovative reworking of genre narrative by an individual author is only recognized as such if the audience has clear expectations of the narrative in the first place. Tudor concludes his definition: "If we imagine a general model of the workings of film language, genre directs our attention to sub-languages within it" (123). Again, this definition would apply to other media. A genre author, regardless of individual skill and intellectual depth, is working with an inherited model—a shared notion that this is the way this kind of story will be told, which the ambitious author typically subverts or transforms in some way to give the genre his or her identifying signature. Serial, or pattern, murder proves to be an apt subject—and metaphor—for the process of genre rewriting. The serial killer, then, becomes a symbolic stand-in for the author working within the constraints of genre.

2. Which is why the *Halloween*-derivative invincible bogeyman—in spite of its run of cinematic popularity to the present day with the release of *Halloween: H20*—soon exhausted itself dramatically. The first *Halloween* avoids this trap by firmly grounding Michael Myers, juggernaut though he is, in a melodramatic but nevertheless clearly human personal history.

3. This strategy also clarifies why Jonathan Demme's undoubtedly well-crafted film *The Silence of the Lambs* is so unbalanced. It pays token lip service to Jame Gumb's victimized past and then proceeds extravagantly to mystify its two villains. Michael Mann's underrated *Manhunter,* also based on a Thomas Harris serial killer scenario featuring two of the same characters, does a much more conscientious job of humanizing its "monster," which might explain why that film did not achieve the success of Demme's.

4. It should be noted, however, that the current subgenre has its definite antecedents, such as the cycle of "stalker films" of the 1970s and 1980s analyzed by Vera Dika; the "Down-Home, Up-Country, Multi-Implement Massacre Movie" such as *The Texas Chainsaw Massacre,* or the *Psycho* imitations, both trends discussed by Kim Newman in *Nightmare Movies*; or the 1920s and 1930s German films, such as *M,* of sexual psychopathology. In the historical periods or waves of popular interest in serial murder as defined by Philip Jenkins, I am analyzing works drawn mostly from the "Thriller Novels" and "New Boom" periods (*Using Murder* 88–91). In that the serial killer is usually male in the majority of these works, I will also

focus on the male serial killer in this study, but it should be noted that a growing number of these characters are female and would form the basis of a fascinating study in and of itself.

5. See Nicole H. Rafter's *Creating Born Criminals* for a detailed overview of the deterministic nineteenth-century conception of the "eugenic criminal"—one who is a "natural-born" criminal incapable of reform. Such rhetoric is still very much with us.

6. However, repetition is action, and thus suggestive of force and will, however limited. If aggressively repetitious movement gains no new ground, it does thoroughly plow up the old and gain some temporary, pleasurable sense of mastery over loss, as Freud says of the *fort/da*. Hence the central insight of traditional psychoanalysis: that by exploring the primal formative events in a traumatic past, one may ideally rewrite one's present through the self-knowledge so gained. Just as likely, however, the unguided rememberer may become hopelessly mired in a solipsistic cycle of remembrance and regret, which is where our fictional serial killers are. In any event, by retelling or reliving a familiar if painful story, the teller gains at least the illusion of increasing personal control over the "text" with each retelling. Peter Brooks parallels the act of repetition to the "grammar of plot" (291).

7. Douglas L. Rathgeb places the serial killer as metaphor into the larger context of the Bogeyman central to popular horror narrative:

> From the suburbanite's paranoia of the Bogeyland that is the city, to our justified fears of an all-encompassing nuclear winter, to the inevitability of daily headlines proclaiming the insidious spread of some new and incurable contagion, or the twisted and bloody path of the latest serial killer whose vile thoughts are but one step removed from our own, we continue to see the bogeyman everywhere we look. (43)

8. The difference between the literary romantic criminal and the Gothic deviant (more directly a prototypical serial killer) is that the latter reflects a deep authorial skepticism of human nature.

9. As Gemini, the demon-possessed serial killer of the film *Exorcist III,* cackles, "It's the giggles that keep us going." Freddy Krueger of the *Nightmare on Elm Street* series is as famous for his one-liners as he is for his murder technique. Hannibal Lecter loves to play jokes on his gullible audiences with anagrams. But given the seriousness of the subject matter, very few mainstream novels and films dare to treat serial murder itself as humorous, with some notable exceptions like John Waters's 1994 film *Serial Mom* or 1998's *There's Something about Mary.*

1. The Gothic Legacy and Serial Murder

1. Something about the Knight theory appeals to students of the case. Its trendy conspiracy theory overtly implicates the evils of a repressive society and gives some measure of larger meaning to the depredations of a lone misogynist butcher. In some way, it is more "comforting" for the paranoid to believe in a state conspiracy to murder women in the signature style of a maniac than to settle for the existence of a lone, privately motivated killer. Besides West's intricate novel, at least two movies have been based on variations of the Knight conspiracy theory. (There is even a comic-art series, entitled *From Hell,* based on it.) The 1979 Bob Clark film *Murder by Decree* features Sherlock Holmes and Dr. Watson in pursuit of not only Netley and Gull (their names have been changed) but also the whole British government. Clark is quoted as saying he consciously wanted to invoke an atmosphere of Watergate- or Chinatown-type conspiracy in his film (McCarty 41). His goal is accomplished

during the film's final scene, in which a visibly beaten Sherlock Holmes appears before a secret royal committee meeting, chaired by none other than Lord Salisbury himself, and wearily acquiesces to their demands for his continued silence on the affair as long as they promise not to harm Eddy and Annie's child. The spectacle of the formidable Holmesian intellect admitting any degree of defeat before the legislative weight of government bureaucracy is a relatively novel addition to the canon of apocryphal Holmes narratives, though in the literary subgenre that we might call "Sherlock Holmes versus Jack the Ripper," the mute fact that the Ripper was never captured must be reckoned with. Usually, of course, Holmes privately unmasks the killer but is compelled for various pressing reasons to keep his public silence, lending him a negotiated victory of sorts. In Clark's film, the private victory is small consolation, as the two women Holmes is consciously attempting to save (Annie Crook and Mary Kelly) meet with a disaster he is unable to avert. Gull, known in this narrative as Sir Thomas Spivey, again escapes punishment.

The 1988 David Wickes television "docudrama" (called, simply enough, *Jack the Ripper*) similarly accuses Gull of murdering prostitutes, this time in order to understand and chart the evolution of his own misogynistic senile dementia, catalyzed into active life through a stroke. Netley is present in this one as well, a lower-class Gollum whose allegiance has been bought by the highbrow Sir William with bogus promises of career advancement. The nearly illiterate coach driver fancies himself to have the makings of a good surgeon if only someone would miraculously whisk him past medical school admission standards. In this version, Gull is acting on his own private initiative. The governmental cover-up is only imposed after the fact in order to prevent medical science from falling into disrepute and to protect Gull's prestigious family. Though the film's protagonist, Inspector Abberline, shouts the customary moral protestations against this proposed policy, he too finally signs on to the cover-up, much as Sherlock Holmes did in Clark's film. Thus, Knight's patriarchal-conspiracy theory remains somewhat intact in Wickes's narrative, though John Leonard also notices the script's insistence on clearing Prince Eddy of the portion of blame assigned him by Knight's original scenario, "as if to curry favor with the regnant Thatcherites" (108): a not unlikely political agenda, as the miniseries was coproduced with Thames Television.

2. Of course, in the contemporary serial killer variations on the Gothic theme, usually written by a male, the active agent in the game of seduction may very well be a woman—a monstrous femme fatale who destabilizes gender boundaries as she pursues and beds the object of her (fe)male gaze. Note, for example, Sharon Stone's serial murderer in 1992's *Basic Instinct,* or Andrei Codrescu's rendition of Countess Elizabeth Bathory in *Blood Countess.* Other dangerous, sexualized female serial killers appear in films such as *Sea of Love* (1989), *Gorgasm* (1990), and *Praying Mantis* (1993). On topics related to this discussion, Joseph Andriano traces the genre development of the female Gothic demon in *Our Ladies of Darkness,* while Barbara Creed analyzes the male fear of sexually aggressive females in contemporary horror films in *The Monstrous-Feminine.*

3. For example, it is the rare true-crime account that can resist throwing in a subplot or two concerning a psychic's visions of the killer or murders, starting with the after-the-fact addition of queen's medium Robert Lees to the Jack the Ripper mythos, and some fictional accounts also follow suit. An example is Stephen King's *The Dead Zone,* in which psychic detective Johnny Smith is based on Dutch psychic Peter Hurkos, a special "consultant" in the Boston Strangler investigation.

4. One of the most famous examples is *Psycho*'s androgynous, easily intimidated Norman

Bates, who literally dons women's garb as he imaginatively transforms into his strong, domineering mother.

    5. Saltzman argues that

> the impossibility of Sickert's maintaining a detached, resolute vantage point
> may be read as an implicit critique of the modernist aesthetic, which, like the
> self-legitimating and imperial focus of the aristocracy, is predicated upon the
> subordination of tensions and disharmonies (in art, in politics) and the recu-
> peration of contradictions. (par. 37)

This is certainly true of Gull, and to a lesser extent Sickert, and suggests that a true postmodern aesthetic such as that possessed by Mary Kelly celebrates the "messy" quality of life without attempting to frame it in a closed system. Saltzman's observation also implies that serial killers (or at least Gull and Sickert) are neoconservative modernists stressed out by the contradictions of a postmodern world. I would add only that some forms of postmodernism seek the kind of recuperation of contradictions that Saltzman speaks of.

    6. As the film later makes clear, Megan has either been, or is about to be, literally raped to death.

    7. For example, he doesn't entrance or hypnotize his lovers—he injects them with Sistol.

    8. However, in spite of the book's title that privileges the women over the Ripper, a male (Sickert) still occupies its centermost focus.

    9. The theme of prostitutes banding together for self-protection against a serial killer when law enforcement is unable or unwilling to do the job is found in movies such as *Angel,* the British TV mini-series *Band of Gold,* and Pat Barker's novel *Blow Your House Down.*

    10. Several of the film's reviewers comment unfavorably on the narrative's punishment of women. Bruce Diamond, noting all the times Kate is reduced to weeping as the narrative progresses, writes:

> [Kate is] an intern and a kickboxer—her medical knowledge and her martial
> arts prowess enable her to escape, but not before we see her break down and
> blubber before her captor like a broken love-slave. . . . [T]o see her break down
> so many times just reinforces the stereotype of a "weak woman." (par. 3)

Rita Kempley also points to the film's misogyny:

> For all its feminist posturing, there's something about targeting willful women
> that suggests there's an especially ugly agenda lurking beneath the surface of
> this all-too-familiar scenario. The more self-assured and accomplished a woman
> becomes, the more likely she will be stalked, kidnapped, imprisoned, raped,
> and tormented. (par. 2)

Finally, John Wrathall observes:

> The only notable feature of Casanova's *modus operandi,* rather conveniently for
> the film-makers, is his preference for pretty and in some way "exceptional"
> women—which is all the more titillating for a male audience. As a result, this
> film leaves a very unpleasant taste. (Rev. of *Kiss* 53).

2. THE PSYCHO PROFILERS AND THE INFLUENCE OF THOMAS HARRIS

    1. After a wait of more than ten years since *The Silence of the Lambs,* Harris's fans finally saw the publication of *Hannibal* on June 8, 1999. The novel features not only the return of Hannibal Lecter but also Special Agent Clarice Starling. Controversy quickly devel-

oped over the novel's ending, wherein Starling becomes not only Lecter's lover but a canni- bal. As of this writing, the ending is proving quite problematic for the novel's adaptation into film. Reportedly, Jodie Foster turned down a reprise of her Oscar-winning role as Star- ling because of the character's transformation.

2. For a fuller picture of these databases, refer to the August 1985 *FBI Law Enforcement Bulletin,* or Ressler, Burgess, and Douglas's 1988 *Sexual Homicide: Patterns and Motives.*

3. During this time, male writers have also created female detectives, with varying de- grees of success. Some merely recreate hardboiled male detectives in female form, as does Peter O'Donnell with Modesty Blaise, but others have written more plausible characters, as Thomas Harris has done with Clarice Starling.

4. Consider, for example, the best-selling novels of Patricia Cornwell, whose female protagonist, medical examiner Kay Scarpetta, softens the narratives' obsessive, typically masculine emphasis on catching serial killers with her empathy not for the killer but for the murder victims. In this, she parallels Clarice Starling, whose concern for victims Catherine Martin and Frederica Bimmel, not her identification with killer Jame Gumb, provides her the necessary clues to find Gumb's house.

5. Given the thematic prominence of the outcast vigilante in American detective fic- tion, this adherence to protocol may seem a contradiction at first, but it isn't. The vigilante is still doggedly clinging to a code, a list of prescribed procedures which he must follow, alone if necessary: the institutionalized regulations that he flouts are seen as aberrations, or devia- tions from the narratively privileged "real" code of conduct. See Slotkin's essay "Detective," p. 99.

6. In Bernard Rose's 1992 film *Candyman,* for example, a female graduate student seeks to find a public-housing serial killer in Chicago.

7. To be fair, however, it should be noted that the lay journalistic chroniclers of profil- ing are far more laudatory of its virtues than the profilers themselves. Note Bruce Porter's claim: "But the day does not seem far off when the police will be able to identify a criminal by the psychic loops and whorls he left at the scene, just as quickly and as surely as if he had covered the wall with fingerprints" (52).

8. It makes even more incredible the existence of journal articles like "The Real 'Silence of the Lambs,'" by Clinton R. Van Zandt and Stephen E. Ether, which compares the FBI's actual investigative strategies against those depicted in Jonathan Demme's film and concludes, presumably optimistically, on this basis that "like the character of Clarice Starling . . . the exact prediction of human behavior is still fictional, but the FBI's ISU [Investigative Sup- port Unit] is rapidly closing the gap between the art and the science" (52). The rhetorical nonchalance concerning the merging of reality and representation is quite revealing in this passage. The authors are self-aware of the artifice of their discourse; they have accepted it and have devised a metatextual way of reading it.

9. Ideology or political agendas are often also concealed, though on occasion the rheto- ric of the profilers and their journalistic muses betrays its reactionary theoretical foundations. Some of the texts place sole blame for serial murder on the individual and deny any larger social contributions to the killer's development: "The offender's aggression is self-generated from his own fantasies, not from any societal model of strength or power" (Ressler and Burgess 6). Other texts admit that classification of people into clinical types, however hopeless a task, is still a desirable goal in order to exert social control: "Human behavior is much too com-

plex to classify, yet attempts are often made to do so with the hope that such a vastly complicated system can be brought into some control" (Ault and Reese 24). A few of the texts are even more explicit in their slant. One profiler, for example, states unequivocally that "interviewing offenders who have perpetrated the unspeakable is an extremely stressful undertaking. In order to comprehend such evil, one must possess a strong belief in a higher power and implement appropriate coping mechanisms" (Geberth 110). Pundit Eugene Methvin blames the supposed ease by which serial killers circumvent the heroic profilers on the Warren Court's "due process revolution" (36).

10. The most recent example of profiling's inadequacy is the investigative debacle centered around Richard Jewell, initially a suspect in the 1996 bombing of the Olympic Park in Atlanta, Georgia, and now exonerated. Jewell, who discovered the bomb and alerted authorities to its location shortly before its detonation, apparently fit long-standing profiling wisdom that as a so-called law-enforcement "groupie" who "sought out" media attention in the hours following the explosion, he might be the bomber. When Jewell's similarity to the profile type was leaked to the media, the subsequent furor over the highly visible case embarrassed law enforcement and damaged Jewell's reputation.

Other examples of the shortcomings of profiling abound, such as the controversy that exists to this day over whether Wayne Williams is the Atlanta Child Murderer. Williams was convicted largely on the basis of his hostile courtroom reaction to the prominence of FBI profiling that zeroed in on him. The 1989 Congressional investigation of a fatal gun-turret explosion aboard the USS *Iowa* was another low point for profiling zealots; an FBI profile that more or less blamed a sailor who died in the explosion was severely criticized for its unsubstantiated conclusions. (See Jeffers, pp. 177–229, for a detailed account of the case.) In their various media appearances, the federal profilers themselves are understandably reluctant to dwell on these ambiguities in profiling history and instead prefer to embrace the valorization accorded to them, at least at the surface level of reading, by the fiction of Thomas Harris and derivative television serials such as *The X Files, Millennium,* and *Profiler.* However, as even the profilers will admit, most serial criminals are captured by luck rather than skillful detection or profiling.

11. Philip Jenkins calls the contest between killer and detective "a personalized, almost gladiatorial combat between individual heroes and villains" (*Using Murder* 111).

12. Glenn D'Cruz maintains that these fictional tales are stitched together out of fragments of discourse drawn from highly specific fields of knowledge—criminology, psychoanalysis, forensic science and so on—and are usually deployed in the service of the detective/protagonist's quest to solve the enigma of the serial killer. . . . The "factual," "real" knowledges of criminology and psychoanalysis attempt an explanation. (326–27)

The psychiatrist's exegesis of Norman Bates's psychopathology at the end of *Psycho* is prototypical.

13. Three brief examples will suffice: not long after *The Silence of the Lambs* was released, Ron Howard's film *Backdraft* featured several scenes with an imprisoned arsonist interviewed by a young fireman—who just happens to be wrestling with the memory of his dead firefighter father—in an attempt to create a profile of an arsonist still on the loose. More recently, a nonfiction book entitled *The Riverman* was published, in which "superstar" profiler Robert Keppel details his series of Death Row interviews with Ted Bundy as both engage in a spirited give-and-take of privileged information, ostensibly for the purpose of finding the still-

unknown Green River Killer. Finally, in *Just Cause* (1995), Ed Harris as serial killer Blair Sullivan advises the law professor played by Sean Connery on his investigation to clear a suspect in the murder of a child.

14. She is also a convincingly female character envisioned by a male author who appeals to a large number of women. Of course, there are differences of opinion on just how "feminist" Thomas Harris is. Sara Paretsky, another detective fiction writer, complains bitterly about Harris's "cross-gender" popularity (17).

15. Christopher Lehmann-Haupt characterizes the ideological construction of Harris's second novel in this way:

> There really are monsters out there in the streets, Mr. Harris seems to be saying—destructive lunatics who may not be worth even trying to understand. . . . That's why it's so peculiar that the author of "Red Dragon" seems to be going knee-jerk liberal halfway through his story. . . . Is Mr. Harris kidding? Is he trying to make fun of liberals who seek all explanations for evil in unhappy childhoods? Actually not, because the most obvious effect of this flashback is to develop a sufficiently good side of Dolarhyde to attract a blind woman who falls in love with him. (*"Red Dragon"* 11)

In contrast, Thomas Fleming sees the flashback as a reductive dramatic flaw: "its construction, especially in the point-by-point correspondence of Dolarhyde's mania to his early psychic wounds, is too machinelike in its symmetry. Real life is more various, less predictable" (14).

16. Contrast this bleak ending with that of Michael Mann's *Manhunter,* based on this novel; in Mann's version, the Graham family unit is optimistically restored by Graham's professional activities, a sentiment more in keeping with neoconservative culture.

17. Again, Michael Mann's film softens this crucial plot development to the point that much of its disturbing ambiguity is purposefully lost, probably in the commercial interests of making Graham a more sympathetic character for a mainstream audience.

18. This is not the only time we will encounter the virus metaphor in the serial killer subgenre. The film *Copycat* (1995), for example, specifically equates serial murder with viruses. Again, the virus as an invasive external corruption suits the deterministic agenda of much of the subgenre, and calls attention to one of the paradoxes of conservative notions of evil: its belief in moral choice and free will, on the one hand, and an opposing belief in the contaminating influence of external factors. Referring to Harris's closing image of Shiloh, Christopher Lehmann-Haupt neatly gives voice to the paradox:

> The more I think about this [image], the less I like it, if only because, connected as it is to the story it embellishes, it suggests that evil is a matter of biology, and has little to do with moral choice. But I have to acknowledge my gut response to Mr. Harris's thriller. It hits us in our outrage, and titillates the part of us all that would like to get rid of evil with a gun. (*"Red Dragon"* 11)

19. This is not to suggest that child abuse doesn't play a part in the formation of a serial killer. But it is only one among what must doubtless be multiple factors.

20. The dialectic, at times, portrays Lecter in deliberately diabolical or satanic terms. For example, Christopher Lehmann-Haupt refers to a specific descriptive passage of Lecter "going to and fro in his suite and walking up and down in it" as a parallel to an almost identically worded passage about Satan in the biblical Book of Job ("Return" 16).

21. Tony Magistrale points out that Lecter as psychiatrist "employs a kind of psychic

cannibalism in the transference of one individual's feelings, thoughts, and wishes to another" (33). Lecter is a contemporary incarnation of an older genre type—what Kim Newman in *Nightmare Movies* calls the evil asylum keeper who torments his helpless wards (94–95), such as the prototypical Dr. Caligari in 1919's *The Cabinet of Dr. Caligari.* According to Newman, the horror genre reserves deep mistrust for the psychiatric profession.

22. Some representative analyses include James Conlon's "Silencing Lambs and Educating Women"; Adrienne Donald's "Working for Oneself: Labor and Love in *The Silence of the Lambs*"; Greg Garret's "Objecting to Objectification: Re-Viewing the Feminine in *The Silence of the Lambs*"; Judith Halberstam's "Skinflick: Posthuman Gender in Jonathan Demme's *The Silence of the Lambs*"; Janet Staiger's "Taboos and Totems: Cultural Meanings of *The Silence of the Lambs*"; David Sundelson's "The Demon Therapist and Other Dangers: Jonathan Demme's *The Silence of the Lambs*"; Julie Tharp's "The Transvestite as Monster: Gender Horror in *The Silence of the Lambs* and *Psycho*"; and Elizabeth Young's "*The Silence of the Lambs* and the Flaying of Feminist Theory."

23. The spelling of some key character names in *Manhunter* is different than Harris's. In the film, "Dolarhyde" becomes "Dollarhyde" and "Lecter" becomes "Lektor." For the sake of continuity, I will privilege Harris' spellings.

24. Perhaps the most (in)famous example of this link is found in Michael Powell's 1960 British film *Peeping Tom,* which practically ruined its director's career.

25. Another film that portrays a blind woman jeopardized by a serial killer is 1992's *Jennifer Eight.*

3. DETECTIVES VERSUS SERIAL KILLERS

1. It is no stretch to claim that Scarpetta and Cornwell are quite similar; Cornwell herself makes this plain in her interviews. (See McElwaine; Tangorra.) In addition to being a crime reporter for the *Charlotte Observer,* Cornwell was a computer analyst for six years in the office of the Virginia chief medical examiner. She brings an undeniable authenticity to her descriptions of forensic procedure. She also shares Scarpetta's paranoia about personal security (O'Shaughnessy C10).

2. Sandra McElwaine summarizes the dark but appealing mood of Cornwell's work in this way: "For all its scarifying power, however, the technical milieu of the novels barely masks what one critic called a poetry of melancholy, an unease about the meaning of death in a violent world that gives the works a powerful undertow" (46). Elise O'Shaughnessy parallels this sentiment: "The world of Kay Scarpetta, the chief medical examiner of the State of Virginia, is frightening and almost unbearably sad. Death is as random as a wrong phone number. The killer could be anyone: the man delivering lost luggage or the dispatcher who answers a call to 911" (C10).

3. For example, Robert Walker's *Instinct* series, centered around medical examiner Jessica Coran, or forensic anthropologist Kathy Reichs's novel, *Deja Dead,* which introduces forensic anthropologist Temperance Brennan.

4. Cornwell says: "Some people [in this genre] write horrible, sadistic scenes. . . . [But] Death and pain are not sexy. They leave terrible marks that are ugly and last forever. My stories are filtered through the feelings and sensitivity of an intelligent woman" (qtd. in McElwaine 148).

5. A common genre convention of made-for-cable-or-network-television movies. Some of the more recognizable TV movies based on "fact" about dedicated detectives chasing evil

serial killers include: *The Deliberate Stranger* (Ted Bundy); *Manhunt: The Search for the Night Stalker* (Richard Ramirez); *To Catch a Killer* (John Wayne Gacy); and *The Limbic Region* (the California Zodiac Killer).

6. His trial led to an explosion of Western interest, giving many Russians their first direct exposure to the capitalistic fascination with true crime stories, as Ivan Solotaroff writes: "In Russia, where the idea of life as something private—and privatizable—is absurd, the sudden influx of hard currency for exclusive rights to the lives of the generals, detectives, and psychiatrists who had pursued him was shocking. They adjusted quickly" (96).

7. Compare to descriptions from Solotaroff's article describing the effects of the investigation on the real Burakov (100) or in Cullen's book (154). There is no denying that the stress of a serial killer investigation exacts a debilitating toll upon law enforcement professionals.

8. The film's brief but graphic images of the desiccated corpses hint at the extent of Chikatilo's savagery. In eighteen cases, he carved out the eyes of his victims. He also directed attention to the genital areas, cutting off testicles, biting through penises, and carving out uteruses. It is also believed that he ate parts of his victims, either raw or cooked over campfires, at the crime scenes. See Peter Conradi's *The Red Ripper* for a case study of Chikatilo.

9. In that later scene, Bondarchuk accuses Burakov of being a perfect suspect in the murder series, which causes Burakov to break down in tears. Fetisov ends the meeting and consoles the overcome Burakov, then confronts Bondarchuk in private. Fetisov threatens to send the secretary's wife evidence of Bondarchuk's longtime homosexual affair with a teenage boy. By committing to Burakov's cause and rebelling against his former patron in the corrupt system, Fetisov redeems his earlier cowardice by symbolically slaying the communist Dark Father and taking over the local government power vacuum left by the collapse of the Party.

10. Though it is unfair to compare Bukhanovsky the fictional character to Bukhanovsky the actual Russian psychiatrist, it is still interesting to see the extent to which the real Bukhanovsky embraced the capitalist mind-set.

11. Stephen Dobyns diagnoses this imbalance of setting and voice as a function of a peculiar first-person narrator:

> John Schuyler Moore, for all of his turn-of-the-century trappings, is basically a contemporary voice. His values and cultural background are of the 1990's more than the 1890's. He is our representative through the world that Mr. Carr creates, but because of Moore's limitations—the chat, the hipness—he also becomes an obstruction. (C19)

12. Carr's demystification project did not sit well with at least one reviewer, who obviously wants his fictional killers to embody a metaphysics of evil:

> The only real weakness of [*The Alienist*] lies in the stringent rationality of Kreizler's investigation. The more his logic makes sense the less threatening his quarry seems, at least to the reader. For if the murderer is purely the product of negative conditioning, then he or she is somehow drained of evil. . . . [T]he story's fatalism grows tedious. You begin to long for a touch, say, of bad old Hannibal Lecter. (Lehmann-Haupt, "Erudite" 17)

13. As was the case with Cornwell, Carr invites biographically based criticism of his work by saying things such as this: "Frankly, what interested me about serial killers . . . was that if I had gone four or five steps in another direction, I could have been one of these guys—the anger they had, the way they chose to embody it" (qtd. in Dubner 60). Though Carr fudges

on the details, in interviews he often hints at an abusive family history and says only "that elements of his life story are in the book" (D. Ellis 76).

4. Serial Killers and Deviant American Individualism

1. It is at this shocking point that Henry paradoxically elicits audience sympathy by preventing Otis from sexually molesting the dead woman's body: a classic example of what Kenneth Burke in part 2 of *Permanence and Change* calls "perspective by incongruity."

2. Taubin makes a point of lamenting Becky's narrative reduction to object but herself does not get Becky's name right. She calls her "Luanne."

3. Most of Ellis's first critics saw very little in the novel beyond the rare but extremely violent descriptions of Bateman's murder of women. These are the same scenes that simultaneously horrified and angered prepublication reviewers and ultimately led to publishing company Simon & Schuster's decision to cancel the book's publication. Perhaps recognizing the financial value of controversy, Vintage Books editor Sonny Mehta quickly picked up the novel and provided Ellis with another payday. As the backstage wrangling between the publishing companies and Ellis's agent continued, literary pundits were quick either to praise Simon & Schuster's good taste and social responsibility or condemn the company's corporate cowardice. Battle lines formed immediately around the First Amendment, as the admittedly scarce Ellis advocates claimed "censorship" and more numerous opponents cried "pornography" and as yet another work of questionable moral influence ran afoul of public decency. On the sidelines, understandably nervous booksellers were given a question-and-answer checklist by *Publishers Weekly* informing them how to handle customer challenges, protests, and picketing if they decided to stock the book ("For Booksellers" 9). Of course, most of the arguing parties had no idea exactly what the novel described, apart from their fevered perusal of two graphic excerpts in *Time* and *Spy* magazines.

Many of those who actually bothered to read the Simon & Schuster manuscript or the Vintage edition some months later soon confirmed in their various printed forums that, indeed, *American Psycho* was not only pornographically violent but badly written at that. According to most, Ellis managed to be irredeemably offensive and boring at the same time. The critical savaging of the novel quickly escalated, most of it personally directed at the author, as if he had literally committed the horrors detailed within the novel. For example, Roger Rosenblatt, in the *New York Times Book Review,* headlined his scathing review: "Snuff This Book!" (3). *Time* magazine, in one of the articles that eventually compelled Simon & Schuster CEO Dick Snyder to drop *American Psycho,* called its forthcoming publication "A Revolting Development" (Sheppard 100). In the *National Review,* Terry Teachout chose a more dignified tone but a nevertheless self-righteous approach when he speculated that

> Ellis spent his undergraduate years steeped in the modish brand of academic nihilism that goes by the name of "deconstruction," a school of criticism in which works of art are verbally hacked to pieces in order to prove that nothing means anything. He seems to have learned his lessons well, if a bit too literally. (46)

Even Norman Mailer, who has not been above using graphic violence in his own work and admits some admiration for Ellis's talent in the March 1991 *Vanity Fair,* nevertheless concludes sadly in the same piece that he could not "forgive" Ellis for botching a potentially Dostoyevskian theme (221).

If Mailer, often considered to be no friend of feminism, could not forgive Ellis, one can imagine the feminist reaction to scenes in the novel such as the one where Bateman introduces a live, starving rat into a dying woman's vagina; or the one where he explodes a woman's breasts by clamping jumper cables to her nipples; or the one where he orally rapes a severed female head; or the one where he cannibalizes a female corpse, first by ripping raw flesh from the bone and later by cooking what's left. And there's much, much more, all equally graphic. As potential victims of the brand of extreme violence detailed in Ellis's narrative, many female commentators obviously felt personally threatened (or in some cases attacked) by what they perceived as Ellis's incitement of real-life, misogynistic psychopaths. Barbara Grizzuti Harrison's is typical: "For days after I read *American Psycho,* I watched men on the street . . . and I wondered: Does that one harbor fantasies of killing me? Mr. Ellis poisoned my days; don't let him poison yours" (149). Ellis became a literary villain unparalleled in recent American publishing history. Indeed, as Pagan Kennedy notes, he became the temporary American equivalent of the hiding Salman Rushdie, who had been condemned to death by Islamic extremists. For an excellent overview of the entire *American Psycho* controversy, refer to Carla Freccero's article, "Historical Violence, Censorship, and the Serial Killer."

4. Somehow, one is reminded of Mr. Brown's critical interpretation of the Madonna song "Like a Virgin" from Quentin Tarantino's 1992 similarly excessive "splatter" film *Reservoir Dogs.*

5. On the other hand, because characters in the novel are always mistaking each other for someone else, Carnes *could* have had lunch with someone other than Owen. Nothing is certain in this novel.

6. This doesn't even take us into the far more subtle area of *emotional* violence, which male and female alike inflict on one another with equal abandon.

7. Reviewers of the novel tend to praise its abandonment of traditional narrative form to give a more realistic, in-depth psychological portrait of a homosexual serial killer. Nancy Pearl's comment is typical: "What gives this novel its awesome power is Oates's ability to convince us Quentin [the killer] might be anyone: a casual acquaintance, a friend or a brother" (121–22). Richard Flood writes: "it is Oates' stylistic combativeness that offers the thrills. Using a terrifyingly deadpan voice, she conjures up the rot that is destined to destroy all our neighbors' perfectly nice kids—the killers and the killed. *Zombie* is numbing but necessary" (24). Even reviewers who were less impressed by the novel pointed to its welcome focus on psychological realism: "this depressing narrative . . . incorporates crude drawings and typographic play to evoke the hermetic imagination of a psychopath" (Steinberg 217).

8. Though in an interview about the novel, Oates does betray a certain slippage between fact and fiction, as well as a reductiveness in her basic adherence to the "profile" construct of the FBI:

> Ted Bundy is actually—this sounds a little bizarre—less realistic in terms of the serial killer profile than my Zombie. My Zombie is much more representative. Though I think of him as a real person and he has his own unique identity, he fits the profile much more than Ted Bundy did, who was so charming, so intelligent . . . sort of free enterprising, you know. A serial killer is the ultimate Darwinian, after all. It's a free market kind of thing.

She also reveals a predilection toward false universalization:

> Jack the Ripper—he's the archetype of the male, the misogynist, who takes his revenge against the female. It's almost like a figure out of mythology. Men have traditionally liked those figures—they stand for the repressed or the buried hostilities that quite normal men feel toward women. It's probably not abnormal

to have those feelings—and Jack the Ripper is kind of the archetype. (qtd. in
"Inhabiting")

Yet very little of this reductiveness comes through in the novel. The novel climaxes the exploration of serial murder Oates undertook in novels such as *Mysteries of Winterthurn* and *The Rise of Life of Earth*.

9. Or, depending on one's perspective, Quentin P. could be yet another homosexual criminal demonized in the popular media.

10. Quentin reserves the use of all-capital-letters nicknames for his victims. It is also significant that women receive no such dehumanization in Quentin's reconfigurations of other people's identities.

11. Toward the end of the novel, Quentin is privately amused when his father's old mentor, a Nobel Laureate at the Washington Institute, is revealed by the newspapers to have engaged in secret and harmful radiation experiments on mentally retarded children and adult prisoners for the Atomic Energy Commission during the 1950s. Professor P___ is publicly humiliated by the disclosure that his intellectual "father" committed such atrocities. The disclosures reveal another moral failure at the private heart of benign paternalism, analogous to the emotional distance between Professor P___ and his son. One can only speculate about the future reaction of Professor P___ when the inevitable happens and his son is arrested for serial murder.

12. Oates is undoubtedly referring here not only to the fact that Dahmer's murders of black and Asian men in Milwaukee went unnoticed for many years but also to the incident that finally brought John Wayne Gacy in Chicago to justice: his murder of a 15-year-old suburban boy, instead of the runaways and male prostitutes that comprised Gacy's normal "fare."

13. Steven Marcus identifies Quentin as representative of two cultures—the punitive and the therapeutic:

> In other words, Ms. Oates's abhorrent protagonist seems to be, on one side, little more than an individualized and monomaniacally focused version of what American society itself is capable of on its legitimate scientific and medical side. Similarly, the liberal, therapeutic culture in which the narrator, his family and everyone else in the work is immersed—"Remember nobody's judging anybody else. That's the bottom line, guys"—is as inane, phony and ultimately abhorrent as the old punitive culture that the contemporary ethos of nonjudgmental therapy and undiscriminating unsympathetic acceptance has largely replaced, with exceptionally indifferent success.

Marcus is ultimately critical of Oates's allegorical character: "America today, for all the violence and brutality we have come both to fear and sometimes to deny, has not quite yet descended into collective madness" (13).

5. The Serial Killer, Myth, and Apocalypse in 1990s Cinema

1. See Michael Stein, "The New Violence, or Twenty Years of Violence in Films: An Appreciation."

2. Then–Senate majority leader Bob Dole came out against the film, for example, as did other public figures. Author John Grisham, no stranger to fictional mayhem himself, argued that Stone could and should be held legally liable for any violent acts that could be attributed to the influence of the film. At least one such suit was filed, by a Louisiana woman

wounded in a robbery by an attacker who had allegedly seen the movie many times. See Ann Oldenburg, "Suit Blames 'Killers' for Woman's Injuries," *USA Today,* 10 July 1996, p. 5D. On March 8, 1999, the United States Supreme Court refused to block the lawsuit, so as of this writing, the case continues to go forward.

3. Of course, "apocalypse" is not a Judaeo-Christian invention. Mircea Eliade has written extensively of the prevalence of apocalyptic myth among "primitive" people. The "primitive" view of apocalypse is optimistic in that the complete destruction of the old order allows for a rebirth—a second chance. A return to chaos does not end there; it is only a state of flux before the next creation. There is no one final judgment but rather a series of them. No end point is ever reached in the sequence of transitions from one state to the other. John May asserts that the Judaeo-Christian apocalypse takes this basic mythic pattern and transforms it by claiming "the end will come only once because, in the Judaeo-Christian worldview, time is linear and irreversible" (11–12).

4. The film's hyperkinetic, fetishized visuals seem a too-literal expression—a form of imitative fallacy not uncommon to this subgenre—of Stone's surface protest against a violence-begetting media. Indeed, what hurts *Natural Born Killers* the most is its over-reliance on its technocratic gimmickry, which makes it "the most sensationalistic attack ever made on sensationalism" (Powers 296). The film's studied simulation of channel-surfing becomes just another exercise in channel-surfing, to paraphrase Nick James. James elaborates:

> For all the hallucinogenic frenzy with which this film shuffles the full range of image-gathering options, it is a curiously second-hand experience. Its pictorial exuberance feels forced, a slap-dash imitation of music video and infotainment style. . . . Stone is clearly so afraid that his audience won't get the fact that he's engaged in parody, that he restates everything over and over, repeatedly cutting from wielded gun, to reacting victim, to entry wound, to gun again. (45)

The net effect is to render the audience weary of the film's subject, simply because Stone's imagistic complexities are clearly impossible to keep pace with and the viewer may give up all the decoding or character-identification strategies so often a part of the viewing experience. Paradoxically, it is exactly this kind of narrative dehumanizing technique that Stone attacks. Added to this is a lack of thematic unity, which Christopher Sharrett notes: "The movie's confusion makes it enervating and passionless, surprising for an Oliver Stone project, but this flows naturally from the director's failure to find a single, focused concept and a style to carry it" ("Killers" 84). The collage of images becomes the story, rather than a support for the story. On the basis of this fetishization of technique, John Simon concludes that the film "is manifestly far too enamored of what it pretends to satirize, even if it knew how to do it" (72). As is evident from these negative critical assessments, Stone is injured here by his embarrassment of images, which are so vertiginous as to be nearly ineffectual. Of course, other critics hail the film as a masterpiece for exactly the same reasons. Chris Salewicz, for one, praises it as "perhaps the most astonishing picture of the Nineties" (101).

5. Possibly a reference to the man who, in the film's opening scene in the diner, magically disappears from one of the booths as Mallory walks by him, and then much later reappears to lead Mickey and Mallory to safety during the prison riot. In one of the film's alternate endings, ultimately not chosen for the theatrical release but available on the director's cut video, this supernatural entity shoots Mickey and Mallory. As a greater force, he is the only one who can put an end to Mickey's earthly evil.

6. The film's token academic, played to deadpan perfection by comedian Steven Wright, is a ludicrous caricature of a psychoanalyst, revealing Stone's intent to dethrone Freud for Jung.

7. Significantly, Mallory is also excluded from Mickey's homosocial mystical interlude, capable only of standing outside the sacred hoop and berating Mickey in stereotypical nagging-wife style ("Bad!" "Bad!" "Bad!") when he fails his vision-quest.

8. The "less evil" Mallory does not begin this narrative as a killer; rather, it is her seduction by Mickey that transforms her into first a patricide and then a spree killer. During the "I Love Mallory" flashback, Mallory is presented as a waiflike innocent whose skimpy attire nevertheless hints at her sexual desire for a male who can rescue her from the domestic prison established by her sexually abusive father. Her desires are soon fulfilled by the appearance of her "dream" man—in this case, Mickey the "meatman," who significantly asks Mallory if she is a "big meat eater." Mallory indicates her willingness to assume Mickey's predatory nature through her reply: "I could be."

9. In respect to the film's relentless attack on liberal and conservative hypocrites, Norman Kagan writes, "the characters standing roughly for society's law, community, and understanding are all Swiftian nightmare figures" (244–45).

10. Oliver Stone says of Scagnetti: "[He] does some heavy shit in this movie, some bad things, because he is Mickey's alter ego and wants to live Mickey's life—but he wants to live it on the side of the law" (qtd. in D. Williams, "Analyzing" 53).

11. As the character of Mallory demonstrates, women are only slightly less susceptible.

12. For an amusing behind-the-scenes account of the filming of the riot in an actual prison using real prisoners as extras, as well as a detailed overview of the film's entire history, refer to producer Jane Hamsher's *Killer Instinct*.

13. See, for example, G. W. Kennedy's critical survey of early American "cataclysmic" novels.

14. In fact, on the basis of his brush-cut hair, fine features, and chic black garb, Brian is called a "cum-swizzling faggot" by a pathologically masculine drunk. Only Early's violent intercession (smashing a beer bottle into the drunk's face without warning) saves Brian from a beating.

15. The name "Dreamland" is also often assigned to the now-infamous Area 51, located in the Nevada desert near Las Vegas. Area 51, believed by some to be the site where military testing of top-secret warplanes or captured extraterrestrial vehicles occurs, has taken on wider mythical importance in the American post-atomic era and features prominently in the fictional cosmology of popular films and television programs such as *Independence Day* and *The X Files*. By consistently denying that the military base exists when in fact something is obviously there, the federal government only enhances Area 51's mystique for those want to believe that aliens and U.S. leaders are engaged in clandestine activities of decidedly sinister bent against the citizenry. "Dreamland," then, is a desert staging area for predatory extraterrestrials and murderous humans, as well as magical but deadly technology, in contemporary America's geo-mythology.

16. Detective David Mills, one member of a two-man team transporting prisoner Doe to a remote desert locale on a search for victims' bodies, discovers that Doe has killed Mills's wife, Tracy, and even worse, cut off Tracy's head and sent it in a parcel to Mills. The detective, always an impetuous hothead at his best, succumbs to his rage and prepares to shoot Doe. The meekly submissive Doe goads Mills: "Become vengeance . . . become wrath." Mills's older and much more insightful partner, Detective William Somerset, implores David not

to shoot: "David, if you do this, he will win." Anguished, bereaved, howling in denial, Mills wavers for only a few seconds, then levels his gun at Doe. Doe closes his eyes in acceptance; Mills shoots and provides Doe with his posthumous victory. The film ends with Mills, career and family destroyed, driven away as prisoner in Doe's place.

17. Janet Maslin takes it to task for being at once dull and "uncommonly nasty" (C18). Beverly Buehrer compares watching the film to "gawking at an accident. . . . We . . . try to justify this staring by dressing up these gory contents with the intellectual works of Dante and Chaucer and St. Augustine, but their cerebral depths are constantly being countered by stomach-churning superficialities" (par. 7). Noting *Seven's* intellectual pretensions, a *New York* reviewer verges on calling the film hypocritical: "The intellectualism of *Seven* hides the true nature of the movie's hideous appeal from filmmakers and audience alike" (Rev. of *Seven* 89). Kenneth Turan weighs in with: "When you add a level of pretension that indicates somebody believed this picture had profound things to say about the human condition, the results are regrettable" (1).

18. Earlier, lesser-known films have also focused on the religious fanatics who serially murder according to parameters set down by religious texts or instruction, such as 1981's *Day of Judgment*, 1988's *Freeway*, or 1992's *Mortal Sins*.

19. David Mills, in spite of his refusal to grant Doe any degree of sanity, also doubles (to a lesser extent) for Doe. Mills and Doe share a desire, however at odds with one another's practice, to "clean up" the city.

20. Though Somerset's transgression of regulations is less spectacular than Mills's brand, the fact remains that both men share a common tendency to operate outside of approved criminal justice practice in the belief that the end justifies the means—a standard convention in Hollywood crime drama.

21. The pro-choice movement is subtly criticized by scenes that associate Somerset's natural regret with Doe's savage murder of a pregnant woman.

22. Although one does wonder what grand finale Doe had in mind before Mills bumbled onto Doe's stage.

23. It is valid to claim that Mills's self-destructive action completely undermines most genre treatments of the same vigilante scenario, a point made by John Wrathall: "It's hard to imagine even the most degraded audiences cheering when Mills shoots Doe . . . because *Seven* leaves us in no doubt that in doing so he has succumbed to Doe's power, and is now irredeemably damned" (Rev. of *Seven* 50). However, the apocalyptic associations that accompany this subversive moment still suggest that a final divine judgment—salvation or damnation—is the only way out of the human moral dilemmas posed by the existence of Others such as Doe, or even Mills.

24. On a limited number of the original theatrical prints, Fincher intensified the darkness by utilizing a special photographic process called CCE, or Color Correction Enhancement, that deepens the black areas of the final print (Summer 67) and plunges Somerset and Mills into oppressively dark crime scenes and killing lairs that weak flashlights do little to relieve. Of the unceasing rain, Fincher says: "I liked the idea of the rain. . . . I was looking for something so that there wasn't any escape. You couldn't go, 'I'm in this horrible, cramped, dark room and I'm going to go outside' because outside isn't that much better" (qtd. in Sloane 35).

25. Of course, the apocalyptic voice provides no material recommendations—only spiritual ones—to achieve social reform.

Works Cited

Rev. of *American Psycho*, by Bret Easton Ellis. *Film Comment* 27.3 (May/June 1991): 55–56.

Andriano, Joseph. *Our Ladies of Darkness: Feminine Daemonology in Male Gothic Fiction.* University Park: Pennsylvania State UP, 1993.

Arnzen, Michael A. "Who's Laughing Now? . . . The Postmodern Splatter Film." *Journal of Popular Film and Television* 21.4 (Winter 1994): 176–84.

Atkinson, Michael. "Crossing the Frontiers." *Sight and Sound* ns 4.1 (Jan. 1994): 14–17.

Ault, Richard L., and James T. Reese. "A Psychological Assessment of Crime Profiling." *FBI Law Enforcement Bulletin* 49.4 (Apr. 1980): 22–25.

Baker, James N. "Stalking a Victorian Killer." *Newsweek* 11 Apr. 1994: 76.

Bakhtin, Mikhail. *Rabelias and His World.* Trans. Helene Iswolsky. 1965. Bloomington: Indiana UP, 1984.

Barthes, Roland. *The Pleasure of the Text.* Trans. Richard Miller. New York: Hill, 1975.

Bates, Peter. "Lost and Found." *Cineaste* 17.4 (1990): 56–57.

Baudrillard, Jean-François. *Simulacra and Simulation.* 1981. Trans. Sheila Faria Glaser. Ann Arbor: U of Michigan P, 1994.

Baym, Nina. "Melodramas of Beset Manhood: How Theories of American Fiction Exclude Women Authors." *American Quarterly* 33.2 (Summer 1981): 123–39.

Begg, Paul. *Jack the Ripper: The Uncensored Facts.* London: Robson, 1988.

Bellamy, Joe David. "Introduction." *Superfiction; or, The American Story Transformed: An Anthology.* Ed. Joe David Bellamy. New York: Vintage, 1975. 3–20.

Bentley, Michael. Rev. of *Kalifornia*, dir. Dominic Sena. *Cineaste* 20 (Jan. 1994): 64.

Binyan, T. J. *Murder Will Out: The Detective in Fiction.* Oxford: Oxford UP, 1989.

Birkerts, Sven. "London Psycho." *New Republic* 6 May 1991: 37–40.

Black, Joel. *The Aesthetics of Murder.* Baltimore: Johns Hopkins UP, 1991.

Blau, Herbert. *The Eye of Prey: Subversions of the Postmodern.* Bloomington: Indiana UP, 1987.

Blennerhassett, Richard. "The Serial Killer in Film: An Archetype for Our Time." *Irish Journal of Psychological Medicine* 10.2 (June 1993): 101–4.

Bloom, Clive. "The House That Jack Built: Jack the Ripper, Legend and the Power of the Unknown." *Nineteenth Century Suspense: From Poe to Conan Doyle.* Ed. Clive Bloom, Brian Docherty, Jane Gibb, and Keith Shand. New York: St. Martin's, 1988. 120–37.

Borchardt, Edith. "Criminal Artists and Artisans in Mysteries by E. T. A. Hoffman, Dorothy Sayers, Ernesto Sabato, Patrick Suskind, and Thomas Harris." *Functions of the Fantastic: Selected Essays from the Thirteenth International Conference on the Fantastic in the Arts.* Ed. Joe Sanders. Westport: Greenwood, 1995.

Boss, Pete. "Vile Bodies and Bad Medicine." *Screen* 27.1 (Jan./Feb. 1986): 14–24.

Bridgstock, Martin. "The Twilit Fringe-Anthropology and Modern Horror Fiction." *Journal of Popular Culture* 23.3 (Winter 1989): 115–23.

Britton, Andrew. "The Myth of Postmodernism: The Bourgeois Intelligentsia in the Age of Reagan." *CineAction* 12/13 (Summer 1988): 3–17.

Brock, Leigh. "Distancing in Brett Easton Ellis' *American Psycho.*" *Notes on Contemporary Literature* 24.1 (Jan. 1994): 6–8.

Brooks, Peter. "Freud's Masterplot." 1977. *Contemporary Literary Criticism.* Ed. Robert Con Davis and Ronald Schleifer. 2nd ed. New York: Longman, 1989. 287–99.

Brophy, Philip. "Horrality: The Textuality of Contemporary Horror Films." *Screen* 27.1 (Jan./Feb. 1986): 2–13.

Brunvand, Jan. *The Vanishing Hitchhiker: American Urban Legends and Their Meanings.* New York: Norton, 1981.

Buehrer, Beverly. Rev. of *Seven,* dir. by David Fincher. *Magill's Survey of Cinema.* 1995. Electric Library. 15 May 1997.
<http://www.elibrary.com/>

Bunnell, Charlene. "The Gothic: A Literary Genre's Transition to Film." *Planks of Reason.* Ed. Barry Keith Grant. Metuchen: Scarecrow, 1984.

Burke, Kenneth. *Permanence and Change: An Anatomy of Purpose.* 1935. 3rd ed. Berkeley: U of California P, 1984.

Cameron, Deborah, and Elizabeth Fraser. *The Lust to Kill: A Feminist Investigation of Sexual Murder.* New York: New York UP, 1987.

Campbell, Colin. "Portrait of a Mass Killer." *Psychology Today* (May 1976): 110–19.

Caputi, Jane. *The Age of Sex Crime.* Bowling Green: Bowling Green State U Popular P, 1987.
———. "The New Founding Fathers: The Lore and the Lure of the Serial Killer in Contemporary Culture." *Journal of American Culture* 13.3 (Fall 1990): 1–12.

Carr, Caleb. *The Alienist.* New York: Random, 1994.

Carroll, Noel. *The Philosophy of Horror; or, Paradoxes of the Heart.* New York: Routledge, 1990.

Carter, Margaret. *Shadow of a Shade: Vampirism in Literature.* New York: Gordon, 1975.

Chang, Chris. "Feed the Reaper." *Film Comment* 30.4 (July/Aug. 1994): 38–39.

Clover, Carol. *Men, Women, and Chainsaws: Gender in the Modern Horror Film.* Princeton: Princeton UP, 1992.

Colby, Cosh. "A Gruesome Cross-Country Ride Argues for Capital Punishment." *Alberta Report/Western Report* 21 (1994): 44.

Collins, Gail. "Wages and Sin." *Working Woman* March 1991: 134.

Conlon, James. "Silencing Lambs and Educating Women." *Postscript* 12.1 (Fall 1992): 3–12.

Conradi, Peter. *The Red Ripper.* New York: Dell, 1992.

Conrath, Robert. "The Guys Who Shoot to Thrill: Serial Killers and the American Popular Unconscious." *Revue Française d'Etudes Américaines* 60 (May 1994): 143–52.
———. "Serial Heroes: A Sociocultural Probing into Excessive Consumption." *European Readings of American Popular Culture.* Ed. John Dean and Jean-Paul Gabilliet. Westport: Greenwood, 1996. 147–57.

Cornwell, Patricia. *From Potter's Field.* 1995. New York: Berkley, 1996.

Creed, Barbara. *The Monstrous-Feminine: Film, Feminism, and Psychoanalysis.* New York: Routledge, 1993.

Cullen, Robert. *The Killer Department.* New York: Ivy, 1993.

Dahmer, Lionel. *A Father's Story.* 1994. New York: Avon, 1995.

Dargis, Manohla. "Pulp Instincts." *Sight and Sound* ns 4.5 (May 1994): 6–9.

Darke, Chris. Rev. of *Kalifornia*, dir. Dominic Sena. *Sight and Sound* ns 4.4 (Apr. 1994): 45–46.

Davenport, Gary. "True Merchants of the Untrue." *Sewanee Review* 101.2 (Spring 1993): 300–307.

Davis, David Brion. *Homicide in American Fiction, 1798–1860: A Study in Social Values.* Ithaca: Cornell UP, 1957.

D'Cruz, Glenn. "Representing the Serial Killer: 'Postmodern' Pedagogy in Performance Studies." *Southern Review* 27.3 (Sep. 1994): 323–32.

Derber, Charles. *Money, Murder, and the American Dream: Wilding from Wall Street to Main Street.* Winchester: Faber, 1992.

Derrida, Jacques. *Of Grammatology.* Trans. G. C. Spivak. Baltimore: Johns Hopkins UP, 1976.

Diamond, Bruce. "*Kiss the Girls, The Matchmaker,* and *U-Turn.*" *Hollywood Online* 5 Oct. 1997. Miningco. 20 June 1998.
<http://hollywoodmovie/miningco.com/library/weekly/99100597.html>

Dika, Vera. *Games of Terror: Halloween, Friday the Thirteenth, and the Films of the Stalker Cycle.* Rutherford: Fairleigh Dickinson UP, 1990.

Dobyns, Stephen. "New York Was a Heck of a Town." *New York Times Book Review* 3 Apr. 1994: 19.

Donald, Adrienne. "Working for Oneself: Labor and Love in *The Silence of the Lambs.*" *Michigan Quarterly Review* 31.3 (Summer 1992): 346–60.

Douglas, John, and Alan E. Burgess. "Criminal Profiling: A Viable Investigative Tool Against Violent Crime." *FBI Law Enforcement Bulletin* 55.12 (Dec. 1986): 9–13.

Douglas, John, and Mark Olshaker. *Journey into Darkness.* New York: Pocket, 1997.

———. *Mindhunter: Inside the FBI's Elite Serial Crime Unit.* 1995. New York: Pocket, 1996.

Dubner, Stephen J. "Serial Killing for Fun and Profit." *New York* 4 Apr. 1994: 58–62.

Dundes, Alan. "Folk Ideas as Units of Worldview." *Toward New Perspectives in Folklore.* Ed. Americo Paredes and Richard Bauman. Austin: U of Texas P, 1972. 93–103.

Dworkin, Andrea. "Books: What Writers Are Reading." *Ms.* July/Aug. 1991: 82.

Dyer, Richard. "Kill and Kill Again." *Sight and Sound* 7.9 (Sep. 1997): 14–17.

Ebert, Roger. Rev. of *Kiss the Girls*, dir. Gary Fleder. *Chicago Sun-Times Online* October 1997. 20 June 1998.
<http://www.suntimes.com/ebert/ebert_reviews/1997/10/100301.html>

Egger, Steven A. "Serial Murder: A Synthesis of Literature and Research." *Serial Murder: An Elusive Phenomenon.* Ed. Steven A. Egger. Westport: Praeger, 1990. 3–34.

Eliade, Mircea. *The Myth of the Eternal Return.* 1971. Princeton: Princeton UP, 1991.

Ellis, Bill. "Cattle Mutilation: Contemporary Legends and Contemporary Mythologies." *Contemporary Legend* 1 (1991): 39–80.

Ellis, Bret Easton. *American Psycho.* New York: Vintage, 1991.

Ellis, David. "Time Traveler." *People* 20 June 1994: 75–76.

Faludi, Susan. *Backlash.* 1991. New York: Anchor, 1992.

Fiedler, Leslie. *Love and Death in the American Novel.* 1960. New York: Dell, 1969.

Fleming, Thomas. "Hunting Monsters." *New York Times Book Review* 15 Nov. 1981: 14.

Flood, Richard. "Real Life Rock: Richard Flood's Top Ten." *Artforum* 34.6 (Feb. 1996): 24.

"For Booksellers, Questions and Answers about 'American Psycho'." *Publishers Weekly* 15 Mar.
    1991: 9.

Foucault, Michel. *The Order of Things: An Archaeology of the Human Sciences.* 1970. New
    York: Vintage, 1973.

Foust, R. E. "Monstrous Image: Theory of Fantasy Antagonists." *Genre* 13 (1980): 441–53.

Fraser, John. *Violence in the Arts.* Cambridge: Cambridge UP, 1974.

Frazer, Sir James. *The New Golden Bough.* 1890. Ed. Theodor H. Gaster. New York: Men-
    tor, 1964.

Freccero, Carla. "Historical Violence, Censorship, and the Serial Killer: The Case of *American
    Psycho.*" *Diacritics* 27.2 (Summer 1997): 44–58.

French, Sean. "The Death of Nick Ingram Barely Made News in the U.S.—Where the Hatred
    of Woolly Liberalism Is Revealed Through the Wild Success of the Novels of Patricia
    Cornwell." *New Statesman & Society* 21 Apr. 1995: 33.

Fuchs, Cynthia. "'Man-Made Weather': Media, Murder, and the Future in *Natural Born
    Killers.*" *Viet Nam Generation* 6.3/4 (1995): 62–68.

Garrett, Greg. "Objecting to Objectification: Re-Viewing the Feminine in *The Silence of the
    Lambs.*" *Journal of Popular Culture* 27.4 (Spring 1994): 1–12.

Geberth, Vernon J. "Serial Murder: A Psychology of Evil." *Law and Order* 40.5 (May 1992):
    107–10.

Girard, Rene. *Violence and the Sacred.* Baltimore: Johns Hopkins UP, 1979.

Gonshak, Henry. "'The Child Is Father to the Man': The Psychopathology of Serial Killing
    in Caleb Carr's *The Alienist.*" *Notes on Contemporary Literature* 25.1 (Jan. 1995): 12–13.

Goodman, Mark. "Cops, Killers and Cannibals." *People* 1 Apr. 1991: 62–70.

Grant, Edmond. Rev. of *Henry: Portrait of a Serial Killer*, dir. John McNaughton. *Films in
    Review* 41.6/7 (June/July 1990): 367–68.

Green, Daniel. "*Natural Born Killers* and American Decline." *The Films of Oliver Stone.* Ed.
    Don Kunz. Lanham: Scarecrow, 1997. 259–71.

Grixti, Joseph. "Consuming Cannibals: Psychopathic Killers as Archetypes and Cultural
    Icons." *Journal of American Culture* 18.1 (Spring 1995): 87–96.

Gross, Louis S. *Redefining the American Gothic: From Wieland to Day of the Dead.* Ann Arbor:
    UMI Research, 1989.

Habermas, Jurgen. "Modernity—An Incomplete Project." *The Anti-Aesthetic: Essays on
    Postmodern Culture.* Ed. Hal Foster. Seattle: Bay, 1983. 3–15.

Halberstam, Judith. "Skinflick: Posthuman Gender in Jonathan Demme's *The Silence of the
    Lambs.*" *Camera Obscura* 27 (Sep. 1991): 36–53.

Hampton, Howard. "American Maniacs." *Film Comment* 30.6 (Nov./Dec. 1994): 2–4.

Hamsher, Jane. *Killer Instinct.* 1997. New York: Broadway, 1998.

Hantke, Steffen. "Deconstructing Horror: Commodities in the Fiction of Jonathan Carroll
    and Kathe Koja." *Journal of American Culture* 18.3 (Fall 1995): 41–57.

Harris, Thomas. *Red Dragon.* 1981. New York: Bantam, 1982.

———. *The Silence of the Lambs.* New York: St. Martin's, 1988.

Harrison, Barbara Grizzuti. "*American Psycho:* Bestseller from Hell." *Mademoiselle* (May 1991):
    148–49.

Hazelwood, Robert R., and John E. Douglas. "The Lust Murderer." *FBI Law Enforcement
    Bulletin* 49.4 (Apr. 1980): 18–22.

Heilbrun, Carolyn. "Keynote Address: Gender and Detective Fiction." *The Sleuth and the*

Scholar. Ed. Barbara A. Rader and Howard G. Zettler. New York: Greenwood, 1988. 1–8.

Hoban, Phoebe. "'Psycho' Drama." *New York* 17 Dec. 1990: 32–37.

———. "The Silence of the Writer." *New York* 15 Apr. 1991: 49–50.

Hogan, David J. *Dark Romance: Sexuality in the Horror Film.* Jefferson: McFarland, 1986.

Holquist, Michael. "Whodunit and Other Questions: Metaphysical Detective Stories in Postwar Fiction." *The Poetics of Murder: Detective Fiction and Literary Theory.* Ed. Glenn W. Most and William Stowe. New York: Harcourt, 1983. 149–74.

Horsley, Lee. "The Founding Fathers: 'Genealogies of Violence' in James Ellroy's L.A. Quartet." *Clues* 19.1 (Spring/Summer 1998): 139–61.

Humm, Maggie. "Feminist Detective Fiction." *Twentieth Century Suspense: The Thriller Comes of Age.* Ed. Clive Bloom. New York: St. Martin's, 1990.

Hutchings, Peter. "Tearing Your Soul Apart: Horror's New Monsters." *Modern Gothic: A Reader.* Ed. Victor Sage and Allan Lloyd Smith. Manchester: Manchester UP, 1996. 89–103.

"Inhabiting the Mind of a Zombie Killer: Joyce Carol Oates." *Salon* 1995. 11 Dec. 1997. <http://www.salon.com/06/departments/litchat.html>

Jacobowitz, Florence. "Feminist Film Theory and Social Reality." *CineAction* (Winter 1986): 21–31.

James, Nick. Rev. of *Natural Born Killers,* dir. Oliver Stone. *Sight and Sound* ns 5.3 (Mar. 1995): 44–45.

Jameson, Fredric. *The Geopolitical Aesthetic: Cinema and Space in the World System.* Bloomington: Indiana UP, 1992.

———. *The Political Unconscious: Narrative as a Socially Symbolic Act.* Ithaca: Cornell UP, 1981.

Jeffers, H. Ron. *Who Killed Precious?* 1991. New York: St. Martin's, 1992.

Jenkins, Philip. "Myth and Murder: The Serial Killer Panic of 1983–5." *Criminal Justice Research Bulletin* 3.11 (1988): 1–7.

———. "Serial Murder in the United States 1900–1940: A Historical Perspective." *Journal of Criminal Justice* 17.5 (1989): 377–92.

———. *Using Murder: The Social Construction of Serial Homicide.* New York: de Gruyter, 1994.

Juchartz, Larry, and Erica Hunter. "Ultraviolent Metaphors for (Un)Popular Culture: A Defense of Bret Easton Ellis." *Popular Culture Review* 7.1 (Feb. 1996): 67–79.

Kagan, Norman. *The Cinema of Oliver Stone.* New York: Continuum, 1995.

Kehr, Dave. "Heartland." *Film Comment* 26 (May/June 1990): 61–62.

Kempley, Rita. "'Kiss the Girls': Clever Creep Show." *Washington Post Online* 3 Oct. 1997. 20 June 1998. <http://washingtonpost.com/wp-srv/style/longterm/movies/review97/kissthegirlskemp .htm>

Kennedy, G. W. "Early Cataclysmic Novels." *Journal of American Culture* (Fall 1978): 584–97.

Kennedy, Pagan. "Generation Gaffe." *Nation* 1 Apr. 1991: 426–28.

Keppel, Robert. *The Riverman: Ted Bundy and I Hunt for the Green River Killer.* New York: Pocket, 1995.

Ketterer, David. *New Worlds for Old.* Bloomington: Indiana UP, 1974.

Kilgour, Maggie. *From Communion to Cannibalism: An Anatomy of Metaphors of Incorporation.* Princeton: Princeton UP, 1990.

Kiss the Girls Website. 1997. Paramount Pictures. 20 June 1998.
   <http://www.cinema1.com/movies97/kissthegirls/us.html>

Klawans, Stuart. Rev. of *Natural Born Killers,* dir. Oliver Stone. *Nation* 19 Sep. 1994: 284–86.

Klein, Kathleen. *The Woman Detective: Gender and Genre.* Urbana: U of Illinois P, 1988.

Knight, Stephen. *Jack the Ripper: The Final Solution.* 1976. London: Granada, 1981.

Lawrence, Barbara. "Female Detectives: The Feminist–Anti-Feminist Debate." *Clues* 3.1 (Spring/Summer 1982): 38–48.

Lehman, David. *The Perfect Murder.* New York: Free Press, 1989.

Lehmann-Haupt, Christopher. "Of an Erudite Sleuth Tracking a Madman." *New York Times Book Review* 29 Mar. 1994: 17.

———. "*Red Dragon.*" *New York Times Book Review* 10 Nov. 1981: 11.

———. "The Return of Hannibal the Cannibal." *New York Times Book Review* 15 Aug. 1988: 16.

Leonard, John. "Murders Most Foul." *New York* 24 Oct. 1988: 106–8.

Madden, Dave. *Understanding Paul West.* Columbia: U of South Carolina P, 1993.

Magistrale, Tony. "Transmogrified Gothic: The Novels of Thomas Harris." *A Dark Night's Dreaming: Contemporary American Horror Fiction.* Ed. Tony Magistrale and Michael A. Morrison. Columbia: U of South Carolina P, 1996. 27–41.

Mailer, Norman. "Children of the Pied Piper." *Vanity Fair* Mar. 1991: 154–59, 220–21.

Malin, Irving. "A Letter to Joyce Carol Oates." *Michigan Quarterly Review* 35.3 (Summer 1996): 570–73.

———. *New American Gothic.* Carbondale: Southern Illinois UP, 1962.

Marcus, Steven. "American Psycho." *New York Times Book Review* 8 Oct. 1995: 13.

Maslin, Janet. "A Sickening Catalogue of Sins, Every One of Them Deadly." *New York Times* 22 Sep. 1995: C18.

Mathews, Jack. "Trailing Another Serial Killer in 'Kiss'." *Los Angeles Times Online* 3 Oct. 1997. 20 June 1998.
   <http://www.hollywood.com/movies/kissthegirls/review/index.html>

May, John. *Toward a New Earth: Apocalypse in the American Novel.* Notre Dame: U of Notre Dame P, 1972.

McCarty, John. *Psychos.* New York: St. Martin's, 1986.

McCay, Mary A. "The Soul of the Serial Killer." *New Orleans Review* 21.1 (Spring 1995): 86–88.

McDonough, John. "Director Without a Past." *American Film* May 1991: 42–49.

McElwaine, Sandra. "Autopsy, She Wrote." *Harper's Bazaar* Aug. 1992: 46, 148.

McKinney, Devin. "Violence: The Strong and the Weak." *Film Quarterly* 46.4 (Summer 1993): 16–22.

Meehan, Brian. "Son of Cain or Son of Sam? The Monster as Serial Killer in Beowulf." *Connecticut Review* 16.2 (Fall 1994): 1–7.

Methvin, Eugene H. "The Face of Evil." *National Review* 23 Jan. 1995: 34–44.

Modleski, Tania. "The Terror of Pleasure: The Contemporary Horror Film and Postmodern Theory." *Studies in Entertainment: Critical Approaches to Mass Culture.* Ed. Tania Modleski. Bloomington: Indiana UP, 1986. 155–66.

Moore, Suzanne. "A Serial Story." *Sight and Sound* ns 1.2 (June 1991): 71.

Morrison, Michael A. "After the Danse: Horror at the End of the Century." *A Dark Night's Dreaming: Contemporary American Horror Fiction.* Ed. Tony Magistrale and Michael A. Morrison. Columbia: U of South Carolina P, 1996. 9–26.

Mulvey, Laura. "Visual Pleasure and Narrative Cinema." *Screen* 16 (Autumn 1975): 6–18.

Murphy, Kathleen. "Communion." *Film Comment* 27.1 (Jan./Feb. 1991): 31–32.

Newitz, Annalee. "Serial Killers, True Crime, and Economic Performance Anxiety." *Cine-Action* 38 (Sep. 1995): 38–46.

Newman, Kim. Rev. of *Henry: Portrait of a Serial Killer,* dir. John McNaughton. *Sight and Sound* ns 1.3 (July 1991): 43–44.

———. *Nightmare Movies: A Critical History of the Horror Film, 1968–88.* London: Bloomsbury, 1988.

Nicolaisen, W. F. H. "Definitional Problems in Oral Narrative." *The Questing Beast: Perspectives on Contemporary Legend IV.* Ed. Gillian Bennett and Paul Smith. Sheffield: Sheffield Academic P, 1989. 77–89.

Oates, Joyce Carol. "'I Had No Other Thrill or Happiness.'" *New York Review of Books* 24 March 1994: 52–59.

———. *Zombie.* 1995. New York: Plume, 1996.

Oldenburg, Ann. "Suit Blames 'Killers' for Woman's Injuries." *USA Today* 10 July 1996: 5D.

Olsen, Lance. *Ellipse of Uncertainty: An Introduction to Postmodern Fantasy.* Westport: Greenwood, 1987.

O'Shaughnessy, Elise. "Anatomy of a Murderer." *New York Times Book Review* 20 Aug. 1995: 10.

Paretsky, Sara. "Soft Spot for Serial Murderers." *New York Times* 28 Apr. 1991: section 4, p. 17.

Pearl, Nancy. Rev. of *Zombie,* by Joyce Carol Oates. *Library Journal* Aug. 1995: 121–22.

Pederson-Krag, Geraldine. "Detective Stories and the Primal Scene." *The Poetics of Murder: Detective Fiction and Literary Theory.* Ed. Glenn W. Most and William Stowe. New York: Harcourt, 1983. 13–20.

Pence, Jeffrey S. "Terror Incognito: Representation, Repetition, Experience in *Henry: Portrait of a Serial Killer.*" *Public Culture* 6.3 (1994): 525–45.

Persons, Dan. "*Silence of the Lambs*: The Making of Director Jonathan Demme's Instant Horror Classic, A Chiller for the '90s." *Cinefantastique* Feb. 1992: 16–38.

Polan, Dana B. "Eros and Syphilization: The Contemporary Horror Film." *Planks of Reason.* Ed. Barry Keith Grant. Metuchen: Scarecrow, 1984. 201–11.

Porter, Bruce. "Mind Hunters." *Psychology Today* Apr. 1983: 44–52.

Powers, John. "Lost Innocence." *Vogue* Sep. 1994: 293–96.

Propp, Vladimir. *Morphology of the Folktale.* 1928. Ed. Louis A. Wagner. Austin: U of Texas P, 1968.

Punter, David. *The Literature of Terror: A History of Gothic Fictions from 1765 to the Present Day.* New York: Longman, 1980.

Rafferty, Terrence. Rev. of *Henry: Portrait of a Serial Killer,* dir. John McNaughton. *New Yorker* 23 Apr. 1990: 91.

Rafter, Nicole Han. *Creating Born Criminals.* Chicago: U of Illinois P, 1997.

Rathgeb, Douglas L. "Bogeyman from the Id: Nightmare and Reality in *Halloween* and *A Nightmare on Elm Street.*" *Journal of Popular Film and Television* 19.1 (Spring 1991): 36–43.

Reddy, Maureen T. *Sisters in Crime: Feminism and the Crime Novel.* New York: Continuum, 1988.

Ressler, Robert, and Ann W. Burgess. "Violent Crime." *FBI Law Enforcement Bulletin* 54.8 (Aug. 1985): 2–31.

Ressler, Robert K., Ann W. Burgess, and John E. Douglas. *Sexual Homicide: Patterns and Motives.* Lexington: Lexington Books, 1988.

Ressler, Robert, and Tom Shachtman. *Whoever Fights Monsters.* New York: St. Martin's, 1992.

Rich, B. Ruby. "Art House Killers." *Sight and Sound* ns 2.8 (Dec. 1992): 5–6.

Richter, David R. "Murder in Jest: Serial Killing in the Post-Modern Detective Story." *Journal of Narrative Technique* 19.1 (Winter 1989): 106–15.

Ringe, Donald. *American Gothic: Imagination and Reason in Nineteenth-Century Fiction.* Lexington: UP of Kentucky, 1982.

Rockett, W. H. "The Door Ajar: Structure and Convention in Horror Films That Would Terrify." *Journal of Popular Film and Television* 10.3 (Fall 1982): 130–36.

Rohrich, Lutz. *Folktales and Reality.* 1979. Trans. Peter Tokofsky. Bloomington: Indiana UP, 1991.

Rosenblatt, Roger. "Snuff This Book! Will Bret Easton Ellis Get Away with Murder?" *New York Times Book Review* 16 Dec. 1990: 3, 16.

Rubin, Martin. "The Grayness of Darkness: *The Honeymoon Killers* and Its Impact on Psychokiller Cinema." *Velvet Light Trap* 30 (Fall 1992): 48–64.

Rubins, Josh. "Serial Murder by Gaslight." *New York Times Book Review* 12 May 1991: 11–12.

Rumbelow, Donald. *Jack the Ripper: The Complete Casebook.* New York: Berkley, 1990.

Salewicz, Chris. *Oliver Stone.* New York: Thunder's Mouth, 1997.

Saltzman, Arthur M. "Beholding Paul West and the Women of Whitechapel." *Twentieth Century Literature* 40.2 (Summer 1994): 256–71. Electric Library. 15 Sept. 1996. <http://www.elibrary.com/>

Sanders, Joe. "At the Frontiers of the Fantastic: Thomas Harris's *The Silence of the Lambs.*" *New York Review of Science Fiction* 39 (Nov. 1991): 1–6.

Schechter, Harold, and David Everitt. *The A to Z Encyclopedia of Serial Killers.* New York: Pocket, 1996.

Schiff, Stephen. "The Last Wild Man." *New Yorker* 8 Aug. 1994: 40–55.

Seltzer, Mark. *Serial Killers: Death and Life in America's Wound Culture.* New York: Routledge, 1998.

Senf, Carol. *The Vampire in Nineteenth-Century English Literature.* Bowling Green: Bowling Green State U Popular P, 1988.

Rev. of *Seven,* dir. David Fincher. *New York* 13 Nov. 1995: 89.

Sharrett, Christopher. "The Horror Film in Neoconservative Culture." *Journal of Popular Film and Television* 21.3 (Fall 1993): 100–110.

———. Rev. of *Natural Born Killers,* dir. Oliver Stone. *Cineaste* 21.112 (1995): 83–84.

Sheppard, R. Z. "A Revolting Development." *Time* 29 Oct. 1990: 100.

Simon, John. Rev. of *Natural Born Killers,* dir. Oliver Stone. *National Review* 26 Sep. 1994: 72–73.

Sloane, Judy. "David Fincher." *Film Review* Feb. 1996: 34–35.

Slotkin, Richard. *Gunfighter Nation: The Myth of the Frontier in Twentieth-Century America.* New York: Harper, 1992.

———. "The Hard-Boiled Detective Story: From the Open Range to the Mean Streets." *The Sleuth and the Scholar.* Ed. Barbara A. Rader and Howard G. Zettler. New York: Greenwood, 1988. 91–100.

———. *Regeneration Through Violence: The Mythology of the American Frontier.* Middletown: Wesleyan UP, 1973.

Smith, Allan Lloyd. "Postmodernism/Gothicism." *Modern Gothic: A Reader.* Ed. Victor Sage and Allan Lloyd Smith. Manchester: Manchester UP, 1996. 6–19.

Smith, Gavin. "Mann Hunters." *Film Comment* 28.6 (Nov./Dec. 1992): 72–77.

———. "Oliver Stone: Why Do I Have to Provoke?" *Sight and Sound* ns 4.12 (Dec. 1994): 8–12.

Solotaroff, Ivan. "The Terrible Secret of Citizen Ch." *Esquire* 119.3 (Mar. 1993): 95–100.

Staiger, Janet. "Taboos and Totems: Cultural Meanings of *The Silence of the Lambs.*" *Film Theory Goes to the Movies.* Ed. Jim Collins, Hilary Radner, and Ava Preacher Collins. New York: Routledge, 1993. 142–54.

Stein, Michael. "The New Violence, or Twenty Years of Violence in Films: An Appreciation." *Films in Review* 46 (Mar. 1995): 40–54.

Steinberg, Sibyl S. Rev. of *Zombie,* by Joyce Carol Oates. *Publishers Weekly* 17 July 1995: 217.

Stewart, Susan. "The Epistemology of the Horror Story." *Journal of American Folklore* 95.375 (Jan./Mar. 1982): 33–50.

Stratton, Jon. "(S)talking in the City: Serial Killing and Modern Life." *Southern Review* 27.1 (Mar. 1994): 7–27.

Summer, Edward. "No Bleach: The Return of Darkness." *Films in Review* 48 (Jan./Feb. 1996): 66–67.

Sundelson, David. "The Demon Therapist and Other Dangers: Jonathan Demme's *The Silence of the Lambs.*" *Journal of Popular Film and Television* 21.1 (Spring 1993): 12–17.

Symons, Julian. *Bloody Murder.* Middlesex: Viking, 1985.

Tangorra, Joanne. "Patricia D. Cornwell: Life Imitates Art in the Career of the Mystery/Thriller Author." *Publishers Weekly* 15 Feb. 1991: 71–72.

Tani, Stefano. *The Doomed Detective.* Carbondale: Southern Illinois UP, 1984.

Tatar, Maria. *Lustmord: Sexual Murder in Weimar Germany.* Princeton: Princeton UP, 1995.

Taubin, Amy. "The Allure of Decay." *Sight and Sound* ns 6.1 (Jan. 1996): 22–24.

———. "Killing Men." *Sight and Sound* ns 1.1 (May 1992): 14–19.

Teachout, Terry. "Applied Deconstruction." *National Review* 24 June 1991: 45–46.

Telotte, J. P. "The Doubles of Fantasy and the Space of Desire." *Film Criticism* 7.1 (Fall 1982): 56–68.

Tharp, Julie. "The Transvestite as Monster: Gender Horror in *The Silence of the Lambs* and *Psycho.*" *Journal of Popular Film and Television* 19.3 (Fall 1991): 106–13.

Thompson, G. R. "Introduction: Romanticism and the Gothic Tradition." *The Gothic Imagination: Essays in Dark Romanticism.* Pullman: Washington State UP, 1974. 1–10.

Tithecott, Richard. *Of Men and Monsters: Jeffrey Dahmer and the Construction of the Serial Killer.* Madison: U of Wisconsin P, 1997.

Tompkins, Cynthia. Rev. of *Zombie,* by Joyce Carol Oates. *World Literature Today* 70.3 (Summer 1996): 693.

Travers, Peter. "When Shock Has Value." *Rolling Stone* 8 March 1990: 69.

Tropp, Martin. *Images of Fear: How Horror Stories Helped Shape Modern Culture (1818–1918).* Jefferson: McFarland, 1990.

Tudor, Andrew. "Genre and Critical Methodology." *Movies and Methods: An Anthology.* Ed. Bill Nichols. Berkeley: U of California P, 1976. 118–26.

————. *Monsters and Mad Scientists: A Cultural History of the Horror Movie.* Cambridge: Blackwell, 1989.

Turan, Kenneth. "*Seven* Offers a Punishing Look at Some Deadly Sins." *Los Angeles Times* 22 Sep. 1995: home ed., F1.

Turner, Patricia. "The Atlanta Child Murders: A Case Study of Folklore in the Black Community." *Creative Ethnicity: Symbols and Strategies of Contemporary Ethnic Life.* Ed. Stephen Stern and John Allan Cicala. Logan: Utah State UP, 1991.

Twitchell, James. *Dreadful Pleasures: An Anatomy of Modern Horror.* Oxford: Oxford UP, 1985.

Van Zandt, Clinton R., and Stephen E. Either. "The Real 'Silence of the Lambs'." *Police Chief* 61.4 (Apr. 1994): 45–52.

Walkowitz, Judith. *City of Dreadful Delight.* Chicago: U of Chicago P, 1992.

Warner, Michelle. "The Development of the Psycho-Social Cannibal in the Fiction of Bret Easton Ellis." *Journal of Evolutionary Psychology* 17.2 (Mar. 1996): 140–46.

Waxman, Barbara Frey. "Postexistentialism in the Neo-Gothic Mode: Anne Rice's *Interview with the Vampire.*" *Mosaic* 25.3 (Summer 1992): 79–97.

West, Paul. *The Women of Whitechapel and Jack the Ripper.* 1991. New York: Overlook, 1992.

Wetzsteon, Ross. "Macho Manner." *Rolling Stone* 22 May 1986: 34–35, 86, 88.

Widdowson, John. "The Bogeyman: Some Preliminary Observations on Frightening Figures." *Folklore* 82 (Summer 1971): 99–115.

Wilkinson, Peter. "Hot Director." *Rolling Stone* 14 May 1992: 74–75, 118.

Williams, David. "Analyzing Oliver Stone." *Film Threat* 18 (Oct. 1994): 52–55.

————. "Overkill." *Film Threat* 18 (Oct. 1994): 36–48.

Williams, Linda. "Film Bodies: Gender, Genre, and Excess." *Film Quarterly* 44.4 (Summer 1991): 2–13.

————. "When the Woman Looks." *Revision: Essays in Feminist Film Criticism.* Ed. Mary Ann Doane, Patricia Mellencamp, and Linda Williams. Los Angeles: U Publications of America, 1984. 83–99.

Williams, Tony. *Hearths of Darkness: The Family in the American Horror Film.* Rutherford: Fairleigh Dickinson UP, 1996.

————. "Through a Dark Mirror: *Red Dragon*'s Gaze." *Notes on Contemporary Literature* 25.1 (Jan. 1995): 8–10.

Wilt, Judith. *Ghosts of the Gothic: Austen, Eliot, and Lawrence.* Princeton: Princeton UP, 1980.

Wrathall, John. Rev. of *Kiss the Girls*, dir. Gary Fleder. *Sight and Sound* ns 8.3 (Mar. 1998): 51–53.

————. Rev. of *Seven*, dir. by David Fincher. *Sight and Sound* ns 6.1 (Jan. 1996): 50.

Young, Elizabeth. "*The Silence of the Lambs* and the Flaying of Feminist Theory." *Camera Obscura* 27 (Sep. 1991): 4–35.

Zamora, Lois Parkinson. "The Myth of Apocalypse and the American Literary Imagination." *The Apocalyptic Vision in America.* Ed. Lois Parkinson Zamora. Bowling Green: Bowling Green U Popular P, 1982. 97–138.

Zipes, Jack. *Fairy Tale as Myth: Myth as Fairy Tale.* Lexington: UP of Kentucky, 1994.

Index

Philip L. Simpson received his bachelor's and master's degrees from Eastern Illinois University and his doctorate from Southern Illinois University. He is now an assistant professor of communications and humanities at the Palm Bay campus of Brevard Community College in Florida, where he teaches writing, literature, humanities, philosophy, and film.